Small Voice, Big City:

The Challenge of Urban Mission

By Howard A. Snyder

Howard A. Snyder
168 Seamands Drive
Wilmore, KY 40390

Urban Loft Publishers | Skyforest, California

Small Voice, Big City: The Challenge of Urban Mission

Urban Loft Publishers
P. O. Box 6
Skyforest, CA 92385
www.urbanloftpublishers.com

ISBN — 978-0692656556

Made in the U.S.A.
Copy Editor: Kara Hardin
Graphics: Elisabeth Clevenger

Table of Contents

SERIES PREFACE

Urban Ministry in the 21st Century is a series of monographs that addresses key issues facing those involved in urban mission whether it be in the slums, squatter communities, *favelas*, or in immigrant neighborhoods. It is our goal to bring fresh ideas, a theological basis, and best practices in urban mission as we reflect on our changing urban world. The contributors to this series bring a wide-range of ideas, experiences, education, international perspectives, and insight into the study of the growing field of urban mission. These contributions fall into four very general areas: 1. the biblical and theological basis for urban mission; 2. best practices currently in use and anticipated in the future by urban scholar/activists who are living, working, and studying in the context of cities; 3. personal experiences and observations based on urban mission as it is currently being practiced; and 4. a forward view toward where we are headed in the decades ahead in the expanding and developing field of urban mission. This series is intended for educators, graduate students, theologians, pastors, and serious students of urban mission.

More than anything, these contributions are creative attempts to help Christians strategically and creatively think about how we can better reach our world that is now more urban than rural. We do not see theology and practice as separate and distinct. Rather, we see sound practice growing out of a healthy vibrant theology that seeks to understand God's world as it truly is as we move further into the twenty-first century. Contributors interact with the best scholarly literature available at the time of writing while making application to specific contexts in which they live and work.

Each book in the series is intended to be a thought-provoking work that represents the author's experience and perspective on urban mission in a particular context. The editors have chosen those who bring this rich diversity of perspectives to this series. It is our hope and prayer that each book in this series will challenge, enrich, provoke, and cause the reader to dig deeper into subjects that bring a deeper understanding of our urban world and the mission the church is called to perform in that new world.

Dr. Kendi Howells Douglas and Stephen Burris,

Urban Ministry in the 21st Century Series Editors

Other Books In The *Urban Ministry in the 21ˢᵗ Century Series* Include:

Crossroads of the Nations, Jared Looney

Mind the Gap, Colin Smith

Sowing Seeds of Change, Michael D. Crane

The Urbanity of the Bible, Sean Benesh

City Church: Working Together to Transform Cities, Kelly Malone

Small Voice, Big City, Howard Snyder

Forthcoming:

The Lord Is My Shepherd: I Have Everything I Need, John Perkins, Kendi Howells
Douglas, & Stephen Burris

Lay People Are Ministers Too: The City-Changing Power of Called Christians, Robert
Linthicum

Christ Centered Civic Renewal, Randy White & H. Spees, Editors

Modern Legends in Urban Mission, Kendi Howells Douglas

*Somebody's Calling My Name: The Power of Voice in Transforming the Lives of African
American Youth*, Reginald Blount

Eat What Is Set Before You: Critical Capacities for Congregational Mission, Scott Hagley

An Urban Introduction to Los Angeles, Randy Lovejoy

Engaging Muslims and Islam: A Helps-Based Approach to Ministry, Amit Bahtia

Conjured Faith: Neopaganism in Christian Perspective, Andrew Wood

Mission Improv: Acting In Character as Church for the World, Greg Perry

Women in Urban Mission, Kendi Howells Douglas

The Community Pastor Leading People Beyond the Institutional Church, Randy Lovejoy

New Awakenings: The Mission of God and the Changing Landscape of North America, Jared
Looney, Editor

Leadership, Character, and Calling: A Multiethnic Perspective, Yucan Chiu

INTRODUCTION

Isaiah prophesies of the coming Messiah: "He will not cry or lift up his voice, or make it heard in the street." Yet "he will not grow faint or be crushed," and in God's own way and time he will establish "justice in the earth" (Isa 42:2–4).

The small voice of Jesus, heard by the poor and humble and by honest truth-seekers, is still the key to justice in the city. This is how, in the Apostle Paul's words, God chooses "what is foolish in the world to shame the wise; . . . what is weak in the world to shame the strong." God works through "what is low and despised in the world, things that are not, to reduce to nothing things that are, so that no one might boast" before him (1 Cor 1:27–29).

This is the wisdom of God in the city.

Years ago Viv Grigg, "Companion to the Poor," as a young urban missionary heard God's voice. "I was in my little slum house in Tatalon, Manila," he writes, when the small voice of mission "called, as clearly as the voice of a child: 'Go up the river and preach.' And like Philip, I went wandering, preaching, casting out demons—I had never done that before!—and caring for a drug addict. I went, seeing what God would do next."[1] What God did next, through a series of steps of faith and obedience, was raise up an international movement of church planting and social transformation among the urban poor, including a Masters Degree in Transformational Urban Leadership now being offered in eight locations around the world.

Believing and acting this way requires audacious faith—faith that can be enlivened and nurtured only in vital communities of Jesus followers who live out the Jesus Good News in the cities of the world.

This book focuses on the power of the gospel—often outwardly weak, small, foolish—to heal the nations and redeem earth's cities. The gospel proved powerful in the first-century world, when the church was born; it still is today.

Though a small-town boy, I have spent over twenty-five years in urban mission of one sort or another—mainly in Detroit, Chicago, Toronto, Dayton, and São Paulo,

---

[1] Viv Grigg, "Hovering Spirit, Creative Voice, Empowered Transformation: A Retrospective," *New Urban World Journal* 1:1 (November 2012), 18. See Viv Grigg, *Cry of the Urban Poor* (Monrovia, Calif.: MARC, 1992); Viv Grigg, *Companion to the Poor: Christ in the Urban Slums*, 3rd ed. (Auckland, New Zealand: Urban Leadership Foundation, 2014); Viv Grigg, *The Spirit of Christ in the Postmodern City* (Auckland, New Zealand: Urban Leadership Foundation, 2009).

Brazil. Ministry has included pastoring, teaching, and coordinating an urban ministry program for college and seminary students. I draw on this experience as well as biblical, historical, and cultural studies in presenting this volume.

Small Voice, Big City sets urban mission, the mission of Jesus, in a broad context: people, land, and the kingdom of God. Look through any number of books on urban mission and you'll likely find nothing on land, ecology, or creation (in the sense of God's ongoing relationship with the physical created order). The fine book *Urban Church: A Practitioner's Resource Book*, for instance, is nearly silent about the actual physical creation as an aspect of urban reality. Ronald Peters's helpful book *Urban Ministry: An Introduction* has some passing references to ecological concerns and refers to the city as "a microcosm of God's creation." But it does not really view the city or urban mission ecologically.[2] This is typical of books on urban mission.

Small Voice, Big City attempts to correct that oversight, that blind spot. It discusses people and their relationships,

---

[2] Michael Eastman and Steve Latham, eds., *Urban Church: A Practitioner's Resource Book* (London: SPCK, 2004); Ronald E. Peters, *Urban Ministry: An Introduction* (Nashville: Abingdon, 2007), 175.

including their gifts, their culture, their worldviews, and their modes of thinking. In particular, we focus on the relationship between people and land, since this is a vital bond we need in order to survive. This relationship is the focus especially of Chapter One, but it extends throughout the volume.

The book sets all aspects of urban mission within the context of the kingdom of God. Whatever the specific context, people faithfully involved in urban ministry serve a transcendent mission and work within a transcendent hope. That hope is the kingdom of God; that God's will be done on earth, in our cities, as in heaven. In victories, we see signs of the kingdom. In setbacks, sorrows, and defeats, we learn to trust God's kingdom promises.[3]

A working premise of this book is that urban mission isn't just about cities. Urban mission is about the Good News of Jesus Christ. Although the focus here is Jesus's Good News in urban contexts, the book's scope is as wide

---

[3] "Kingdom of God" in the sense used here is shorthand for God's overall plan of redemption in all its dimensions, past, present, and future. At one level, "Kingdom of God" is a metaphor based on the image of an earthly king and kingdom, and grounded in Old Testament history. The concept "Kingdom of God" may not serve well in all contexts; some other terminology, such as "economy of God" (which Paul uses in Eph 1:10 and elsewhere) may prove more useful or powerful in some settings. These issues, including the adequacy of kingdom language today, are explored in my book *Models of the Kingdom* (Nashville: Abingdon, 1991).

as the gospel and God's overall plan of reconciliation. In other words, this book sets urban mission in the larger context of the gospel in the whole world. This means recognizing and facing all the challenges of our world, viewing them through the lens of the gospel, and asking about their relevance for urban mission. Many books on urban ministry focus specifically on urban history and dynamics, such as demographics, urban cultures, and ethnic diversity. Assuming the usefulness of such books, this one employs a wider scope.

This is a book mainly for practitioners, not academics. Although it engages the mind, concepts, and thought processes, the book's chief burden is actual on-the-street practice of redemptive urban mission. Precisely because of the book's broad scope, however, I believe it helpfully contributes to the academic study of urban mission and may prove useful in university and seminary settings.

Overview

The book begins with "The Ecology of Urban Mission" (Chapter One). Here is the main thesis of the book. Often urban mission is discussed as if land were irrelevant. Conversely, those who write about land sometimes rail against the big, bad city. This division is not only silly and unnecessary, it is toxic, whether you're looking biblically or scientifically. Land and city are part of one ecology. We need to think and serve ecologically.

The chapter outlines five elements of a comprehensive and global model of urban mission, tying this to a vision of God's reign. It does this partly in dialogue with Timothy Keller's vision of "Center Church."

Chapter Two, "The Church as Community," looks at the familiar image of *community* and asks what that really means in the context of mission in today's urban world. I argue that both the city and the church are suffering a crisis of community. By exploring key biblical texts, we discern the way to genuine *Christian* urban community that redemptively impacts other dimensions of human life and culture.

Chapter Three, "MacroTrends of the Twenty-First Century," highlights several key aspects of the world that urbanites inhabit today. We all know the world is changing at increasing speed. Is there a way to make sense of such change from a kingdom of God perspective? This chapter outlines ten large trends that are shaping and reshaping the church in relation to culture, beginning with the shift away from homogeneous churches and ending with emerging ecological sensitivity. It also notes countertrends, the challenge of Islam and other world religions, and the promises and perils of Christian "insider movements."

Chapter Four, "The Kingdom of God Index," asks: Can we know empirically whether urban mission is having any real long-term impact or not? Is it more true or less true that year by year God's will is actually being done on earth as it is in heaven? Can we know?

This is a serious question that raises foundational issues. Today's world abounds in global indicators of all sorts—a corruption index, freedom index, quality-of-life index. Is it unspiritual or heretical to propose a kingdom of God index? This chapter offers five reasons such an index, if carefully grounded biblically and missionally, could help dissipate fog and fuzzy claims, adding realism to urban witness.

Chapter Five, "Strategic Planning in Urban Mission," asks about the role of planning in faithful witness and discipleship. The chapter shows how planning can (and should) be done, insisting that it must be carried out in ways consistent with the kingdom itself. The solution is to plan in light of the present and the near future while forming a "prophetic ideal" that looks ahead to the "eschatological horizon" (the kingdom of God in fullness) for orientation. Planning should be an integral part of urban mission and discipleship, aimed not at institutional success but at faithful witness to Jesus and his reign.

Chapter Six investigates "The Loss of Prophetic Christianity." We note five critical signs of global crisis in Christian faith today, including the church's historic decline in the West, the problem of mere cultural Christianity, and the major discipleship gap afflicting many churches globally, not just in the West. Part of the problem is the church's loss of ancient wisdom. We also note the dawn of the Anthropocene Age. For the first time in history, humans have gained such technological mastery and such numbers that we are harming the planet itself. Urban mission must face this.

Chapter Seven, "Recovering Prophetic Christianity," points the way forward. The end of Christendom may mean the rebirth of prophetic Christian witness in cities and nations of the world. I argue that recovering radically prophetic Christian faith requires understanding the earth, uncompromising biblical monotheism, robust Trinitarian faith, seeing salvation in a fully biblical way, present hope of God's kingdom, and living visibly as the body of Christ in today's cities.

Chapter Eight, "Renewing the Church, Restoring the Land," returns to the theme of land introduced in Chapter

One and discussed briefly in other chapters. Much "missional" literature is superficial because it ignores the biblical concern for *the land.* Such writing often reflects a very deficient understanding, biblically speaking, of creation and (therefore) new creation. Yet a theology of salvation is not biblical and urban mission is not holistic if it ignores the land. The chapter concludes with a new vision of mission that takes both *story* and *ecology* seriously, as Scripture in fact teaches us to do.

Chapter Nine, "Thinking Straight in a Tangled World," discusses the different ways people think and how that affects urban mission. Conflicts and misunderstandings arise partly because of different thinking modes—which in turn reflect cultural and personal differences. Unconsciously, we have been raised to think according to one set of assumptions. I explain four models of the ways we all think and act, and thus the things we take for granted: *hierarchical, linear, cyclical,* and *ecological.* These thinking modes are embedded in and reflect culture. From a different angle, we can read all of human history through these models.

In the last chapter, we revisit the question of models of the church and their relevance for urban mission. I argue that the ancient concept of *sacrament,* biblically grounded and contextualized to urban realities, can give urban Christians in a profound sense of what urban mission is and can be today.

I have added an afterword which I call "Mission Theology 2.0 – the Blogification of the Kingdom"—a collection of a dozen short blogs which amplify some of the themes in the book.

Note: All biblical citations in the book are from the New Revised Standard Version (NRSV) unless otherwise indicated.

ACKNOWLEDGEMENTS

Some of the chapters in this book are adapted from material published previously. In these cases I have substantially revised and reworked the material to advance the book's central message.

Chapter One, "The Ecology of Urban Mission," is republished from *The New Urban World Journal* 2:1 (May 2013), 47–60.

Chapter Two, "The Church as Community," first appeared as Chapter Five in *Liberating the Church: The Ecology of Church and Kingdom* (Downers Grove, Ill.: InterVarsity, 1983), 112–31. In 2015 it was substantially revised for publication in *Plough Quarterly* as a chapter in *Called to Community: The Life Jesus Wants for His People* (Walden, N.Y.: Plough Publishing House, 2016).

Chapter Three, "MacroTrends of the Twenty-First Century," has not been published previously.

Chapter Four, "The Kingdom of God Index," first appeared as "Do We Need a Kingdom of God Index?"—Chapter Eight in Rob Clements and Dennis Ngien, eds., *Between the Lectern and the Pulpit: Essays in Honour of Victor A. Shepherd* (Vancouver, B.C.: Regent College Publishing, 2014) and appears here in revised and expanded form.

Chapter Five, "Strategic Planning in Urban Mission," is an expanded version of my brief article "Strategic Planning and the Kingdom of God," *Revitalization* 14:2 (Fall 2007), 2.

Chapters Six and Seven, "The Loss of Prophetic Christianity" and "Recovering Prophetic Christianity" have not been published previously other than digitally on Academia.edu.

Chapter Eight, "Renewing the Church, Restoring the Land," is here published for the first time. However it is based upon and summarizes material found in my book with Joel Scandrett, *Salvation Means Creation Healed: The Ecology of Sin and Grace* (Eugene, Ore.: Cascade, 2011).

Chapter Nine, "Thinking Straight in a Tangled World," incorporates material previously published in "Thinking Theologically, Thinking Biblically," in Maxie D. Dunnam and Steve G. W. Moore, *A Thoughtful Faith: Cultivating Thinking Theologically* (Franklin, Tenn.: Providence House, 2005), 51–65, and in "Thinking Biblically, Thinking Missionally," in Howard A. Snyder, *Yes In Christ: Wesleyan Reflections on Gospel, Mission, and Culture* (Toronto: Clements Academic, 2011), 127–42.

Chapter Ten, "The Church as Sacrament and Sacrifice in the City," is based upon Chapter Four, "The Church as

Sacrament," in *Liberating the Church: The Ecology of Church and Kingdom* (Downers Grove, Ill.: InterVarsity, 1983), 96–111.

I wish to thank the publishers of this material for permission to reprint it here in revised form.

CHAPTER 1
The Ecology of Urban Mission

A chill winter's night has fallen as we walk out of the Hauptbahnhof, Cologne's central rail station along the Rhine. Entering the wintry plaza, we are awestruck by the massive, looming spires of Cologne Cathedral—black, white, gray, illuminated by hidden lights high on the spires.

The vision dominates everything. We and the crowds filling the square seem little crawling things, light snow falling on us all.

I think of Jacques Ellul's words, "The city is man's greatest work"—the pinnacle of human technical achievement.

Technic city. In the case of Cologne Cathedral, the technology dates back to the 1200s. The technical breakthroughs—pointed arch, ribbed vaulting, flying buttress—birthed Gothic architecture. The technology was religious, theological: a monument to glorify God.

But of course the cathedral was also commercial (think relics, pilgrimages, fund-raising), as well as political, social, cultural.

In other words, there is an *ecology* to it all: the cathedral, the city, a river, a people; birds and animals; pigeons and rats; air, food, plague, and pollution. All part of the story— and *all best grasped ecologically.*

Cologne, one of Europe's oldest cities, became a Roman colony in the days of the first Apostles. From early on the town had a Christian community. After the bones of the Three Wise Men came to Cologne as relics, the town attracted thousands of pilgrims. Building a cathedral made increasing economic, ecclesiastical, and political sense.

My wife and I visited Cologne shortly before Christmas. We were fascinated by the cathedral, the Christmas markets, and the crowds. Then incidentally we discovered that the large building next to our hotel was Gestapo headquarters from 1935 to 1945; now a museum. Displays on the rise of Nazism and basement cellblocks alerted me to other realities of urban ecology through space and time.

Urban Ecology

Ecology is a concept in space and time. Ecosystems thrive in particular places and localities; they emerge and change constantly with time. This is true of the ecology of the city and also of urban mission. We can best grasp the challenges of urban mission, in fact, if we view them ecologically.

There is such a thing as an urban ecosystem. Like all ecosystems, it involves inputs, throughputs, outputs, with complex interrelationships and feedback loops.

This is true in a city's every dimension. It is true physically with material goods, fuel, food, waste, and the networks linking them. It is true socially, with the complexity of urban social systems of all sorts. It is true economically, politically, technologically, and culturally.

I learned this in the 1980s when I pastored and worked at Olive Branch Mission in Chicago, on what was then Skid Row. Teaching urban intern students from mostly non-urban campuses, I stressed three key points: (1) Chicago is a city of neighborhoods; (2) each neighborhood is unique; yet (3) each neighborhood is enmeshed in a complex web of urban systems. You won't understand urban mission if you don't understand neighborhoods, diverse as they are. And you won't understand neighborhoods if you don't look *ecologically*, examining the complex interactions of people and systems, of physical and material things (water, roads, electricity, garbage); the whole range of life from microorganisms to dogs and cats to the flora and fauna of parklands.

Must then the urban missioner really understand all these things, be an expert in everything? No. That is impossible. It means this: Effective urban mission requires an ecological mindset, an ecological sensitivity, and at a practical working level, ecological knowledge.

An Ecological Approach to Urban Mission

Every city is an ecosystem intimately linked with a vast array of larger and smaller ecosystems. And Christians know the key, essential secret: The urban ecosystem can truthfully be understood only spiritually, in light of the revealed gospel of Jesus Christ.

What then is an ecological concept of urban mission? It is an approach that makes the concept of ecology central to every dimension so that mission can be as comprehensive as is the Christian gospel.

Formally, *ecology* is defined as the branch of science that deals with the relations of living things to one another and to their physical surroundings. This includes the study of human interaction with the environment in all its complexity. As a character in Barbara Kingsolver's novel *Flight Behavior* comments, ecology means studying "biological communities. How populations interact. It does not mean recycling aluminum cans."

Christians know that our human environment is more than just the physical world, or even the social-physical world. It includes all God has made—all things, visible and invisible, on earth and in heaven, as the Apostle Paul emphasizes (Col 1:16 and Eph 1:10, for example). The key biblical phrase "all things" opens a window into the ecological character of the biblical worldview and hence of all Christian mission.

What I mean, therefore, is that we must define Christian mission as comprehensively as the breadth and depth of the Christian gospel, and as deeply and broadly as the actual nature of the urban environment in all its dimensions; in its "all-things-ness." This is my key point.

Unless we thus think ecologically, we will forever be battling half truths, lopsidedness, over-emphasis in some areas and under-emphasis in others.

An ecological concept of urban mission has five key elements:

1. *Ecological sensitivity and awareness in considering every aspect and dimension of urban mission.* Ecology is a mindset; a sensitivity—almost like awareness of music. It's a lens; a way of seeing; as much caught as taught.

Ecological alertness means seeing *every aspect* of urban mission (no exceptions) through an ecological lens. One is forever asking: How does *this* relate to *that*? How does this action affect that situation, or those people, or that piece of urban landscape? It means knowing that every effect has multiple causes, and every cause births multiple effects— not all perceived or understood—and also multiple feedback loops.

Effective urban mission requires thinking, planning, and acting ecologically.

2. An ecological concept of urban mission means *recognizing the essential, critical role of spiritual realities in every urban ecosystem.* Ecology is the sworn enemy of dualisms and compartmentalization. Nothing in the city is *not* spiritual, one way or another. Probably at some deep level every urbanite senses this, if not during the day then in wakeful nighttime hours. The spirituality of the city stirs musicians and artists and poets.

Here enters the uniquely Christian contribution. Christians recognize not only the reality of the spirit; they know how to name the spirits. They know that the key reality is Jesus Christ made real to people by the Holy Spirit. Centered in this reality they know, or can learn, how to pull all other spiritual strands into proper perspective and relation to each other.

In other words, Christians are Christians. They dwell in the city not just with human resources, but with divine revelation. They proclaim and seek boldly to embody Jesus Christ in the city. Since they understand this revelation ecologically, they present not a one-dimensional gospel or church or mission, nor certainly a "spiritual" gospel that denies the reality and legitimate priorities of the "physical." They embody an ecological gospel that is as multidimensional and multidimensionally relevant as is the living Jesus Christ, present now in the power of the Spirit.

Effective urban mission means Christians serving as channels of "the one thing needful," the reality of spiritual life and illumination that comes uniquely through Jesus Christ.

3. An ecological approach to urban mission means *recognizing the importance of physical, social, economic, and cultural dimensions in urban mission.* Again, no dualisms. If

Christians insist on the reality and priority of things spiritual, they also insist on the reality and proper role of things physical. This of course means things cultural in all dimensions, for culture begins with physical things—food, weather, water, the materials from which we build or homes and literature and social spaces.

The unique Christian contribution involves the recognition of the constant flow between things spiritual and things material. An ecological concept of urban mission opens missional space to talk about and mess with politics, economics, poetry, technology, healthcare, water quality, building codes, orchestras, poverty, education, family life, gender relationships, and everything else. It is constantly saying: "This, and also that."

Effective urban mission means connecting the spirit to everything that is (or appears to be) non-spirit and recognizing the reality and priority of every physical dimension of God's good creation.

4. An ecological conception of urban mission means *recognizing the essential role of face-to-face community.*

Ecology is all about relationships. Ecosystems of living things are social communities. What then is human community? It is a kind of ecosystem embedded in other ecosystems. Human communities are biological communities. They are of course much more than this, so we resist reductionism. Any human community—family, neighborhood, city, church—is much more than a biological community, but it is *not less than* this.

Human community exists at many levels. The ancient Greeks understood this; witness their various terms based on *oikos* (family or household), from *oikonomos* (household steward), to *oikonomia* (economy or plan of a household or city), to *oikomene* (the inhabited earth). Hence our terms *economy* and *ecology*.

Christians stress face-to-face community for both sociological and theological reasons. Sociological, because we recognize the social power of face-to-face community. Theological, because we believe humans are created uniquely in the image of God and profoundly reflect Trinitarian truth. At heart these two reasons are one, for the very sociology of human being is theologically based: our creation in the image of Holy Trinity.

An ecological concept of urban mission means recognizing the priority of face-to-face community because that's the way we are created and how we function. In community. Life in community may often be dysfunctional, but life without community becomes suicidal. We are social beings.

Effective urban mission requires attention to all kinds of community, but especially to face-to-face community. This is where our identity is formed or malformed. Now that the Internet and various forms of virtual community are ever present, this is newly urgent. In her prophetic book *Reclaiming Conversation,* sociologist Sherry Turkle shows how cellphones and social media undercut real face-to-face community: "frequent use of social media leads to feelings of depression and social anxiety" and robs us of empathy toward others. The cure is face-to-face conversation.[1]

In an ecological conception of urban ministry, four forms of face-to-face community are most essential: Family, neighborhood, church, and small-scale communities such as clubs and civic organizations. These form the all-important infrastructure of society and are key to its health or its dysfunction. They are key, in other words, to urban ecology. So they necessarily play a large role in effective urban mission.

Redemptive urban witness will engage a whole range of issues, no doubt, from the micro to the macro level. Not only neighborhoods but also systems and macrostructures. If not grounded in face-to-face community, however,

---

[1] Sherry Turkle, *Reclaiming Conversation* (New York: Penguin, 2015), 25.

mission will ultimately be ineffective and will burn out from lack of oxygen.

Face-to-face community is, humanly speaking, the life-source of effective urban mission.

5. An ecological conception of urban mission will be *based in a functional, biblical ecclesiology.* It will teach and embody expressions of the body of Christ that reflect New Testament teaching.

There are big debates about "biblical ecclesiology," of course. What I mean is fairly simple: a focus on the church as the visible community of Jesus followers in particular places. Despite variations reflecting different traditions, I find much consensus across the spectrum of Christianity as to the essentials of (at least) local Christian community. My own take on this (in *Community of the King*) focuses on the three key elements of *worship, community,* and *witness* as the ecology of congregational life.[2]

Whatever the tradition, effective urban mission today will be grounded in local, living communities of *koinonia,* worship, and varieties of witness. Its shared life will be more organic than institutional; more relational than programmatic. But it will also find forms and structures

---

[2] Howard A. Snyder, *The Community of the King* (rev. ed., InterVarsity, 2004).

that effectively build the church and help it engage the surrounding urban context.

Key here is a focus on the priesthood of believers, the gifts of the Spirit, and (accordingly) equipping believers for ministry, as taught especially in Ephesians 4:1–16. In my experience, without fail urban churches that redemptively engage their world have figured out how to practice spiritual gifts and the ministry of all believers; how to embody the "one-another" teachings of the New Testament and to equip all believers for ministry even as they grow in grace.

Effective urban mission must be grounded in visible, redemptive Christian community.

How to embody the powerful gospel of Jesus Christ transformingly in cities today? The answer: Urban mission marked by (1) an ecological mindset, (2) focus on spiritual realities, (3) attention also to physical and cultural realities, (4) face-to-face relationships, and (5) visible Christian community that resembles in its essence the body of Christ as pictured in the New Testament. Together, these five components constitute the ecology of redemptive urban mission. These elements all function in ecological interconnection, with constant feedback loops.

Three Big Objections

This ecological approach to urban mission raises a raft of questions. Here are three:

1. *This is all too overwhelming.* If ecology necessary involves *everything*, we drown in the totality of it all. It's too big to be practical. Don't we risk losing sharp focus by looking at everything? How do we keep balance, establish priorities, keep fresh the gospel's transforming, redemptive edge?

Answer: We must see the big picture, and this is *in fact* the big picture. Theologically we can interpret it through biblical teachings, models, and metaphors. Particularly crucial are passages such as John 1, Ephesians 1, Colossians 1, and Hebrews 1. We start where those books start, with the big picture, viewed in light of the large economy and ecology of God.

From the big picture, constantly reiterated, we move to the actual practice of Christian community. This is what Paul does in his letters. We take our cue from Ephesians 4:4–7:

> There is one body and one Spirit, just as you were called to the one hope of your calling, one Lord, one faith, one baptism, one God and Father of all, who is above all and through all and in all. [The big picture.] But each of us was given grace

according to the measure of Christ's gift. [The particularization and application.]

This is how the ecology of urban mission works. It is what Paul does all the time. In Romans he begins with "the gospel of God, which he promised beforehand" (Rom 1:1–2) and ends with Priscilla and Aquila and their house church (Rom 16:3–4). We best find the particular and specific within the ecology of the big picture.

This is what Jesus did, showing the big picture (the Kingdom of God) and bringing this home to specific people and needs and building community.

In the actual practice of Christian community, working with the fruit and gifts of the Spirit in local contexts and neighborhoods, we learn how to strategize and determine priorities. The Spirit leads, joining the big picture to specific times, places, and persons. This is why I stress ecclesiology.

Ecological lenses help us here. We find ourselves nurtured by a complex ecology of grace where we neither fully understand nor control everything. So we strive to be faithful and trust the Spirit to weave the particular into the larger ecology of his redemptive purposes within the complex ecology of our world.

2. Second objection: *This approach requires major professional expertise.* Where can we find specialists in urban ecology in all its complexity? The necessary skills and knowledge are way beyond most churches, especially poor ones, those with small voices.

Two answers. One involves clarification and the other networking.

Clarification: An ecological concept of urban ministry does not mean people have to be academically trained in ecology. Ordinary people can develop practical ecological sense. Some may already have it intuitively, or as a spiritual gift. We learn, and learn to feel, that everything is tied to everything else both by immersing ourselves in Scripture and by paying attention to what we're increasingly learning about the world around us.

Second, networking. We need each other. Every church needs other churches, and may need specialized ministries that provide resources for particular challenges. Most cities, as well, are full of resources of various sorts. The key is networking on the basis of and out of the strength of local, living Christian community.

3. *Isn't this ecological approach pressing an analogy way too far?* Is it legitimate actually to take a concept from science

and apply it to urban mission? Isn't this a mismatch of categories?

No. This approach makes sense for three reasons. First, the ecological sensitivity we learn from studying living systems helpfully illuminates urban life and ministry, *both* by way of analogy and *in actual fact,* since urban mission exists within and is part of the real ecology of cities.

Second, the Bible itself radiates an ecological sensitivity based in the very nature of creation and gospel. Modern ecological science actually appropriates realities already embedded in the biblical revelation. The Bible is ecological.

Third, bringing this biblical ecological sensitivity into conversation with today's ecological science births new insights. Ecology as applied to the church and ministry is more than metaphor. It illuminates realities long overlooked.

The smallest microorganisms and micro-ecosystems reveal dynamics that function on much larger scales. Ecological principles run all through God's magnificent creation. To repeat: The city and urban mission are much more than ecological phenomena, but they are not less. We will understand both city and mission better, at more profound levels, as we view them ecologically.

The Ecology of the City

The city is an ecosystem interacting with multiple other ecosystems. This is the reality that underlies an ecological view of urban mission.

The City as Ecosystem. The city is an ecosystem physically, socially, culturally. But Christians know, as Jacques Ellul discerned, that the city is also a spiritual reality. Better: It is a spiritual ecosystem. It is the locus of principalities and powers of all sorts. Its dynamics are affected by prayer, by worship, by Christian community, and by multiple forms of Christian witness. Its life is shaped as much by spiritual things as by physical things— probably more.

This is fact, not theory. The city is a complex interplay between its physicality and its spirituality. This is what makes the church of Jesus Christ unique. As body of Christ, the church knows the secret. "We wrestle" in multiple dimensions. And the church's impact — redemptively or not—flows in all these directions; follows all these paths and byways. The church's impact is both physical and spiritual, with the two in constant interaction—as we know personally, with our own body-spirit struggles. So urban mission necessarily touches everything, including how we do or do not care for creation.

The city, in other words, is inescapably and necessarily part of the non-urban environment. City and no-city depend upon each other for their very existence. You can't have Chicago without downstate Illinois and Lake Michigan, nor Singapore without oceans. *They are all part of one ecology.* The literal, watery connection between Lake Michigan and earth's oceans reminds us that every urban ecosystem is connected with the global ecosystem.

The City and the Land. Today much of the world is rapidly urbanizing. Usually urbanization is treated however as though it were only a matter of cities.

But urbanization is always only half the story. The other story, of equal ultimate importance, concerns the land—the land that remains and does not move to the city. People move to cities and leave the land behind, but they do not leave their *dependence upon* the land. Yet as people move to cities they lose ancient wisdom about the land.

Urban ecology therefore must include the land and its wisdom. So urban mission, viewed ecologically, will include the land in its scope.

Our grandparents or great-grandparents understood much about the land. Most knew how to farm, of course.

But equally important: They knew about birds, plants, animals, the flow of rivers, the changing of seasons, the stars, and the cycles of nature. They knew about medicinal plants. They knew how to grow food, and they enjoyed the fresh tang of fruits and vegetables straight from the garden rather than food formulated in factories.

This is no longer the case for city dwellers the world over. Yet we know—both theologically and, increasingly, scientifically—that human flourishing requires living in contact with the land, with nature, and with the created order. It's built into us; part of God's plan.

Without this bond with the land and its creatures we suffer what Richard Louv calls "nature-deficit disorder." Human development, and especially childhood development, is hampered by lack of unstructured interface with the world of nature.[3]

If we speak of urbanization we must speak also of the land, and what has been lost in the move to the cities. In the study and practice of urban mission we must heed the land as well as the city. We learn that our cities depend for

---

[3] Richard Louv, *Last Child in the Woods: Saving Our Children From Nature-Deficit Disorder* (Chapel Hill, N.C.: Algonquin Books, 2008). Louv's book and Sherry Turkle's *Reclaiming Conversation* should be read together, because together they show synergistically how direct, unprogrammed interaction with both people and the land promote human wellbeing.

their very existence on land—both the land they occupy and often pollute, and the land that supplies their food and water.

This doesn't mean Christians should move out of cities and into rural areas. What must happen, rather, is the recovery of ancient wisdom about the land, and thus the recovery of a harmony between land and people. We must come to understand the real, actual ecology of our relationship with the beautiful but vulnerable created order (urban and non-urban) that God has given us.

This has big meanings for urban mission. No person and no church is healthy without healthy interaction with the land. No mission is holistic if it does not include the biblical, covenantal relationship with the land and all God's creatures (Gen 9). No city can be healthy and sustainable over time if it does not learn to live in sustainable harmony with the land.

Here is a call for creativity. It raises issues of urban farming, cooperatives, community markets, trees and flowers, artwork, music, and poetry. It presents the challenge of getting city people out to the country from time to time and country people into the cities.

Center Church: The Gospel in New York

New York City has been the scene of much effective urban mission over centuries. Some of America's earliest and most creative city ministries began there. In its great complexity, New York to this day offers varied examples of redemptive urban mission, ranging from creative church multiplication to specialized ministries of many sorts.[4]

One of the most creative and comprehensive is Redeemer Presbyterian Church in Manhattan, led by senior pastor Timothy Keller. Founded in 1989 without a building, the church grew rapidly. Today it attracts some 5,000 people to multiple services at three different sites. But much of its emphasis is on discipleship and church multiplication. Its conception of discipleship is serious but broad, for the church aims "to renew the city socially, spiritually and culturally." Redeemer has helped plant over a hundred other congregations throughout the New York area.

In his book *Center Church: Doing Balanced, Gospel-Centered Ministry in Your City,* Keller sets out a strategy for reaching cities multidimensionally, using ecological models. Keller outlines a vision embodying three core

---

[4] See for example Mark R. Gornik, *Word Made Global: Stories of African Christianity in New York City* (Grand Rapids: Eerdmans, 2011).

commitments: Gospel-centered, city-centered, and movement-centered. He understands this vision ecologically.

Keller argues that cities can be transformed when a tipping point is reached—"when the number of gospel-shaped Christians in a city becomes so large that Christian influence on the civic and social life of the city—and on the very culture—is recognizable and acknowledged." Keller writes:

> There is no scientific way to precisely determine a city's tipping point—the point at which the gospel begins to have a visible impact on the city life and culture. In New York City, we pray for and work toward the time when 10 percent of the center city population is involved in a gospel-centered church. In Manhattan, this would amount to about 100,000 people.[5]

Keller's proposals breathe the spirit of Gospel optimism—based not on human ingenuity, but in the power of God working through Christians who are savvy both about the gospel and about urban dynamics.

There is nothing unrealistic or outlandish about this vision. The Gospel is powerful enough. Where sin abounds, grace can visibly abound yet more.

---

[5] Timothy Keller, *Center Church: Doing Balanced, Gospel-Centered Ministry in Your City* (Grand Rapids: Zondervan, 2012), 376.

Keller's vision and proposals are worth considering, particularly in light of Redeemer Church's impact and given Keller's sensitivity to the dynamic of movements and of ecological realities. The book is a good resource in developing an ecological conception of urban mission.

Keller's approach is limited in some respects; people from other theological traditions may not be comfortable with aspects of the church's conservative Reformed perspective. Keller's emphasis on the ecology of church, city, and movements, however, acknowledges the complexity of urban mission and the fact that God works through various church forms and traditions.

I celebrate Keller's ecological approach, but would press it further. Keller uses the concept of ecology only analogically. "Likening a gospel city movement to a biological ecosystem is an analogy," he writes. The church and Gospel ministry are different from "a biological ecosystem." Yet he notes that "The image of the ecosystem conveys how different organisms are interdependent, how the flourishing of one group helps the other groups flourish."[6]

True, but we must push the ecological paradigm further, beyond analogy. Effective urban mission requires

---

[6] Keller, 378.

that we break through to a real ecological awareness of church, city, and mission.

Much of the dynamic of Viv Grigg's prophetic ministry among the world's urban poor, highlighted in his article "Hovering Spirit, Creative Voice, Empowered Transformation: A Retrospective" in the first issue of *The New Urban World Journal,* springs from his large-scale ecological sensitivity and models. Though Grigg does not generally use the term *ecology* in the sense I mean here, his ministry in its comprehensiveness can best be understood by viewing it through an ecological lens.[7]

Conclusion: Ecology of the Church in Mission

Urban mission is more comprehensive and effective the more it's viewed ecologically. Just as the city is an ecosystem so in another sense the church, body of Christ, is an ecosystem—globally, regionally, locally. How the two interact defines the shape of mission.

Christians without ecological awareness miss key dimensions of mission just as surely as secular ecologists miss key dimensions of the spirit. As ecology is more than metaphor, so body of Christ is more than metaphor. The

---

[7] Viv Grigg, "Hovering Spirit, Creative Voice, Empowered Transformation: A Retrospective," *New Urban World Journal* 1:1 (November 2012), 17–26.

church is an organism that partakes of the mystery of the very body of Jesus Christ and the mystery of the Trinity—and as such, is called into mission.

In the New Testament, body of Christ and Christian community are intertwined truths. In the next chapter we look more deeply at the meaning of Christian community.

CHAPTER 2
The Church as Community

By definition, the body of Christ is a community.

In my book *Liberating the Church: The Ecology of Church and Kingdom* (InterVarsity, 1983) I described what I called four liberating models of the church: The church as sacrament, as community, as servant, and as witness. The Bible provides some basis for all these models. We'll consider the church as sacrament at the end of this book.

But the central New Testament model of the church is *community*: a community of disciples gathered around Jesus, committed to him, his way, and his kingdom. This is a core meaning of the dominant New Testament image of the church: body of Christ. Though "body of Christ" means more than community, Christian community is its genius and key dynamic.

Hunger for community is an inborn need and appetite. Drawing toward intimacy is fundamental to human personality and a central aspect of God's image in us. But in today's society many people avoid community because they fear it or simply have never really experienced it. Rather than drawing together into nurturing groups, they are "cluster-phobic."

Deep hunger for human intimacy raises the question of community for the church. Many people, Christians as well as nonbelievers, long for more intimate and meaningful relationships with other persons. They want to find a group whose meaning and mission transcend the daily grind and the routine rat race. Something within them says there must be something more, a level of sharing and common life that goes beyond what they have known.

Crisis of Community in Society

Significant social indicators point to a breakdown of community today—in the home, the school, the neighborhood, the church. This goes hand in hand with the advance of a technological society which focuses either on the individual or on the mass even as it speeds the disintegration of small, intimate groupings. The illusion of total, unrestricted individual freedom ("Have it your way") in fact leads to totalitarian mass society in which close-knit intermediate communities of meaning—the glue of society—are dissolved, as Jacques Ellul wrote prophetically in *Propaganda*.[1]

Obeying the enticing commands of ever-present, constantly repeated ads, people fail to perceive that the freedom offered is the freedom to do what someone else wants (for a price) and what everyone else is doing. So "Have it your way" really means "Do it our way—and feel good about it!"

Now digital social media—especially ubiquitous cellphones and constant use of texting and apps—adds a whole new dimension. I mentioned earlier Sherry Turkle's remarkable new book, *Reclaiming Conversation*. "When we have our mobile devices with us, we see that we turn away from our children, romantic partners, and work colleagues," Turkle notes. "Studies show that the mere presence of a phone on the table (even a phone turned off) changes what people talk about. If we think we might be interrupted, we keep conversation light, on topics of little controversy or

---

[1] Jacques Ellul, *Propaganda: The Formation of Men's Attitudes* (New York: Alfred A. Knopf, 1971; original French edition 1962), especially pp. 6–9.

consequence." Real understanding and empathy don't develop. Turkle cites evidence of a sharp decline in empathy among college students that seems linked to the rise of digital communication.[2]

But social media and technological materialism, with their morality of means, are only part of the problem. Many forces are at work to undermine community, both in society and in the church. This can be clarified by playing a little game. How would one go about undermining community, isolating people from each other and from shared life with others?

The first thing, of course, would be to fragment family life. The family is the fundamental unit and microstructure of society, the first form of human community. Undermining community begins with undermining the family. One would fragment the family by drawing off its members in different directions and into different worlds.

Another way to break down community would be to move people away from the neighborhoods where they grew up. Cut the roots. Instead of allowing people to live near relatives and friends and among familiar landmarks and symbols, move them to new neighborhoods. And then,

---

[2] Sherry Turkle, *Reclaiming Conversation* (New York: Penguin, 2015), 17, 21.

for further disintegration, separate the places people work from where they live. Partition off people's lives into as many worlds as possible.

Another way to undermine community is to move people gradually farther and farther apart through larger and larger yards, bigger houses, or through walls, fences, and "apartments." Here affluence is a great aid in dissolving community.

The automobile further extends the process. The more houses, stores, schools, and places of employment or entertainment are physically separated, the more people travel separately to those places in cars, especially in suburbia. Adding a second or third car furthers the process, cutting down even more on the time family members spend together.

If we really wanted to break down community, we would certainly bring TV and the Internet into the home. Television is perhaps the modern world's most effective communication blocker. We think of TV as a means of communication. More accurately, it is a means of blocking communication—if communication means two-way interaction.

The explosion of Internet-based "social media" in recent decades has failed to build genuine community in the biblical sense. It was clear from the beginning that such online media would be used primarily for selling products and services—in other words, for the promotion of what I call technological materialism. On the other hand, social media and other Internet avenues do provide strategic opportunities for Christian witness and the articulation of Christian values in art, music, education, economics, and other areas. (Consider the negative example of the effective use of social media by the ISIS terrorist cult.)

The final clincher, then, in the fragmentation process would be to cut down on family size. Two parents and several children make a small community. But with one or no children in the home, and the circumstances traced above, real community life expires altogether.

We must not underestimate the role of entertainment and social media in this disintegrative process. The role of the visual media in breaking down community in society is twofold. First, visual media undermine community simply because they are passive rather than participatory. They block communication. Second, the visual media push values to the sensate level. Because television and movies are almost totally the tools of technological materialism, programming constantly moves toward the sensate. The media challenge accepted mores of society and push the barriers just beyond what is accepted as normal in real life, titillating. The visual media operate less and less at the level of ideas and concepts; more and more at the emotional and sensual levels. And the less the viewers think, the more they respond at the sensate level.

The media could operate more constructively and responsibly, but in today's culture they largely assist the breakdown of community.

All this is part of the crisis of community in society. And it is both related to and compounded by the crisis of community in the church. The question of the role of the church is significant, for *undermining community in the church destroys the best hope for community in the world*—the best chance for rebuilding community in society. When the church is a genuine community experiencing real *koinonia*, it is the most potent source of community in the world.

Crisis of Community in the Church

We face a crisis of community, of discipling fellowship, in the church today. Lack of community testifies partly to a lack of understanding of the church itself, partly to the individualism, and partly to the pressure of broader social currents. The Western church finds itself in a world where Christian consensus has melted away.

We may of course question whether the consensus that held Western society together was really Christian. But certainly that society was shaped and influenced in large measure by Christian values, even if only partially and imperfectly. In the United States, some Christian values permeated the culture rather thoroughly. At least there's been a strong sense of the worth of the individual. One simply did not snuff out another person's life easily.

In an earlier age, Christians could assume that when a person became a Christian or came up through a Christian family, their basic values were at least compatible with Christian beliefs. It wasn't quite as crucial that the church lacked a real basis in community. A church without a genuine experience of community could at least function as a Christian church with some decree of integrity because society's values reinforced and overlapped those of the church.

No more. Christian consensus is gone. A person growing up in North America or in most of the world's cities today simply does not have either a Christian worldview or set of Christian values instilled by the culture. Someone entering the church from such a background begins almost at point zero in Christian life and understanding. This means that the church must increasingly take seriously its true nature as a community and counterculture that reinforces and perpetuates its own values and virtues. Otherwise the church simply accommodates itself to the culture. This is what is happening, and this is the church's crisis.

In sum, the church is confronted by the breakdown of Christian consensus in society, and this is compounded by the absence of real community in the church. Increasingly we will hear calls for the church to recognize its true situation and danger. It must be a community with the social strength to incarnate values that are antagonistic at key points to the world around us.

Merely *adopting such a viewpoint* will mean nothing, however. The church must in fact *be* a community that experiences and reinforces biblical values. No group with values which differ significantly from its host society can endure long in that society unless the group is a counter-community. Our values and worldview are molded by our community context. A group of Christians cannot exist in society and maintain Christian virtues unless they are part of a community that reinforces those virtues. This is simply a matter of the sociology of knowledge.

I believe this is a crucial point. "Certainly it is not impossible for individual Christians to maintain biblical beliefs even if a hostile majority disagrees," Ron Sider wrote. "But if the church is to consist of communities of loving defiance in a sinful world, then it must pay more attention to the quality of its fellowship."[3] The relation of Christian community not only to kingdom living but also to doctrinal integrity will increasingly have to be examined.

Doctrinal orthodoxy is no defense. If Christians cease to act like Christians, sooner or later they will stop believing like Christians. So community is a crucial concern. To be Christian at the level of virtues and values that influence our behavior means to be part of a community that reinforces Christian virtues and values as they confront non-Christian alternatives.

The New Testament Community

The New Testament pictures the church as the community gathered around Jesus. We see this for example in Matthew 18:15–20, Acts 2:42, Philippians 2:1–11, and Ephesians 4:1–16.

Matthew 18:20 is perhaps the Bible's most compact definition of the church: "Where two or three come

---

[3] Ronald J. Sider, *Rich Christians in an Age of Hunger* (Downers Grove, Ill.: InterVarsity, 1977), 193.

together in my name, there am I with them."[4] What makes a church? One person is not enough. Even one person alone with Jesus ("just me and Jesus") is not the church. Church is community. Where two or three come together in Jesus's name, there church begins. The church is a community of people gathered around Jesus, committed to him, worshiping him, and ready to serve his kingdom in the world, heeding the small voice that calls to Christ-like mission.

People gathered around Jesus is the irreducible minimum of the church. Then arise questions of preaching, sacraments, liturgy, ordination, doctrine, church government, and many other things that divide Christians into denominational families. Some say you can't have the church without the sacraments; others say you can. But Jesus says that at heart the church is the community of people gathered in his name and in his presence, sharing his life.

In its actual history as pictured in the New Testament, the early church was truly the community of Jesus. This is

---

[4] This is a key verse in Karl Barth's ecclesiology. Barth quotes or refers to the verse over a dozen times in his discussion of the church. The verse seems to have appealed to Barth because it suggests the weakness and humility of the church while also stating its glory: Jesus Christ is there. Especially it emphasizes the central fact of the church's being: its gathering together in Jesus's name.

not of course to deny its roots in Jewish culture. On the contrary, the church was born in first-century Jewish society. Its early character and style were largely Jewish. Although the church quickly (but not painlessly) transcended its Jewishness as it crossed racial and national lines, still its strong Jewish roots must be understood.

In fact, the early church drew much strength from these Jewish roots. The church was born in a culture with a strong sense of community and with an ethos of peoplehood. Jews in Jesus's day were keenly aware they were a people. They knew they were a covenant people; they existed as a nation because God had acted in history. The Old Testament writings record this history, showing how God had acted in faithfulness to his covenant, in both blessing and judgment.

The church was born in this Jewish matrix. The new reality believers discovered in Jesus Christ was built on this foundation of community and peoplehood that God had been building through the millennia of Old Testament history, and preeminently through the two thousand years from Abraham to Jesus Christ.

Even though the church outgrew its Jewish character, it brought over understandings, concepts, practices, and even structures from the Jewish community which became basic to the church. For example, the church initially built its worship on the synagogue model. Churches were at first largely Christian synagogues.[5] When we look at the first Christians, we do not see a group of people alienated from their cultural context, but rather a community rooted in a specific culture. This particular cultural context provided the base from which the church moved out to become more than merely the Jewish sect that it initially appeared to be.[6]

From the beginning, however, the church was much more than simply a Jewish sect because it was the community of *Jesus's* disciples. Jesus was the key. Here was not just another rabbi or philosopher, but the incarnate Son of God announcing a new order and kingdom. The impressive thing about Jesus's three years with his disciples is not just the miracles and the teaching and the crowds, but *the embryonic community Jesus himself formed.* This was a new social reality consisting of the Twelve plus a larger community of disciples beyond the apostolic core. Tracing the word *disciple* through the Gospel of Luke reveals a community of several concentric circles of disciples, beginning with the Twelve.

---

[5] On the synagogue pattern see Snyder, *The Problem of Wineskins,* 197–98n6, and *Community of the King* (1977 ed.), 151–52.
[6] See Robert Banks, *Paul's Idea of Community: The Early House Churches in Their Historical Setting* (Grand Rapids: Eerdmans, 1980).

The church pictured in Acts and the Epistles was based on this community Jesus had formed. The disciples after Pentecost simply repeated what Jesus had done with them. Acts 2:42, and in fact the first several chapters in Acts, show the pattern. Jesus himself provided for the many converts of Pentecost by preparing a community of people—not a disconnected corps of experts, but a prepared community of disciples. How different from most missionary and evangelistic methods today!

Picture the Pentecost scene. Your small church of a few hundred members suddenly gains three thousand converts in one day. A few days later several thousand more are added. Soon the church has grown to twenty or thirty thousand. And you don't even have a board of directors, an organizational manual, a budget, a doctrinal statement, committees or buildings. Can you survive?

From our perspective, the church on the day of Pentecost was hopelessly handicapped. It should not have survived. But Jesus had prepared for Pentecost. He had prepared his disciples not only to receive the Pentecostal outpouring of the Spirit; he had also prepared them as a community. The church at Pentecost knew the basics and was not distracted, as we often are, into looking elsewhere.

Jesus could have left a book of instructions or set up an organization. He could have created a readymade system so that when the thousands of converts appeared, the church would have known exactly what to do.

But Jesus worked at a more fundamental level. He gathered a community of believers, working intensively with them so that they would understand who he was and why he had come. God, through Jesus Christ, had such confidence in the Twelve that he left it to them and their fellow disciples to figure out organizational questions. They could handle the problems as they came up, guided by the Holy Spirit and following Jesus's teaching and example. In the book of Acts we see believers using their own intelligence but guided by the Holy Spirit in nurturing the growth of the church.

Here is a vital lesson about church life and structure, about wine and wineskins. It is easy to look at Pentecost and see the Spirit but miss the structure. It is easy to be amazed at what was new but blind to what was old. At Pentecost the disciples clearly got a taste of new wine. But Jesus provided also the basis for new wineskins in the community he had formed—wineskins created not out of thin air but from patterns, customs, and understandings derived from centuries of God's acts in history. As he delights to do, the Ancient of Days did a new thing. Jesus drew on centuries, even millennia, of God's work in forming his new community—and then baptized the little group with his Spirit at Pentecost.

And so the first disciples did what Jesus did. As Jesus had been with them in small groups, and as they had met together outdoors and in homes, so did the first Christians. The early church took shape primarily in the homes of the believers. Its life was nourished in homes in two ways. First, the church was built through normal family life, drawing on the strength of the family in that day. Second, it was fed through *koinonia* groups, cells of people who met together for prayer, worship and the Eucharist and who passed on Jesus's teaching by example and word of mouth.

The church's experience of community as it developed and spread through the Roman world was complemented by the sense of being a distinct people. The Epistles reveal a strong countercultural consciousness in the early church, a consciousness that developed and deepened as the church spread across the empire. Initially Jewish Christians saw themselves simply as Jews who accepted the Messiah. But as the church grew and spread, it learned that God's plan was not just for the Jews. It was for the Gentiles, for all peoples, nations, and classes. The book of Acts shows the gospel spreading beyond Jewish confines and beginning to develop a people consciousness.

This consciousness dawned gradually; it didn't come all at once. Through the ministry of Peter, Paul, Barnabas, Philip and others (Acts 8–15) the church came to see that it was a new community and people. The Holy Spirit was poured out equally on Jew and Gentile (Acts 10:44–47; 11:15–18; 19:5–6). The believing community was not just a subcommunity among the Jews but a new work of God in history. Christians began to think of themselves as a third race: neither Jew nor Gentile, but something new transcending both.[7] They were the new Israel, the new people of God fulfilling Old Testament promises and expectations, but as a new social reality transcending the separate identities and allegiances of Jew and Gentile, slave and free, male and female. The church became not just a subculture within the dominant culture, but a new counterculture in the Greco-Roman world. Christians were "neither Jew nor Greek, slave nor free, male nor female," but "all one in Christ Jesus" (Gal 3:28; note also 1 Cor 12:13; Eph 2:14; Col 3:11). This was not merely spiritual renewal. It was social revolution.

---

[7] W. A. Visser 't Hooft, *The Renewal of the Church* (Philadelphia: Westminster Press, 1956), 54.

The tragedy today is that this consciousness has all but evaporated from the church, especially in North America. Given a test of loyalties, many Christians would place their identity as Americans or Canadians, or as members of a particular socioeconomic, employment, political, racial or ethnic group, above their identity as God's people. A sad symptom of the loss of true community and peoplehood in the church is the way Christians easily accept massive gaps between rich and poor in the church and society as normal, or at least as not a pressing gospel concern. The early Christians took steps so that "there were no needy persons among them" (Acts 4:34) and shared with those in need, even in other countries (Acts 11:28–30; 24:17; Rom 12:13; 15:26; 1 Cor 16:3). Today relatively few Christians are so moved.

In North America and many other places, most of the Christian church is a subculture rather than a counterculture. A *subculture* is in fundamental agreement with the dominant culture on major issues and values, but has distinct secondary values and characteristics. By contrast, a *counterculture* is in tension with the dominant culture at the level of fundamental values, even though it may share many secondary characteristics with that culture. The church functions as a subculture, not as a counterculture, when it fails to oppose the dominant culture at those points where the culture pays allegiance to alien gods rather than to the kingdom of God.

The Church as Countercultural Community

But should the church really be a counterculture? Some say no, wanting to preserve the church's vital, transforming link to society. That's a legitimate concern. But faithfulness both to the New Testament picture of the church and to the church's kingdom mission points to the church as a counterculture. Understood biblically, the model of the church as countercultural community is both dynamic and missiologically faithful.

The term *counterculture* is an inheritance from the Sixties—the days of hippies, antiwar protest, the drug scene and the Jesus Revolution. Observers were quick to see that a sizable number of young people were switching to a set of values which constituted not a mere subculture but rather a counterculture. This development was analyzed in such publications as Theodore Roszak's 1969 book, *The Making of a Counter-culture.*[8]

---

[8] Theodore Roszak, *The Making of a Counter-culture* (New York: Doubleday Anchor, 1969).

Counterculture is a useful term in probing the calling and experience of the church. In his study of the Sermon on the Mount, *Christian Counter-Culture,* John Stott wrote, "If the church realistically accepted [Jesus's] standards and values as here set forth, and lived by them, it would be the alternative society he always intended it to be, and would offer to the world an authentic Christian counterculture."[9] Instead of doing this, the church throughout history has too often developed clever ways of explaining why Jesus didn't really mean what he said or why his teachings no longer apply. Fortunately, there have been prophetic exceptions to this pattern of unfaithfulness.

As applied to the church, counterculture is both a positive and a negative concept. Perhaps the negative side is more obvious: As a counterculture the church takes its stand *against* surrounding culture. The Christian community must be in some sense "other than" the world around it, maintaining fundamental points of antithesis.

But counterculture is also positive. A counterculture offers a genuine alternative to the dominant culture. In fundamental ways, the counterculture claims to be not only other than but also better than the world's culture. In

---

[9] John R. W. Stott, *Christian Counter-Culture: The Message of the Sermon on the Mount* (Downers Grove, Ill.: InterVarsity, 1978), 10.

offering a clearly delineated, visible alternative, the counterculture pushes society to self-examination, self-criticism, and very often self-defense. Hidden or only dimly perceived questions rise to the surface. In this way the counterculture has a significant social impact, good or bad.

Conversely, the counterculture is influenced by its contact with the larger culture and often defines itself in reaction to the prevailing view. If the dominant culture emphasizes a work ethic, for instance, the counterculture may champion "dropping out" of the job market and the economic system generally. If the dominant culture stresses materialism and sensuality, the counterculture may move toward asceticism and mysticism. If "correct" culture wears suits, ties, white shirts, and carefully manicured hair, the counterculture may sport blue jeans, bright colors, beads and beards. Of course, with time the countercultural trends may be taken over, popularized, and exploited by the dominant culture, as happened in the United States from about 1970 to 1975.

In what sense should the church be a counterculture? Is the fidelity of the church to the kingdom a matter of a countercultural existence? Or is this an unwholesomely negative way to picture the church's life?

The answer depends on the biblical image of the church. Does the Bible picture the church counterculturally? Five Scriptures answer the question.

John 15:18–19—In the world, not of it. "If the world hates you, keep in mind that it hated me first. If you belonged to the world, it would love you as its own. As it is, you do not belong to the world, but I have chosen you out of the world. That is why the world hates you." With this we may compare John 17:14–16, "I have given them your word and the world has hated them, for they are not of the world any more than I am of the world. My prayer is not that you take them out of the world but that you protect them from the evil one. They are not of the world, even as I am not of it."

These passages show that Jesus's disciples must maintain a critical tension: *in* the world but not *of* it. Christians are neither to withdraw from the world nor to become one with it. Jesus said, "My kingdom is not of this world" (Jn 18:36), but he made it plain that it is *in* the world (Lk 17:21). Jesus plants us in a place of tension. We are to maintain that tension against the strong pull to a more comfortable position either out of the world or totally of the world. This is the tension of incarnation, and it requires the church to be in some sense a counterculture.

Romans 12:2—Conformed to Christ, not the world. "Do not be conformed to this world, but be transformed by the renewing of your minds." With this we may compare Romans 8:29, "For those whom he foreknew he also predestined to be conformed to the image of his Son, in order that he might be the firstborn within a large family." The church is to avoid conformity to the world by being conformed to Jesus Christ through the renewing work of the Holy Spirit in the minds and lives of Christians. The statement that Jesus is "the firstborn within a large family" suggests that the church is a brother- and sisterhood, a family, a community.

The church is to be a community of people who are conformed to the pattern of Jesus, not the pattern of the world's culture. Is this merely another way of saying that we are to be in the world but not of it? Certainly Paul's statement here presupposes what Jesus said in John 15 and 17. But we find an added note: Jesus calls us to *be* conformed to himself, to be like him. Jesus's disciples are not of the world *just as* Jesus himself was not of the world (Jn 17:16). We are to be conformed to the image of God. We are "in all things" to "grow up into him who is the Head, that is, Christ" (Eph 4:15).

So here conformity to Christ means nonconformity to the world's culture. This also suggests that the church is a countercultural community.

Luke 12:29–32—the flock of the kingdom. "Do not set your heart on what you will eat or drink; do not worry about it. For the pagan world runs after all such things, and your Father knows that you need them. But seek his kingdom, and these things will be given to you as well. Do not be afraid, little flock, for your Father has been pleased to give you the kingdom."

Here Jesus pictures his disciples as the flock of the kingdom, the kingdom community. What an amazing contrast of weakness and strength—a flock and a kingdom! You are a little flock, Jesus says, but in your very weakness and dependence on me you will inherit the kingdom of God, no less! (Compare 2 Cor 12:9.)

The church is the community which has traded the values of the present world for the truth of the kingdom. So the church is a counterculture. It pledges its allegiance to a sovereign different from that of the citizens of this world kingdom, the dominion of darkness.

This goes beyond what has been said already, adding two more elements. First, the church's distinctness from the world is not merely a difference; it is a warfare, a world struggle. A battle is raging between the kingdom of God and the powers of the enemy. Second, in this warfare the church must be faithful to its King and Lord. It must be faithful to the New Covenant. As a covenant community, the church has pledged itself to live by the values of God's reign and to renounce the values of the world's culture. This is the basis for its concern with justice, truth, reconciliation, and God's new order.

John 17:18—Sent into the world. Many Scriptures teach that Christians are sent into the world as Christ's witnesses and ambassadors. In his prayer recorded in John 17 Jesus says, "As you sent me into the world, I have sent them into the world." We are sent to be witnesses and to make disciples in all nations. In other words, the church is to be engaged aggressively with the world in winning the allegiance of increasing numbers of people away from the world and to Jesus as Lord and King. Its task is to win people not just to the church but to the full kingdom and economy of God. This comes about through the regenerating work of the Holy Spirit in human lives. We are called to make disciples, not just converts, and disciples of the kingdom, not just of the church.

As God's counterculture the church is not merely to be in the world; it is to pursue the mission of God in the world. It is the agent of God's kingdom in bringing all things under the headship of Jesus Christ (Eph 1:10).

Revelation 21:23–27—Contributing to Culture. Revelation 21 beautifully pictures the holy city. We read, "The city does not need the sun or the moon to shine on it, for the glory of God gives it light, and the Lamb is its lamp. The nations will walk by its light, and the kings of the earth will bring their splendor into it. On no day will its gates ever be shut, for there will be no night there. The glory and honor of the nations will be brought into it. Nothing impure will ever enter it, nor will anyone who does what is shameful or deceitful, but only those whose names are written in the Lamb's book of life."

We may not understand all this passage means, but one thing is brightly clear. The holy city—the consummated Kingdom of God—will include "the glory and honor of the nations."[10] This suggests a positive evaluation of cultural diversity and of human cultural works. All that is good in human works—whatever is pure, lovely, true, honorable, and harmonious—will be brought into the city of God. Everything false, ugly, and distorted will be rejected. God will somehow gather all our cultural works, purify them, and use them in his kingdom.

---

[10] Isaiah 60 is the background here. Note especially v. 11.

This means Christians themselves have a positive contribution to make to culture. In being a Christian counterculture, the church can legitimately be engaged in cultural works that add beauty, harmony and ecological health to the world. This also is kingdom work. When we speak of the priesthood of all believers and the ministry of all God's people, we must understand that kingdom ministry is not confined to religious things or church work. It includes all good work in the world which holds potential for glorifying God.

The Kingdom Community

The danger of a countercultural model is that it may lead inward, away from worldly engagement. The antidote to this danger is a deep consciousness that the church exists for the kingdom. The model of countercultural community is essentially negative, despite its positive possibilities. It is therefore an inadequate model by itself. But as part of the total picture of what it means to be the church in a hostile world, it is an important perspective. The church can be free for the kingdom only if it is sufficiently detached and distinct from the world's culture to maintain obedience for the kingdom.

The key fact, then, is the church as *kingdom community*. In most cultural settings, a faithful church will be a countercultural church. The more important point however is simply that the church be faithful to the kingdom, whatever this means for its position in society.

Often the church's notion of community is shockingly shallow. It fails to see how radical it is to build a community for the kingdom. It misses the deeply social, economic, and political dimensions of New Testament *koinonia*. Being the *community* of God's people is a social and political reality because to be a Christian is to be part of a social group.

Government controls or regulates people in social groupings. Thus a purely individualistic faith is politically irrelevant, while the shared faith of God's people is a sociopolitical declaration, reality, and threat. Individual, isolated Christians are seldom persecuted. Christian communities which dare to follow an alternate Christian sociopolitical life together constitute a political challenge to the status quo and are always in danger of persecution or extermination, as too many historical examples show.

The church for the kingdom is inevitably political, social, economic, and ecological. *Political,* because it deals with ultimate meaning and allegiance and aims to change the present order. *Social,* because it forms people into close-knit intense social groups organized around questions of values and life meaning, not just around secondary tasks. *Economic,* because it involves the stewardship of money and resources and some level of mutual economic sharing and liability. *Ecological,* because it's a key player in the larger ecology of God's healing of creation.

Biblically, there is no *koinonia* without some form of economic sharing. If the church poses no threat to the enemy in these areas, its allegiance to Jesus Christ is deeply suspect. We are, after all, involved not merely with a religious organization but with the *people* of God, the *community* of the Spirit and the *kingdom* of Jesus Christ, our sovereign Lord.

Years ago Jim Wallis addressed this issue prophetically in his book *The Call to Conversion.* He suggested that we ask Christians, "What is the most important social reality in your life? What place, what group of people do you feel most dependent upon for your survival?" In asking this question, Wallis says, he finds that most Christians respond by indicating their workplace or some other nonchurch organization or institution, "usually something associated with economic livelihood, personal advancement, or social influence." Then Wallis makes his key point:

> If in fact most Christians are more rooted in the principalities and powers of this world than they are in the local community of faith, it is no wonder that the church is in trouble. Clearly, the social reality in which we feel most rooted will be the one that will most determine our values, our priorities, and the way we will live. It is not enough to talk of Christian fellowship while our security is based elsewhere. We will continue to conform to the values and institutions of our society as long as our people's security is grounded in them.[11]

This rings true both spiritually and sociologically. It is important to emphasize Wallis's point. This is not simply the common sermon line that, regardless of our involvements in the world, our deepest commitment *should* be to the church, and we *should* remember to keep that commitment first. That is merely a mental exercise devoid of real historical significance.

The point is the one Jesus makes: Where your security is, there your heart is. Jesus didn't divide people's allegiances into political, economic, and spiritual compartments, merely saying, Don't forget to check the

---

[11] Jim Wallis, *The Call to Conversion* (New York: Harper & Row, 1981), 117.

spiritual box. He said plainly, "Do not store up riches for yourselves here on earth. For your heart will always be where your riches are. You cannot serve both God and money" (Mt 6:19, 21, 24 TEV).

The question is basic loyalties. Do we find our fundamental meaning and security in the kingdom community or in material and economic resources? It is a choice between the Kingdom of God and the kingdom of this world. Wallis says,

> We have to create a base that is internally strong enough to enable us to survive as Christians and to empower us to be actively engaged in the world. The community is the place where the healing of our own lives becomes the foundation for the healing of the nations. The making of community is finally the only thing strong enough to resist the system and to provide an adequate spiritual foundation for better and more human ways to live.
>
> There is no greater moral authority than that given by standing before the world free of its securities. There is no greater threat to the system than that of being free of its rewards and punishments, and therefore free of its control. And there is no greater power than that which comes

from being free to offer ourselves for what we know to be true.[12]

Only one kind of community can possibly have such strength and exercise it redemptively, and that is the community of Jesus that lives for God's reign. This is what it means to discern and live by the economy of God.

Building Urban Community Today

The church has redemptive significance not when community is a theoretical perspective but only when it is an empirical fact—a social and historical reality. It means little to call the church a community if socially speaking it is not. The community model is helpful only if it serves as the basis for building authentic community in the church.

This is where an understanding of local church ecology comes in. Building community means applying basic biblical principles of church life based on the key components of worship, witness, and *koinonia*, shared life. Building genuine Christian community today involves especially the following aspects.[13]

---

[12] Jim Wallis, "Rebuilding the Church," *Sojourners* 9:1 (January 1980), 12.

[13] By "building community" here I mean building the total Christian community, including the aspects of worship and witness. The basic elements of worship, community, and witness are ecological, influencing each other. Here I am speaking more particularly of the aspect of community (discipline, gifts, and sanctification), but more

Commitment and Covenant. Christian community starts at the point of commitment and covenant. There is no genuine Christian community without a covenant. Whether this is a formal or an informal commitment is secondary. The point is, Christian community cannot exist without commitment to Jesus as Lord and to each other as sisters and brothers. And this must be more than a general mental commitment. It must be specific and explicit involving our time, energy, and resources. Covenant is not a nebulous feel-good commitment to each other; it takes specific shape in history.

Shared Life. This means, first of all, spending time together. The church exists in time and space and must necessarily come together in time and space. Real community means shared time, shared meals, shared priorities, plus some level of economic sharing, some genuine economic mutual interdependence. While specific patterns of such sharing may vary, *koinonia* in the New Testament sense does not exist without this level of shared life. Such life finds its real meaning in the balance of shared worship, nurture, and witness.

---

broadly of the total life of the church, including all aspects of the model, viewed from the perspective of community.

The Dimension of Transcendence. It is possible to have *human* community based on covenant and shared life without having *Christian* community. But we are talking about building the church, the community of Jesus and his kingdom. Human community is kingdom community only when it is formed around Jesus and lives by the Spirit for the sake of God's reign.

The church transcends mere human community when the horizontal, human dimension is married to the vertical dimension through Jesus Christ. This transcendent dimension constitutes the church and builds the church into a true community of the Spirit. It causes the Christian community to look not just inward or outward but also upward to God and ahead to God's future in the promised kingdom. The presence of Jesus Christ through the Holy Spirit creates true New Testament *koinonia* in the church.

To be the community of the Spirit the church must live in the atmosphere of worship. The first priority of the church is always worship. If community itself, or the church's witness in the world, takes the place of worship, the dimension of transcendence may be lost. The church then forfeits both its unique character and its peculiar power.

Service in Community Building

Servanthood is an essential mark of authentic Christian community and should characterize the church's internal life and its life in the world. The church is called to be a community in the world at the service of God's reign.

The church's most potent role as community is in community building, particularly at the levels of family, church, and neighborhood. Although society's macrostructures must be changed or replaced before universal justice can reign, much of the battle for justice today takes place at the level of the microstructures of family, church, and neighborhood. These structures are the building blocks of a just society and the school where justice, mercy, and truth are learned. Christians can and must work in other areas, but if the church fails to make its unique contribution in building community at these foundational levels, it will have little significant impact at broader levels.

If the church is seen primarily as an institution, its ministry will be largely institutional and program-oriented. But if the church is viewed as community, its ministry will be person-oriented, focusing on building structures of human interaction. In this perspective, the structures of family, church, and neighborhood are most basic. All are fairly intimate forms of human community based on face-to-face personal relationships. Together they provide the glue of society.

We can see how these foundational structures are being undermined today. But the church as community has the answer. More specifically:

Family Building. The church builds families first by recognizing that the church is the family of God and that the family is the church of God. Family was the original form of human community. Both in Scripture and in history the family precedes the church. Indeed, the Old Testament initially makes no distinction between church and family.

To understand what this means we must of course think beyond the nuclear family. Mother, father, and two kids, virtually divorced from grandparents, cousins and other kin, may have been the hallowed ideal of mid-twentieth-century Middle America and of church bulletin covers, but it is not the biblical ideal. Effectively building family life today means rediscovering the extended family. With so many fractured and isolated families and so many people living singly, the church should see itself as an extended family where every believer finds a home—not just figuratively but literally. The church must work to build strong homes, exploring extended family models, so that each home truly is a church and the church truly is a family.

Neighborhood Building. Beyond family life, a key ministry for the church is building vital, healthy neighborhoods. This is true especially in the city, but it applies elsewhere, too.

In urban neighborhoods the church has often been guilty of "ecclesiastical redlining"—failing to invest in, or abandoning, neighborhoods which most needed a Christian presence. Neighborhoods decline when the key institutions sustaining their social and economic lifeblood begin to pull out. When a bank refuses to grant mortgages or loans in a particular area or an insurance company refuses to offer policies there, this is called "redlining" (from the practice of either literally or figuratively drawing a red line around areas where service was no longer to be offered). Such practices simply hasten neighborhood deterioration which otherwise could be prevented. For this reason redlining has long been illegal in many U.S. cities.

The church practices redlining when it abandons or bypasses needy communities. Too often it becomes a party to institutional disinvestment, the pattern of pulling from a neighborhood the very institutions most needed for healthy community. In so doing the church fails to live up to its mission as a builder of community.

When biblically faithful, the church has the two things the world needs most: God's love and life in community. When its love extends to the building of healthy community, the kingdom of God is advanced. Then the church meets society's crucial need for functioning communities where people trust one another and everyone is treated fairly and justly.

What happens in a neighborhood when the church takes seriously its commission to serve in Jesus's name in building community? Let us imagine:

Here and there, couples on the brink of divorce discover that God's love can put their homes back together.

Fearful neighbors get acquainted and begin to work on community problems—crime, the schools, energy conservation, discrimination, rent control, gardens, poor city services, or whatever the needs may be. Fear fades and understanding grows as Christians help bring people together.

Poor families find that someone cares as Christians reach out to them in love, giving material aid when needed and working to improve housing conditions and economic opportunities.

Aimless children with no real home life find that God has a plan for them and a loving, caring family where they are welcome as the church opens to them its doors.

Elderly folks with little meaning in life and perhaps no one to look after them find new security and new opportunities for service as Christians care for their needs.

These are but a few examples of what can happen when Christians catch a vision for turning neighborhoods into real communities. In these ways the church can literally transform neighborhoods, and the larger society, for Christ.

Effective urban witness means freeing Christians to be a community of believers that serves as an agent of God's reign. As the church *becomes* a community in the New Testament sense, it is able to *create* community and to enhance existing community not only among Christians but in society at large.

When the kingdom comes in fullness, it will come through genuine community in Christ through the power of the Spirit. Where the church today is truly the community of God's people living for God's glory and mission, there the kingdom is already visibly present as sign, promise, and firstfruit.

CHAPTER 3
MacroTrends of the Twenty-First Century

The church is called by God to be the living, visible body of Jesus Christ in the world. This is central to the ecology of urban mission. So I have argued in the first two chapters.

But what kind of world is the church facing today, in cities and elsewhere? This chapter surveys cultural trends that will likely pressure the church to move in particular directions or force it to face new challenges. Although the focus here is on recent decades, I attempt to set these trends within the larger framework of church history.

A Matter of Perspective

As Christians see culture changing or the church in decline, they look around for fresh expressions or new models of the church. This is not new; it is a constant dynamic of church history.

The history of the Christian church is the story of repeated "reinventions"; of new life breaking forth from what looked like the church's death watch. Church history is in fact best understood as the story of successive renewal movements, as I argue in *Signs of the Spirit*.

Through the centuries, the history of the church has generally been viewed in two main ways: as the progressive history of institutional Christianity, or as the hidden history of a faithful remnant. The first and more dominant view sees church history as the story of ongoing development, progress, and victory despite setbacks.

Others have said: No! The church keeps falling into unfaithfulness. Institutional Christianity is ever in decline. But always there has been a hidden faithful remnant, a small, often underground, often persecuted body of faithful disciples who have kept the faith alive. I call this view the secret history of the faithful remnant. In this view, new movements that pop up from time to time are actually part of an underground stream, a hidden history where God is truly at work among those who pay the price to follow him and who keep the flame alive.

There is truth in both these seemingly contradictory views. Even when the church compromises the gospel and looks massively unfaithful, unless it is completely apostate it still carries some truth and small seeds of renewal. Often these seeds are embedded in the church's doctrine, liturgy, hymns, and the simple profound faith of common people. Above all, it is there in the Bible, which through the centuries continues to reveal the Word of God, even if that revelation be forgotten, eclipsed, ignored, or so encrusted with tradition that Spirit's small voice is quenched.

The secret history of the faithful remnant view does have a point, however. Often throughout history true believers are persecuted and forced underground, sometimes in the name of the church! We easily think of horrendous examples like the Inquisition, but more frequently there have been less violent, less notorious examples in all church traditions—Roman Catholic, Orthodox, Protestant. Examples would be the initial repression of the Charismatic Movement in many church bodies in the twentieth century, strong opposition to Francis of Assisi and his "brothers" in the thirteenth century, persecution of Anabaptists in the sixteenth century, or the seventeenth-century "conventicle acts" in England that outlawed informal religious meetings in homes. New life is always a threat.

But there is a better way to view history—a more helpful angle from which to view the Spirit's work in church and world that can help us in urban mission today. It is this key fact: God is always in the renewal business. The Spirit is always saying to the church: I will do a new thing! Jesus is always potentially present to lead and form a body of disciples who will gather around him, follow his ways, and turn the world upside down.

This is the church renewal view. It is a both–and view. It neither writes off the institutional church nor denies that God also works below the surface, out of sight, in movements that may never be recognized or may in fact be persecuted. The renewal movement view takes as its text Jesus's words: "Every scribe who has been trained for the kingdom of heaven is like the master of a household who brings out of his treasure what is new and what is old" (Mt 13:52). That's the key: things both old and new.

The question for faithful urban churches today, then, is this: How can the church be God's authentic renewal movement—that is, a faithful, redemptive body of disciples—as it discerns and interacts with macrotrends that may push it this way or that?

This means that the key issue is not some "new model of the church," but rather the wisdom to discern, learn from, and engage with larger trends from the sure basis of faithful community in Christ.

Ten MacroTrends, 1985–2015

Here then are ten MacroTrends that will put pressure on urban mission, but also provide redemptive opportunities.

Four points of clarification: First, by MacroTrends I mean overarching currents that transcend geography, culture, particular urban contexts, and church traditions. Second, I am tracing these trends mainly from about 1985—a convenient date to mark the end of Christendom. From the mid-nineteen-eighties, Christendom ceased to exist in the West in the sense of a firm church-state connection or in the sense that Christian values and presuppositions permeated society. Christendom was the traditional context in Europe and the Americas, and many of Christendom's assumptions were carried around the world by missionaries in the nineteenth and twentieth centuries. Christendom has now largely disappeared globally, with just a few exceptions.

Third, some of these trends concern developments mainly within the church, while others are larger cultural trends shaping the context within which the church lives and ministers. The impact of these trends will of course be different in different contexts, yet virtually nowhere in the global urban world are these trends absent.

Finally, the set of trends presented here is selective. Many other cultural, political, economic, and religious currents and cross-currents are flowing today. I focus here on ones that seem particularly pertinent to contemporary urban mission.[1]

1. From Church Growth to "Third Culture"

Church Growth thinking was a product of Christendom. Church Growth began to fade as Christendom presuppositions lost their force. Christendom assumes and attempts to build and enforce a homogenous culture. It tends toward standardization. Variations are considered subversive deviations to be corrected or suppressed. Dig a bit, and you find such assumptions

---

[1] For discussion of other trends and competing worldviews, see Howard A. Snyder with Daniel V. Runyon, *Foresight: 10 Major Trends That Will Dramatically Affect the Future of Christians and the Church* (Nashville: Thomas Nelson, 1986) and Howard A. Snyder, *EarthCurrents: The Struggle for the World's Soul* (Nashville: Abingdon, 1995). Although these analyses are now dated, they are still useful for understanding the challenges of urban mission.

underlying Church Growth theory.

Church Growth thinking and methods thrived briefly where Christendom presuppositions still held sway. Church Growth tended toward and promoted homogeneity ("homogeneous units"), focused on numerical growth of congregations rather than discipleship and comprehensive ministry, and tended to see numerical church growth as synonymous with kingdom growth. These were its Christendom presuppositions, assumptions common to the nearly fifteen-hundred-year reign of Christianity in Western Europe.[2]

It is ironic then that Church Growth theory arose in a missions context (initially, Donald McGavran's ministry in India). Its strength was its recognition that evangelism and church planting had to be tailored to the cultural context. So far so good. Its weakness was precisely its Christendom assumptions, noted above, which undercut its prophetic impact.[3]

---

[2] Similar assumptions held sway in most of Orthodoxy, including Russian Orthodoxy until the Communist Revolution. Basic Christendom presuppositions were not seriously challenged by the Protestant Reformation except in its Radical Reformation form.

[3] This is not the place to fully evaluate Church Growth theory, but see the discussion in *Community of the King.* See also Howard A. Snyder, "Renewal View," Chapter 5 in Gary L. McIntosh, *Evaluating the Church Growth Movement: Five Views* (Grand Rapids: Zondervan, 2004), 209–31.

Church Growth theory tended to argue *against* multicultural or culturally diverse congregations on the grounds that cultural heterogeneity impeded growth. That view has now been discredited. In contrast to a decade or two ago when Church Growth theory emphasized "homogeneous unit" churches, today a mushrooming literature advocates multiethnic and third-culture churches. "Third-culture" here means affirming and celebrating cultural differences and integrating these into the very DNA of the church. Numerous viable examples of such churches can now be found.[4]

Larger cultural and demographic trends spurred by globalization, urbanization, and mass migration have pushed multicultural and third-cultural emphases to the fore. Multicultural churches prompt us to reexamine gospel-and-culture issues in Scripture and in the early church.

Although culture generally is diverse, every viable

---

[4] Some examples: Manuel Ortiz, *One New People: Models for Developing a Multiethnic Church* (Downers Grove, Ill.: InterVarsity, 1996); Stephen A. Rhodes, *Where the Nations Meet: The Church in a Multicultural World* (InterVarsity, 1998); Dave Gibbons, *The Monkey and the Fish: Liquid Leadership for a Third-Culture Church* (Grand Rapids: Zondervan, 2009) and Mark DeYmaz, *Building a Healthy Multi-Ethnic Church: Mandate, Commitments, and Practices of a Diverse Congregation* (San Francisco, Calif.: Jossey-Bass, 2007). See also Gary V. Nelson, *Borderland Churches: A Congregation's Introduction to Missional Living* (St. Louis, Mo.: Chalice Press, 2008).

particular culture is coherent. A living culture "coheres" or holds together by bonds of language, customs, traditions, and worldview. Any viable culture is thus in this sense *homogeneous.* The goal of the gospel however is not to baptize a culture's homogeneity, but rather to introduce the new wine of the gospel and let it do its work—a process of fermentation that brings gospel transformation. One result of this is a kingdom vision. Christians in a particular culture learn to see their Christian sisters and brothers in other cultures as their own kin in Christ. A new basis of transcending homogeneity is introduced: crosscultural reconciliation in the blood of Jesus Christ, as we see in the New Testament.

Dynamic churches are in fact a blend of "homogeneous" and "heterogeneous" elements. Both unity and diversity. Finding oneness in Jesus Christ, they learn to embrace the other, appreciate gracious diversity, and recognize God at work beyond their own cultural realities and assumptions.

All communities by definition must have some degree of homogeneity in order to exist. The gospel in fact has its own principle of homogeneity. It is called *reconciliation* in Christ. Within the church, the degree of both homogeneity and diversity will of course vary from place to place, depending on the cultural context, as we see in the New

Testament.[5] But the key point of commonality, the glue that holds the church together (if it is true to the gospel), is reconciliation through Jesus Christ. Based on that reconciliation, diverse persons of diverse social situations become one community, one body. This diversity-in-oneness is a key, unique feature of the community of the King.[6] In this sense, a church's homogeneity should be its diversity. The key "homogeneous principle" that unites diverse Christians is their oneness in Christ, and a key mark of a faithful church in most contexts is its diversity.

So in the church and in the Kingdom of God, the point is neither homogeneity nor heterogeneity but rather unity and diversity in Jesus Christ—thus hinting at the ultimate transcending reality of Holy Trinity.

---

[5] Note the descriptions of the church in Antioch in Acts 11 and 13. The church in Antioch was much more diverse than the early Jerusalem church, yet "a great number of people believed and turned to the Lord" and Paul and Barnabas discipled "great numbers." In large measure because of its diversity, now including Gentiles as well as Jews, "The disciples were called Christians first at Antioch" (Acts 11:21–26).

[6] Diversity is as much a "mark" of the church as is unity, though of course the precise demographic and sociological contours of that diversity will vary greatly according to the cultural context. (See Snyder and Runyon, *Decoding the Church,* Chap. 1.) Minimally the diversity of the church will normally include differences of age, gender, personality, and spiritual gifts, and usually much more. The greater the range of social heterogeneity united and reconciled in the church, the greater the *visible social demonstration* of the power of the gospel that raised Jesus Christ from the dead. It would be a distortion of the gospel, however, to define acceptable diversity so broadly as to include behaviors that are incompatible with Jesus's teachings.

The church is prophetic when it creates communities that visibly transcend the divisions in society that result from racism, economic or social marginalization, or other forms of injustice and oppression. The New Testament Gospel calls the church to be a community of visible reconciliation. As René Padilla notes, the early apostles "sought to build communities in which Jew and Gentile, slave and free, poor and rich would worship together and learn the meaning of their unity in Christ right from the start, although they often had to deal with difficulties arising out of the differences in background or social status among the converts." The early church "not only grew, but it grew across cultural barriers." Clearly the apostles "never contemplated the possibility of forming homogeneous unit churches that would then express their unity in terms of interchurch relationships. Each church was meant to portray the oneness of its members regardless of their racial, cultural, or social differences."[7]

Today a growing number of urban churches are demonstrating that diverse, multiethnic churches can grow

---

[7] C. René Padilla, *Mission Between the Times* (Grand Rapids, Mich.: Eerdmans, 1985), 160, 167. These points are adapted from and elaborated further in Snyder, *Community of the King* (Rev. Ed.), 125–28.

healthily and reproduce themselves, just as in the days of the early church.

2. From TV Culture to Online Culture

Here we face a larger cultural trend that is already dramatically changing the church. In societies where online access and social media are dominant—which now means virtually every city of the world—Christians are as digitally connected as are non-Christians.

I attended a Sunday evening church service in Port-au-Prince, Haiti. The congregation was a good mix of ages, including a crowd of young folks. At the front of the open-air sanctuary were several electrical outlets where people had plugged in their cellphones, using this opportunity to get them charged. In a very poor community outside Pretoria in South Africa I saw people standing outside their homes, using cellphones. This is new, it is global, and it is somehow transformative.

Television and radio gradually connected much of the world throughout the twentieth century. But the idea of potentially every adult on the planet being connected globally at low cost, able to communicate with other people around the world, was barely the stuff of science fiction. Television of course has not gone away; now it is increasingly being integrated with computers, cellphones, and other devices. This is global online culture.

It is too early to tell what the long-range impact of this shift will be. It is part of the continuing and growing impact of global wireless digital technology on every area of society, from automobiles to surveillance. Most of us sense, at least vaguely, that there are both benefits and negative costs.

For urban mission, some implications are already clear. Resources: More and more information is now at our fingertips. Distraction: People's attention is easily drawn from other things (worship, prayer, duty) to ever-present digital messages or images, games and entertainment. Stewardship: Such connectedness raises questions about the use of time, money, and earth's resources. Awareness: Everyone—urban youth, especially—now has much broader knowledge of what is going on in the world. But also tribalism: People tend to keep in touch with a peer group of folks who share their views and values. This can make them less open-minded and tolerant of difference, not more so. Discipline: Effective urban mission in this context means establishing covenant relationships through which Jesus's disciples *commit* to steward their own focus and time so as to put Christian ministry and discipleship first and maintain this commitment through accountable community.

Christians in urban mission will be particularly sensitive, also, to those who are information-or technology-poor, though they may be rich in personal relationships or ancient wisdom.

3. From Secular Society to Multi-religious Society

Fifty years ago, the West (North America, Western Europe, and Australia and New Zealand, mainly) were thought to be secular or rapidly becoming so. But I agree with Steve Addison: "It's questionable whether 'secularization' was ever a reality outside of the wishful thinking of certain academic and theological circles. The problem is not that people don't believe. It's that they will believe anything."[8]

Rather than secularization, we are seeing resacralization—rejecting secularism and turning alternative beliefs into extreme religious ideologies which in many cases young people are ready to kill or die for.

The most significant new development here is the recognition of the importance and inevitability of religion, whichever that is—Christianity, Islam, Hinduism, Buddhism, shamanism, economism, varieties of "New

---

[8] Personal communication.

Age," scientism, or whatever. Although many secularists and atheists strongly deny it, these views also are forms of faith and substitute forms of religion.

Now virtually every world city except those under the strict control of Islam, Hinduism, or some other ideology is a competitive marketplace of religions and worldviews. In its global scale, this is new compared with fifty years ago. In previous centuries only a few world cities were such crossroads of religion. Today however mosques and temples spring up in small "secular" cities throughout the West. Increasingly one confronts the Muslim next door or the Hindu or Buddhist running the convenience store.

Importantly, this development merges with the first, online connectedness. In seconds virtually anyone can know what's happening within one's own faith community or in other "alien" faiths, whether locally or globally. This can breed either understanding or violence.

It is still true of course that major influential sectors of Western society, and also some sectors in predominantly Islamic countries and in India, are aggressively secular in the sense that they oppose theocracy or attempts to give any religion privileged status within the political structure. We see this struggle being fought out right now in the United States and Canada, Europe, Turkey, India, and to some degree in other places. Although we don't know where this will lead, history suggests that we can anticipate growing reform movements in the world's religions as they interact with each other and with European Enlightenment thought. Within Islam there are small movements toward more religious toleration and pluralism that likely will grow with time. These are prompted in part by reaction to radical terrorist Islamic cults.[9]

Both religious pluralism and religious relativism[10] will likely continue and become increasingly prominent in the world's cities. This trend is fed in turn by global entertainment, advertising, marketing and "branding," and consumerism.

Here is a major (maybe *the* major) challenge for authentic urban mission: Religious/philosophical relativism and the commodification of belief systems and religious "products," including the marketing of religious "experiences." In fact materialistic consumerism, and the forces of global capitalism behind it together with the

---

[9] See for example Ayaan Hirsi Ali, *Nomad: A Personal Journey Through the Clash of Civilizations* (London: Simon & Schuster, 2010), and Ayaan Hirsi Ali, *Heretic: Why Islam Needs a Reformation Now* (New York: HarperCollins, 2015).

[10] Religious pluralism means the accepted coexistence of various religious groups; religious relativism means the belief that all religions are equally true (or false); that no one religion is "true" to the exclusion of others. Thus pluralism and relativism are not the same thing.

increasing commodification of everything, including culture itself, is the new religion which it is now heretical to question.[11] So far the church has not been very effective in challenging this. In the United States, most of the church has capitulated to a consumerist, celebrity-oriented, entertainment culture. This same dynamic will more and more be a main challenge for urban mission in every cosmopolitan city of the world, regardless of size.

4. From "Standard Model" Churches to Megachurch / Microchurch Mix

What is a "regular" or "normal" Christian church? Protestants know, in a general sense. They have an idea or assumed model in their heads. We may call this the Standard Model. It generally has these components, at least: Christians meet Sunday mornings, preferably in a consecrated building which is generally called a "church." Most congregations, it is assumed, will be between fifty and four hundred, though some may be smaller or larger. The church will have a pastor, preferably ordained and full-time, and preferably male. There will be just one pastor unless the church is large or prosperous enough to hire "staff" to carry out various aspects of the church's ministry.

---

[11] Jeremy Rifkin, *The Age of Access: The New Culture of Hypercapitalism Where All of Life is a Paid-For Experience* (New York: Tarcher/Putnam, 2000).

On Sunday mornings the congregation will sit in rows facing an elevated platform, which usually has a pulpit. People will similarly have assumptions about order of worship, preaching, sacraments, music, architecture, and so forth. The primary focus of worship services will be the sermon.

This Standard Model is mainly the fruit of Christendom. It developed over centuries in Western Europe, was reshaped somewhat by the Protestant Reformation, and was then carried around the world by Christian missionaries or emigrants to other lands.

For our purposes here, two key points about the Standard Model: First, this model ceased to be standard with the demise of Christendom. Today there is no Standard Model. The Standard Model has been replaced by multiple nontraditional forms. Of course the Standard Model persists as one of many forms or options. But it is no longer standard.

In the United States, the Standard Model was strongly reinforced by the post-World War II boom of suburban evangelical churches. Hundreds of thousands of church buildings were built, all adhering generally to the Standard Model. This therefore was seen as normal by Baby Boomer

Protestants, that generation which is just now passing into retirement.

Many of the conflicts, controversies, tensions, and church defections of the past twenty years can be traced to the demise of the Standard Model. In its place we now have multiple nontraditional forms. We may call this a megachurch–microchurch mix or continuum, with all kinds of variations in between.[12]

The second but really more pertinent point: the Standard Model has virtually no biblical support. It is almost totally the fruit of accumulated tradition. In the New Testament, although Christians often met on Sundays, they met frequently at other times. There were no church buildings. Most congregations were small and met in homes. They were led by elders who had been discipled but were not formally trained, were generally not full-time employees of the church, often functioned as a team (rather than "solo pastor"), and sometimes included women. There was no formal ordination process. Since Christians met in homes most of the time, there was no standard architecture or seating arrangement. Bible reading, teaching, and shared meals were normal practice. Much of the worship consisted

---

[12] I discuss four variations of the Standard Model and their roots in *Salvation Means Creation Healed*: Traditional-Liturgical, Revivalist, Pentecostal-Charismatic, and Rock Concert Pattern (168–78).

of teaching and admonishing each other and joyfully singing "psalms, hymns, and spiritual songs to God" (Col 3:16). When Christians gathered for worship, one or another believer might have "a hymn, a lesson, a revelation, a tongue, or an interpretation" (1 Cor 14:26).

And most of these churches, it appears, were city churches.

The point here is *not* to say that today's churches should slavishly imitate the New Testament church. It is just to say that, biblically speaking, there is no Standard Model. There are however biblical principles of participatory worship, community, spiritual gifts, and the priesthood of believers that help maintain healthy, effective Christian experience, discipleship, and mission.

Discerning churches today will not look for a Standard Model nor some kind of New Model. They will avoid the temptation to think that either megachurches or microchurches are the new standard. The new standard is neither the megachurch of thousands nor the house church of just a few. Nor is it something in between. There is no Standard Model. This means churches are free, perhaps within the constraints of their particular traditions, to find the form of the church that best faithfully incarnates the gospel in their own contexts.

5. From Megachurches to Emerging Churches

This trend is twin to the previous one. The past decade saw lots of discussion about "emerging churches."[13] Under the illusion that megachurches had become the Standard Model, some argued that the megachurch is now being replaced by the emerging church. A good example was Dan Kimball, *The Emerging Church: Vintage Christianity for New Generations*, which contrasts the two.[14]

This is a misunderstanding on two levels. First, "the emerging church" is too amorphous to be a model. The term covers a wide spectrum of experiments, new church plants, ministry innovations, and online discussions. "Emerging" or "emergent" church is too vague and incoherent to ever become a new model. Second, as already argued, megachurches never were the new Standard Model, and it is vain to expect or look for another.[15]

Wise urban mission leaders will of course want to keep their eyes on trends in church and society (as discussed in the next chapter). But they will be very cautious about

---

[13] I summarize varieties of "emerging churches" in Howard A. Snyder, *Yes In Christ* (Toronto: Clements Academic, 2011), 234–39.

[14] Dan Kimball, *The Emerging Church: Vintage Christianity for New Generations* (Grand Rapids: Zondervan, 2003).

[15] To put megachurches in historical perspective and in relation to other models, see Howard A. Snyder with Daniel V. Runyon, *Decoding the Church: Mapping the DNA of Christ's Body* (Grand Rapids: Baker Books, 2002), 62–72.

adopting "new models" or forms or structures that may be mere fads and may not be compatible either with their context or with biblical principles.

6. From Believing-to-Belong to Belonging-to-Believe

In Standard Model churches, people assumed unbelievers would come to faith in Jesus and join a church. More generally, Christendom assumed that the church consisted of people who believed the Christian message, however vaguely or nominally.

Given this assumption, evangelism naturally focused on gaining "decisions for Christ." The goal was to get individual persons to believe in Jesus and consequently to become church members. The view has two underlying ideas: that people come to faith in Jesus Christ one by one by individual personal decision, and that faith precedes incorporation into the church. This is the believing-to-belong model: Belief comes first, then church membership.

This set of assumptions, largely unquestioned in many Protestant churches for centuries, is giving way to a different approach: belonging-to-believe. For many people, community both precedes and produces faith.

This is not a new discovery; it is an old one. People are won to faith in Jesus Christ and go on to discipleship through personal relationships—not solely a singular "personal relationship with Christ," but rather—first of all—personal relationships with other believers.[16]

If we reflect on this, we know it is true. People who participate in a community tend to adopt the beliefs of that community. This is basic sociology. The idea that a person must first be convinced of their need of Jesus Christ so that they thus believe and join a church runs counter to the way people naturally and normally behave. The believing-to-belong model assumes that the gospel is essentially a set of rational presuppositions that people must be persuaded to believe. Believing, they will then take the logical next step of joining a church.

For the vast majority of people, this is not the way it works.

This is actually an encouraging word for urban mission. Christians should be firm in their Christian faith and belief, but their first task is not to persuade others of their truth claims but to welcome them into community. Any person who becomes lovingly engaged in a community of firm Christian believers and disciples will most likely come

---

[16] John Finney, *Recovering the Past: Celtic and Roman Mission* (London: Darton, Longman and Todd, 1996), especially 46–47; George G. Hunter III, *The Celtic Way of Evangelism* (Nashville, Tenn.: Abingdon, 2000).

to share their faith—that is, come to trust fully in Jesus Christ as Savior and Lord. A few will not, but most will.

Faithful urban mission will develop and multiply welcoming communities that become incubators of Christian transformation in people's lives, while taking care not to neglect solid Christian formation, including its biblical and doctrinal content.

7. From West-to-the-Rest Mission to Global Diaspora Mission

What historian Kenneth Scott Latourette called "The Great Century" of Christian missions—essentially 1800 to 1914—was predominately West-to-the-rest missions. The Great Century was the remarkable period when Protestant missionaries from the North Atlantic region planted churches and Christian institutions throughout much of Africa, Asia, the South Pacific, and Latin America.[17]

This century was "great" because it was fruitful. Today Christian churches are found in most nations and regions of the world. In many places they are vital and growing. This would not be true had it not been for the Great Century and, significantly, Roman Catholic and Orthodox

---

[17] Kenneth Scott Latourette, *A History of the Expansion of Christianity*, especially volumes 4-6, *The Great Century in Europe and the United States of America; The Great Century: The America, Australasia, and Africa*; and *The Great Century: North Africa and Asia* (New York: Harper & Row, 1941–1944).

missions in the sixteenth and seventeenth centuries. Now many churches in other regions of the world are sending missionaries to the North Atlantic nations.

The twentieth century and early twenty-first century however have witnessed a new phenomenon: mass migration from poorer or war-torn regions to places of more stability. By far the largest movement of migrants and refugees has been from South and Central America to North America and, more recently, from North Africa and the Middle East into Europe in unprecedented numbers.

These developments have produced global diaspora mission. Today the face of mission, and thus increasingly of urban mission, is diaspora mission, or mission in diaspora.

Over the last decade, diaspora mission has become a significant new focus mainly for two reasons: the massive numbers of displaced persons involved and increasing Christian witness within and among today's global diaspora. Mission historian Steven O'Malley in the introduction to the book *Revitalization Amid Diaspora* notes that today there are "more than 400 million persons living in a state of permanent diaspora throughout the world." Many of these, "scattered as transnationals outside traditional homelands," are "finding their identity in the people of God being scattered by the Holy Spirit in the unfolding of salvation history." That is, global diaspora mission means not only scattered people finding salvation and a new identity in Jesus Christ, but also a new realization that throughout history God has often worked through diaspora. "Christians trace their genesis as a scattered people of God throughout the earth to their initial expulsion from Jerusalem, whereby they were enabled by the Spirit to actualize the promises bequeathed to them at Pentecost," O'Malley notes. Biblically the roots trace clear back to Abraham. Diaspora mission is "a return to an ancient pattern that God followed from the inception of the biblical narrative of salvation history."[18]

Migrating people usually end up in cities. Throughout history cities have often been cosmopolitan places, and today they are strategic in diaspora mission. In terms of scale, diversity, sheer numbers, and missional reflection, however, today's diaspora mission is new.[19] Diaspora mission thus becomes both an inescapable reality and a

---

[18] J. Steven O'Malley, "Introduction," in J. Steven O'Malley, ed., *Revitalization Amid Diaspora – Consultation Three: Explorations in World Christian Revitalization Movements* (Lexington, Ky.: Emeth Press, 2013), vii–ix. This book presents a number of case studies and interpretations of diaspora mission with particular focus on renewal and revitalization in the church.

[19] See Enoch Wan, *et al.*, *Diaspora Missiology: Theory, Methodology, and Practice,* 2nd ed. (Portland, Ore: Institute of Diaspora Studies of USA, 2014).

nearly unprecedented opportunity for the kind of urban mission that not only assists and heals people but that forces the church to rethink the whole nature of salvation and therefore of mission.

8. From Church Extension/Reproduction to "Insider Movements"

Throughout most of Christian history, the dominant mode of missions has been evangelism and church planting. Missionaries worked hard to produce distinct communities of Christians who publicly self-identified as such. If you were a Christian, people knew it because of your involvement in Christian worship and other activities and by the kind of life you lived. Wherever the church was faithful, Christians modeled the character of Jesus and demonstrated the virtues and priorities of the kingdom of God in their daily lives and in their engagement with society.[20]

In recent decades, however, large numbers of Muslims as well as many Hindus and Buddhists have been turning to Jesus Christ without identifying themselves with existing Christian churches. Generally the reasons are cultural and social, though sometimes missional. Jesus followers within

---

[20] What follows is adapted and updated from Snyder, *Yes In Christ*, 238–40.

other religious communities want to reach as many as possible of their coreligionists with the gospel without alienating them from their social and religious context.

A good introduction is "Appropriate Approaches in Muslim Contexts" by John and Anna Travis in the book *Appropriate Christianity*, edited by Charles H. Kraft. The authors write, "in a number of countries today, there are groups of Muslims who have genuinely come to faith in Jesus Christ, yet have remained legally and socio-religiously within the local Muslim community." Travis and Travis believe that "one way God is moving at this point in salvation history, is by sovereignly drawing Muslims to Himself, revolutionizing them spiritually, yet calling them to remain as salt and light in the religious community of their birth."[21]

In 1998 John Travis developed the C1–C6 spectrum or continuum, distinguishing "six types of Christ-centered communities" according to three factors: language, cultural forms, and religious identity. The C5 position, "Muslim

---

[21] John Travis and Anna Travis, "Appropriate Approaches in Muslim Contexts," in Charles H. Kraft, ed., *Appropriate Christianity* (Pasadena, Calif.: Wm. Carey Library, 2005), 397–414 (quotations from 397).

Followers of Jesus," is approximately equivalent to what have come to be known as "insider movements."[22]

David Garrison defines insider movements as "popular movements to Christ that bypass both formal and explicit expressions of the Christian religion."[23] An extensive discussion quickly emerged over insider movements.[24]

Part of the insider-movement debate involves the question of "churchless Christianity." Herbert Hoefer's 2001 book of that title focused on Hindu followers of Jesus, reporting "research among non-baptized believers in Christ in rural and urban Tamilnadu, India" supplemented by "practical and theological reflections."[25]

---

[22] Travis and Travis, "Appropriate Approaches," 397; see John Travis, "The C1 to C6 Spectrum," *Evangelical Missions Quarterly* 34:407–08. Some however distinguish between insider movements and the C5 category.

[23] David Garrison, "Church Planting Movements vs. Insider Movements: Missiological Realities vs. Mythiological [sic] Speculations," *International Journal of Frontier Missions* 21:4 (Winter 2004), 151–54.

[24] E.g., John and Anna Travis, "Contextualization among Muslims, Hindus, and Buddhists: A Focus on Insider Movements," *Mission Frontiers* (Sept.-Oct. 2005), 12–15 (based on their longer essay cited above); "An Extended Conversation about 'Insider Movements,'" with contributions by John Piper, Gary Corwin, John and Anna Travis, and others, *Mission Frontiers* (Jan.-Feb. 2006), 16–23; Rebecca Lewis, "Promoting Movements to Christ within Natural Communities," *International Journal of Frontier Missiology* 24:2 (Summer 2007), 75–76; Timothy C. Tennent, "The Hidden History of Insider Movements," *Christianity Today* 57:1 (January-February 2013), 28.

[25] Herbert E. Hoefer, *Churchless Christianity* (Pasadena, Calif.: Wm. Carey Library, 2001).

For purposes of current urban mission, the point is that these movements exist and that they pose challenges for traditional ecclesiology. More basically, they raise the question of the meaning of *church*. Are two or three people gathered in Jesus name (Mt 18:20), with no church building and no connection with broader church structures or networks, really churchless?

God's Spirit is at work today beyond groups and ministries that own the name "Christian." Increasingly urban Christians may encounter Muslims, Buddhists, and Hindus—especially young ones—who are searching for truth and may well be attracted to Jesus and open to God's Spirit but are very reluctant, often for good reasons, to identify with Christians or have any involvement with Christian churches.

In today's cities, this is a primary boundary area where God's Spirit is at work. The church in the city needs to be as sensitive as Peter was at Cornelius' house. Peter learned that "God shows no partiality, but in every nation anyone who fears him and does what is right is acceptable to him" (Acts 10:34–35).

9. From Church as Familiar/Traditional to Church as "New Social Reality"

Underlying all these trends is the question of *tradition*. Like every community and culture, churches gradually form traditions. Traditions are useful and necessary, but they are also expressions of the cultural context. Every tradition is the wineskin through which churches attempt to maintain the ferment of the new wine of the gospel while at the same time making it available to those who have not yet tasted of the goodness of the Lord.

Traditions grow, and we become familiar with them. They make us comfortable and allow us to worship God and engage in mission. But since traditions are particular to the cultural context, they feel alien to people from other cultures. Church tradition easily becomes a barrier to mission rather than a vehicle of mission. So ongoing discernment is needed.

Tradition tends to become stable and uniform, whereas urban society is often—and increasingly—dynamic and diverse. Potentially, this is a problem. The answer however is not to throw out tradition nor to prematurely create new forms (birth new traditions). Rather, the approach should be inductive. The way forward is to discern how the Spirit is moving both within the Christian community and beyond, especially in those "borderlands" between Christian community and urban society.

The trend I discern here is a movement of vital urban churches away from holding on to the familiar and traditional toward recognition that at its best and most authentic, the church is always a "new social reality." An authentic community of Jesus followers is always something new, whatever the cultural context. Its genius is found in its center—Jesus Christ—and its power is found in personal relationships more than in doctrine or forms. Yet Christians recognize the vital importance of doctrine and forms because of who Jesus Christ truly is, as revealed in Scripture and often attested in human experience.

So the trend here is not the creation of new forms or attempts to found new traditions. Rather it is a new, enhanced, or recovered awareness that Jesus by his Spirit is always doing something new—that is, something old-but-new—in communities of disciples. In other words, the point is to focus not on traditions and forms, old or new, but on the Center, Jesus Christ. It is to put first the wine and seek the Spirit's discernment *through the Body* when dealing with wineskins.

Vital, faithful urban mission finds its life and dynamic in the creative new social reality of Christian community—

not in either clasping or trashing familiar forms and traditions.

10. From Ecological Ignorance/Indifference to Emerging Ecological Sensitivity

It would be foolhardy to engage these various trends and yet ignore a larger overarching reality that will dramatically affect urban mission worldwide in coming decades, and that is global climate change. The effects of climate change are in fact already with us. One way or another, every city of the world is now being hurt by climate change. Depending on geographical location, this means floods, toxic pollution, coastal erosion, drought, unprecedented fires, environmental refugees, and possibly economic collapse.[26]

Global climate change is not a trend; it is a fact. The macrotrend here is the shift from ecological ignorance and indifference to growing ecological sensitivity. In the face of continuing resistance by some governments and by sectors of the economy whose profits are closely linked with despoiling the land, more and more people worldwide are

---

[26] Sources on this are now abundant. For an overview, see Snyder and Scandrett, *Salvation Means Creation Healed,* 82–92, which discusses not only climate change but such related issues as endangered oceans, deforestation, and species depletion.

recognizing the danger and moving toward support of environmental protection and creation care.

One positive sign here is the development of the Global Compact Cities Programme. This is a cooperative effort among major cities worldwide. It involves "all levels of government, business and civil society" in collaborative efforts "to enhance sustainability, resilience, diversity and adaptation within cities and in the face of complex urban challenges," including climate change.[27]

Within evangelical Protestantism, two examples of growing ecological awareness are the international Lausanne Creation Care Network and Young Evangelicals for Climate Action.[28] Also strategically important is Pope Francis's remarkable encyclical on climate change and creation stewardship, *Laudato Sí: On Care of Our Common Home*. Calling to mind Francis of Assisi, Pope Francis writes, "a healthy relationship with creation is one dimension of overall personal conversion, which entails the recognition of our errors, sins, faults and failures, and leads

---

[27] Information available at http://citiesprogramme.com/aboutus/the-cities-programme

[28] See the websites http://lwccn.com/ and http://www.yecaction.org/

to heartfelt repentance and desire to change." Pope Francis thus calls for "Ecological conversion."[29]

Today faithful urban mission simply must engage with this concern and priority. First of all, as a matter of awareness, of course. But beyond that, as a matter of faithful mission. Urban Christians are partisans in the global struggle to protect, preserve, and heal the planet. Faithful urban missions stands in solidarity with all global citizens who share this concern. God is raising up a number of Christians mission organizations to give leadership in this area, such as Care of Creation, Eden Reforestation, and many others. Urban Christians should do three things: Support such ministries, be good creation-care stewards in their own local and global contexts, and integrate creation care into discipleship, spiritual formation, and doctrinal teaching. Alert pastors and leaders will also watch for signs of the Spirit's charism in gifting young Christians for focused ministry in this area.

Conclusion

Tracing trends in society and in the church, if we do it carefully, brings us round to where we started: Church and

---

[29] Pope Francis, *Encyclical on Climate Change and Inequality: On Care for Our Common Home* (Brooklyn, N.Y.: Melville House, 2015), 132.

mission as revealed in Scripture and supremely in Jesus Christ by the Spirit. Trend analysis may help us discern key boundary areas, the liminal places, where new or newly strategic mission can and should take place. But faithful churches don't go racing after trends. Like New Testament Christians, they ask: What doors of opportunity is God providentially opening for us? Remember the letters to the seven churches in Revelation 2–3.

To summarize: By God's grace, churches can be the new social reality of the Jesus community in urban places, the "new thing" of the Spirit, through eyes-wide-open analysis of what's trending in their world, but then returning to first things, the church's first love.

How can urban churches and Christian ministries know, however, whether or not they are really making any difference for the kingdom of God? That is the focus of the next chapter.

CHAPTER 4
The Kingdom of God Index

Is it *more true* or *less true* year by year that God's will is actually being done on earth as it is in heaven? Can we know?

Does Christ's church in the twenty-first century need a Kingdom of God Index (KGI)? Could urban churches especially, as well as missions and Christian ministries generally, benefit from a compilation of empirical data, regularly updated and global in scope, that gives a quick overview of evidence of kingdom progress?

This is a serious question. It is not frivolous, and in fact raises some fascinating and foundational theological issues.

In business, science, education, government, and other fields, *data* is crucial. What is actually happening? What are the trend lines? The red flags or the positive indicators? And consequently, what if any action should be taken?

Some speak of "dashboard indicators." That is, by analogy with automobiles, a quick summary of key data that says whether things are functioning properly or not and warns of dangers or dysfunctions. A Kingdom of God Index would regularly provide churches and Christian organizations with a snapshot of available data that bear positively or negatively on the progress of the Good News in the world.

Pro and Con

Should and can the kingdom of God, and the church's kingdom mission, be viewed in this way? The pro and con argument can easily be framed:

No! God is sovereign. The Spirit's action is mysterious. "The coming of the kingdom of God is not something that can be observed" (Lk. 17:20 TNIV). It would be hubris, egocentrism, and probably idolatry to ever try to put together a Kingdom of God Index. Think of the trouble Israel got into by taking censuses. God sent judgment.

Yes! In humble submission and full recognition of God's sovereign and mysterious ways, we ask for empirical evidence of God's gracious working in the world. God's grace produces "effects." Just look at the Book of Acts. We are told how many new believers there were after Pentecost, for instance.

For the church, the purpose of such data is the same as in other areas where ongoing indicators are important: to know how to act most effectively now.

Pastors and other church leaders do this all the time in the life of their churches. They keep track of attendance, church membership, finances, and perhaps other areas. Of course such evidence may be misleading, incidental, or missionally irrelevant. It may not reveal the most important things happening in the church. But in the hands of wise leadership with a clear grasp of the gospel of the kingdom, such data is useful in guiding ongoing ministry, including key decision-making.

As Christians, we often do something similar in our own Christian walk. Do we see any "signs of grace" in our lives? Can we locate any evidence that we are "seeking first God's kingdom and righteousness"? Perhaps some see such questions as misguided or even idolatrous, putting the spotlight on ourselves rather than God. Are we left then simply with our own self-perceptions: "I *feel like* I'm growing in grace and faithful discipleship," or not? Or do we rely on the church, or a pastor or spiritual mentor, to guide us here?

How we answer such questions very likely reflects in some measure our particular theological tradition and commitments.

But let us proceed. What good would a KGI do, and how might one be constructed? Then finally we can return to the question of possible dangers and unintended consequences.

Reasons for a KGI

Here are five reasons a Kingdom of God Index could be useful in the church's life and mission.

1. It would raise practically, conceptually, and evidentially the question of the relationship between our church life and our world.

It is clear from Scripture that the gospel of the kingdom is larger than the church itself; broader than our own personal salvation. When Messiah's reign is fully established, "the earth will be full of the knowledge of the Lord as the waters cover the sea" (Isa. 11:19). All nations and the whole earth will praise him. God's will shall be done fully upon earth.

Does the church have a role to play in this? Clearly it does. In mission of God (*missio Dei*) terms, we can affirm the saying: It is not that the church has a mission but that the mission has a church.

How do we know the church is having any impact at all on the world? Certainly signs of authentic conversions and Christ-like discipleship point toward the kingdom. But if our claims about Jesus Christ and his reign are true, certainly there will be signs not just of church success but also of cultural transformation. There should be some correlation, for instance, between growing numbers of conversions and positive changes in society.

Can we identify any empirical signs of this? Any small voices with prophetic resonance? Would it help if we could and did? A serious question.

2. A Kingdom of God Index would raise practical questions about discipleship and church life generally.

Jesus wants his disciples to be doers of the word, not just hearers (Jas 1:22). He said plainly, "Not everyone who says to me, 'Lord, Lord,' will enter the kingdom of heaven, but only the one who does the will of my Father in heaven" (Mt 7:21). Christians are to let their "light shine before others, so that they may see [their] good works and give glory to [our] Father in heaven" (Mt 5:16; cf. Phil 2:15).

Authentic discipleship and genuine Christian *koinonia* should normally have a discernible cultural impact. Absence of this impact raises questions about the depth and genuineness of the church's life and discipleship.

To be more specific: If in a city the church (that is, Christian churches in aggregate) is growing but the crime rate is not dropping, does this indicate a failure of Christian discipleship? It might or might not, since many factors are involved. But this data would at least raise the question. It might prompt Christians to ask why their Christian faith and witness are not having greater social impact. A KGI could help here.

3. A Kingdom of God Index would expand the church's horizons in a way consistent with the biblical gospel.

Churches, like people and all social organizations, tend to focus mainly on themselves—their own life and success. Increasingly so with the passage of time. Even if a church is dedicated to mission in the world, it tends to become preoccupied with its own horizon of mission and its own successes or failures.[1]

---

[1] A great deal of research on institutions and organizational behavior shows that organizations tend over time to become increasingly focused on themselves, insular, self-protective, and in the process to lose sight

A KGI would keep reminding the church of wider horizons. It might help churches broaden their vision, look more globally, see the whole world in all its dimensions, the full scope of the kingdom of God.

In other words, a KGI would raise issues and dimensions of mission and gospel impact that many churches rarely think of, or else consider to be matters beyond Christian or at least their own local concern.

Churches cannot and should not, of course, try to do everything. They must focus on areas of mission to which God especially calls them—their particular calling and *charism*. So careful spiritual discernment is needed. The point here is not to call churches to try to do everything; quite the opposite: To provide data and perspectives that help churches perceive the breadth of kingdom concerns and then seek guidance as to their particular strategic kingdom focus.

The gospel is for the whole world. God's reign and healing plan encompasses "all things." A KGI could serve as a reminder of this key biblical truth, not just conceptually but in practical and even empirical ways.

---

of their original purpose. The church is not immune to these dynamics, especially as it becomes larger, more highly structured, and more "successful" in institutional or worldly terms.

4. A Kingdom of God Index could thus be strategically useful in the church's missional engagement with the world.

We live in an increasingly fast-paced society marked by rapid and nearly constant change. The church should be a rock of security, a place of stability in a changing world. Change is often bad, not good.

But the flip side of this bedrock truth is that the church is called not to withdraw from the world, but to be missionally engaged. Urban churches that have a clear sense of who Jesus Christ is and of the hopeful certainty of the kingdom of God, "rooted and grounded" in Christ's love (Eph 3:17), will seek with high intentionality to engage the world in all its dimensions with the redeeming, transforming power of the gospel. Here the kind of data provided by a KGI could be useful.

Businesses, governments, and organizations of all types make use of a constant and increasing flow of data. Nowhere is this more true than in financial markets. An unending stream of data and forecasts from a constantly expanding universe of financial institutions and analysts feeds into Wall Street, Toronto, London, Shanghai, and other financial centers. In response, stock markets jump up and down like puppets on strings.

This is an extreme. Churches should not be like Wall Street. On the other hand, neither should they be like the monks on Mount Athos (bless them), totally walled off from the world. Churches should indeed be in but not of the world. Relevant and well-selected data can be useful here.

Businesses make strategic decisions based on current data and on future projections, as well as on their own history ("past performance"). Missional city churches can do something theologically similar. That is, well grounded in the gospel and in their Christian identity, urban churches can filter the unending data flow for facts, trends, and insights that can make mission more effective. A Kingdom of God Index raises that possibility.

5. Perhaps most importantly, a KGI would raise and help clarify the relationship between the church and the kingdom of God—between "church business" and "kingdom business."

Churches have a lot of access to data about church growth, church attendance, and so forth. But they have very little data on kingdom growth or impact. Churches generally track their own organizational statistics—attendance, membership, finances, programs. But few if any, to my knowledge, try to track what difference they are making for the kingdom of God. How many even ask the question?

As I have written elsewhere, biblically there is a huge difference between church business and kingdom business.[2] The two may be intimately related, positively and ecologically, or they may be totally divorced. Church history bristles with examples of the church energetically if unwittingly fighting against God's kingdom.

We want our churches to be agents, signs, and outposts of the kingdom of God. It can happen. But how would we know? A KGI would provide, or point toward, some real if still ambiguous answers. If nothing else, it would cause churches and church leaders to ask whether they are in the church business or the kingdom business.

Signs of the Kingdom?

What would a Kingdom of God Index look like? It would bring together a wide spectrum of available data on matters that, biblically, are of kingdom of God import. It would indeed be an *index*, a summary profile of data, frequently updated and also traced back into history as far as possible.

---

[2] Snyder, *Liberating the Church,* 11.

I emphasize here the need for a *wide spectrum analysis.* The natural tendency is to limit our analysis to those markers that are most visible, obvious, traditional, and easily countable. The sustainability-conscious investment firm Generation Investment Management does something different. It employs a full spectrum analysis when making investment decisions. Using the analogy of the spectrum of light—from invisible infrared to invisible ultraviolet—Generation notes that most financial institutions limit their analysis only to the visible portion of the spectrum: what is easily seen and measured, such as short-term profit and loss. Most companies thus miss crucial hidden, "invisible," longer-term factors, such as social and environmental impact. Generation includes "factors deliberately left out of many business measurements," like "a company's environmental effects, the culture it creates internally, and its impact on the societies in which it operates."[3]

Similarly, with the Kingdom of God Index, Christians are, or should be, aware of a much broader range of factors than people who are focused only on the here and now or on material things. This is perhaps the biggest challenge,

---

[3] James Fallows, "The (Planet-Saving, Capitalism-Subverting, Surprisingly Lucrative) Investment Secrets of Al Gore," *The Atlantic* (November 2015), 85–96 (quotation, p. 88). The whole article is relevant to the question of indexing for urban mission.

because not all relevant data or dynamics can be known. But revealed biblical truth can guide us in selecting data that have most long-term gospel relevance.

Importantly, such an index would not require massive amounts of new research. Much relevant research is already being done and is readily available, as I will show. The effort necessary to construct a KGI would mainly be one of compiling, sifting, summarizing, and reporting available data. The most creative part would involve deciding exactly which data to include and how to weight different items. Work would be necessary also to trace the data back into history.

Many Christian research centers now exist all around the world. A competent global KGI could be produced by one of these, or by a new Christian think tank that works collaboratively with and networks existing centers. One obvious candidate would be the Center for the Study of Global Christianity at Gordon-Conwell Theological Seminary, directed by Todd M. Johnson, and its World Christian Database, available online *(http://www.worldchristiandatabase.org/wcd/)*. This database already provides a remarkable range of regularly updated information. In 2009 the Center published the *Atlas of*

Global Christianity 1910–2010, edited by Todd Johnson and Kenneth Ross.[4]

Developing and maintaining a Kingdom of God Index could be undertaken or coordinated by a research center connected with a Christian seminary or university, or carried out cooperatively by several such centers.

The Evidence Exists!

Currently evidence exists in two main forms: Databases that serve the church by providing information useful mainly for evangelism and missions strategizing, and secular databases that publish information used mainly by businesses, governments, NGOs, and educational institutions.

Two examples of the former are the World Christian Database, mentioned above, and Global Mapping (GMI). Global Mapping describes itself as "A global Christian community that practices knowledge stewardship to stimulate, shape, and sharpen outreach for Kingdom impact." Global Mapping "leverages research and

---

[4] Edinburgh, Scotland: Edinburgh University Press, 2009. Some might argue that the World Christian Database already provides in effect a KGI, or at least the raw material for one. But the data provided there would need to be sifted and organized into an actual index, and should be supplemented by additional sources of information not specifically linked to Christianity.

technology to create, cultivate, and communicate mission information leading to insight that inspires Kingdom service." The organization partners with other organizations globally to help assist emerging mission movements and leaders. GMI traces its history to the beginning of the Global Mapping Project at the U.S. Center for World Mission in Pasadena, California, in 1983.[5]

The Evangelical Fellowship of Canada compiles a large amount of statistical data through its research and media relations department that would also be relevant to a KGI. To some degree the Evangelical Fellowship of Canada is also a clearinghouse of other sources of relevant data.

Selected information from these and other Christian databases would form an essential component of a KGI. I am particularly interested however in secular databases that might be drawn upon for kingdom of God purposes. Most Christians are unaware of these or don't see their potential missional usefulness. A top-quality KGI would draw from both Christian and non-Christian data sources.

---

[5] Information from the Global Mapping website (http://www.gmi.org/), accessed December 3, 2015.

A growing number of global databases or information sources now exists that could be particularly useful for a KGI. A few examples:

Transparency International publishes annually its Corruption Perception Index, which lists estimated corruption levels by country. *(See http://cpi.transparency.org/cpi2011/).* The level of corruption, based on a variety of indexes, can thus be tracked year by year.

Global Witness *(http://www.globalwitness.org/)* highlights links between environmental exploitation and human rights abuses, especially where key natural resources are being abused or misused.

Freedom House *(http://www.freedomhouse.org/)* and the Fraser Institute, a Canadian think tank founded in 1974 and based in Vancouver *(http://www.fraserinstitute.org/)*, both attempt to assess levels of freedom in the various nations of the world. Freedom House focuses also on freedom of the press. The Fraser Institute links with about eighty other think tanks around the world.

These and others organizations represent a range of political and economic viewpoints and provide data that can be useful for mission. Wikipedia notes, "There are several non-governmental organizations that publish and maintain assessments of the state of freedom in the world, according to their own various definitions of the term, and rank countries as being free, partly free, or unfree using various measures of freedom, including political rights, economic rights, and civil liberties." Wikipedia provides basic information on these. *(http://en.wikipedia.org/wiki/List_of_freedom_indices).*

The World Values Survey is another source. This organization describes itself as "the world's most comprehensive investigation of political and sociocultural change" *(http://www.worldvaluessurvey.org/)*. The historian Niall Ferguson used this survey to assess the level of religious belief and practice in his enlightening book, *Civilization: The West and the Rest.*[6]

Another source is the Global Peace Index *(http://www.visionofhumanity.org/gpi-data/)* which assesses the degree of peace around the world and publishes reports.

Much of the data from organizations such as these is readily available over the Internet.

The Economist magazine (or newspaper, as it calls itself) publishes annually *The Economist Pocket World in Figures*, also a handy source. It gives data for instance on population size and growth, birth rates, refugees, living standards, quality of life, education, life expectancy, health, and

---

[6] Niall Ferguson, *Civilization: The West and the Rest* (New York: Penguin, 2011), 266-67.

marriage and divorce (among other categories). For example under "quality of life," using the U.N. Human Development Index (HDI), in 2010 Canada had the seventh highest overall ranking globally and South Korea the eleventh, with Norway the highest and Zimbabwe the lowest. The HDI combines data on years of schooling, life expectancy, and income levels. What it tells us is thus quite limited, but it is one data point which could be considered in conjunction with, say, fifty or so others.

A number of governmental agencies also provide data on various countries and issues in the world. The U.S. State Department for instance publishes a wide range of data on countries and on human rights. *(See for example http://www.state.gov/countries/ and http://www.state.gov/j/drl/rls/hrrpt/).*

Globally and internationally, there are many more social, economic, and cultural indices that could offer strategic data. They don't all need to be enumerated here, and doubtless new ones will appear. The point is that a great variety and range of data is now available that could be regularly assessed and updated as a resource for Christian mission and fidelity according to the values and virtues of the kingdom of God.[7]

---

[7] See for example "Ranking the Rankings" (*The Economist* Nov. 8, 2014, 61–62), which notes increasing numbers of such indices and

Kingdom Discipleship Today

Analysis of these kinds of data by Christian researchers could not of course establish precise cause and effect between the church's witness and its impact on society and culture. The *missio Dei* cannot be fed into computers and projected as computer-screen data points.

But we might be able to discern *curious correlations*. For example, if in nations or regions where the church has been growing substantially over many decades we find evidence of less violence, more family stability, improved health, better environmental stewardship, and a lessening of poverty, that might indicate that the church is having a positive impact for the kingdom. If no such evidence can be found, that at least raises the question of *why*. Is the church authentically living out the gospel in wholesome and wholistic discipleship? If so, where's the evidence? And what countervailing factors might possibly be undercutting its social impact? Many factors could impinge: War, ecological changes or disasters, political instability,

---

relative quality or soundness. Other indices include the Multidimensional Poverty Index (MPI), the Heritage Foundation's Index of Economic Freedom, and the Zoological Society of London's Living Planet Index. Howard Steven Friedman's book, *The Measure of a Nation* (Amherst, N.Y.: Prometheus, 2012), compares the U.S. with other countries on five "vital measures."

economic collapse, possibly persecution, could all enter in and would need to be taken into account.

As Jesus's disciples, his Body, we are called to "seek first [God's] Kingdom and his righteousness" and justice (Mt 6:33 TNIV). This is both a moral and a strategic imperative. Pertinent data, viewed longitudinally, brought together in a Kingdom of God Index, could be a provocative tool toward greater kingdom faithfulness. It could also help with missional strategic planning along the lines I suggest in the next chapter, "Strategic Planning and the Kingdom of God."

Does the church need a Kingdom of God Index? In these most critical times, the question is worth serious consideration.

CHAPTER 5
Strategic Planning in Urban Mission

It may seem that strategic planning and the Kingdom of God live on separate planets. Strategic planning is sometimes used in urban mission, but by what criteria and with what theological or worldview assumptions?

In Christian mission, few people seem to see any vital connection between the kingdom of God and strategic planning. Kingdom of God? That's off somewhere else—in the future; in heaven; maybe a little bit in my heart. Maybe reflected dimly in the church. But the Kingdom of God here and now, on Planet Earth? That's a more difficult question.

But Strategic Planning—OK, we're talking Here and Now and in the foreseeable future. We have to plan, and we *can* plan. As Christians, we do our best. We plan, we pray, we ask God to bless our efforts. But the kingdom of God as a realistic *strategic priority* seldom enters our minds or our field of vision.

There is something wrong with this picture. Jesus said specifically: Seek first the kingdom of God with its justice and righteousness. If you do that, everything else will fall into proper place (Mt 6:33). That sounds strategic. It implies planning.

Yet when it comes to our own lives, our churches, our businesses, our Christian colleges and other institutions, the kingdom of God seldom enters the calculation in any practical sense. Perhaps we *assume* that because we're Christians, we are sort of automatically seeking God's kingdom. We worship God, so we can trust him to guide our planning and bless our plans. Or else we think that strategic planning and the kingdom of God are simply unrelated. The Kingdom of God? That's God's business. Strategic planning? That's our business.

This chapter is a natural next step beyond the question of a possible Kingdom of God Index. If strategic planning and the kingdom of God are both important—both priorities for Christians—how may they be integrated? Is there any way that the priorities of God's kingdom can really, realistically, functionally be married? Or are we talking apples and oranges here? Maybe even apples and angels?

Let's Build the Kingdom?

Long ago as people migrated from the east (so we read in Genesis 11); they came to a broad plain that looked like a good place to settle.

They said to each other, "Come, let us build ourselves a city, and a tower with its top in the heavens. Let's make a name for ourselves!" (Gen 11:4).

They did some strategic planning. They figured out how to make bricks and mortar and to design a great tower. The improved the technology. Apparently they figured out how to organize workers and get the project underway— good management.

God was bemused. He "came down to see the city and the tower the people had built" (Gen 11:5). The Lord put an end to the enterprise by confusing the people's language.

So is this God's answer to human planning?

Hardly. Consider all the planning that went into the construction of the tabernacle in the book of Exodus. Not to mention Solomon's temple.

Clearly strategic planning can be either good or bad—either in harmony with God's will or starkly against it. Is there a way to know the difference? Don't we always run the risk of voiding God's Word by our own traditions (Mt 15:6), including the tradition of strategic planning, so much loved in the West?

We don't "build" the kingdom of God. God does. Yet clearly we are called to be kingdom workers. All our work (and play, and rest) is to be oriented, like filings to a magnet, to the kingdom of God.

Strategic planning and the kingdom of God need not be enemies. Jesus says his kingdom "is not something that can be observed" (Lk 17:20 TNIV). It grows silently, by itself, unobserved, like seeds in soil. But we are to sow and work productively and bring in harvest for the kingdom of God. That doesn't happen automatically or under the direct control of the Holy Spirit. It is a matter of planning and of strategy; of knowing seasons and techniques and varieties of seeds and of how things grow, and knowing the difference between good seed and weeds.

Farmers and sowers plan. So do military generals. Jesus said, "What king, going out to wage war against another king, will not sit down first and consider whether he is able with ten thousand to oppose the one who comes against him with twenty thousand?" (Lk 14:31).

Jesus said his disciples should be prudent and provident. Planning is essential.

But how? Here is a thoughtful way planning can be carried out by Christians—not only consistently with, but in fact (bold claim!) actually *contributing to* the kingdom of God.

Here's the thesis: Urban churches should plan in light of the present and the near future, but always with an eye *practically and strategically* on the "eschatological horizon" (the kingdom of God in fullness) for orientation. Realistic but modest planning thus occurs with a shorter-term vision and goals but also with functional orientation toward a *prophetic ideal* that is consistent with and moves in the direction of God's reign.

When I was about fifteen I worked for a farmer who was our next door neighbor in Spring Arbor, Michigan. He was about sixty. Decades earlier he had lost both hands and most of his arms in a corn-shelling machine accident.

But Ollie Pretty was clever and resourceful. With welded hooks and rings he was still able to drive his big spike-wheeled International tractor.

Ollie let me drive the tractor and showed me how to cut a straight furrow when starting to plow a field. "You see that big tree over there, clear on the other side of the field?" he asked. "Head for that! Keep your eye on it."

It worked. The furrow was straight. The field was plowed, prepared.

As Christians, we have to keep our eye on the kingdom of God. Not let anything distract us.

The Kingdom of God is Not General Motors (or Google)

Christian organizations typically elaborate successive plans through a strategic planning process. But they follow a secular, this-worldly model. If Christian churches and missions develop a "prophetic ideal" that is faithful to the mission of God, this could boost strategic planning beyond merely human dreams (or hubris) and begin to embody in some sense God's dreams.

Basic assumption: Planning should be an integral part of our discipleship, aimed not first of all at institutional success but at faithful witness to Jesus Christ and his reign.

I once heard Christian strategic planning defined something like this: "An interactive process in which constituents formulate the optimal way to achieve God's agenda for kingdom impact." That's pretty good. But how, and with what larger assumptions?

From a Christian standpoint, the ultimate goal of faithful urban mission is nothing less than the kingdom of God—God's will being done on earth as in heaven right here on our streets, in the neighborhoods, in both the microstructures and macrostructures of the city and its larger context. Yet the kingdom is in large measure a mystery, as we have emphasized. Jesus said, "The kingdom of God is not coming with things that can be observed" (Luke 17:20 NRSV) or "with observation" (KJV).

Christian leaders however, like most leaders, are planners. Institutions, especially, like to plan. Many Christian organizations have a planning process. Christian colleges and universities make medium- and long-range projections.

Is there any connection between planning and truly redemptive ministry? Or is planning a merely human or "secular" predilection? Can strategic planning *in fact* contribute to the coming of the kingdom of God? If not, then for Christians is it a waste of time, maybe even an idol?

Strategic planning for urban mission that is faithful to the kingdom of God can in fact be done. Here is a visual model of how planning and the kingdom of God might be strategically linked. The basic *thesis* is this: If Christian organizations think of their future in terms of the priorities of the kingdom of God (Mt 6:33) and let those priorities shape their planning process, strategic planning *can* contribute to (not build) God's kingdom. The basic *assumption* is this: Planning, if done, should be an integral part of our discipleship, aimed not at institutional success but at faithful witness to Jesus Christ and his reign.

Strategic Kingdom Planning in Urban Mission

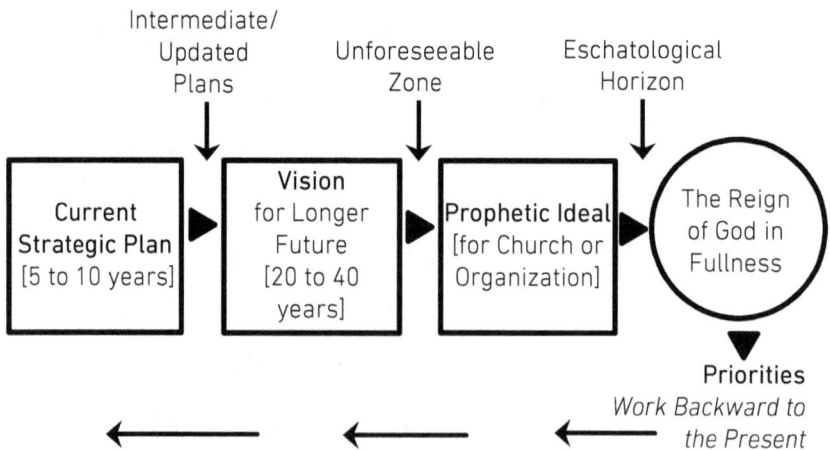

Intermediate/
Updated
Plans

Unforeseeable
Zone

Eschatological
Horizon

↓   ↓   ↓

| Current Strategic Plan [5 to 10 years] | ▶ | Vision for Longer Future [20 to 40 years] | ▶ | Prophetic Ideal [for Church or Organization] | ▶ | The Reign of God in Fullness |

▼
Priorities
Work Backward to the Present

←   ←   ←

Essential Critical Questions:

- Is the **current strategic plan** sufficiently open and flexible to allow and facilitate the longer-term **vision?**
- Is this **vision** consistent with and shaped by our **prophetic ideal?**
- Would the **prophetic ideal** actually contribute to, or move in the trajectory of the kingdom of God?

How it Works

Note that the thee key components here are *Current Strategic Plan, Vision for the Longer Future,* and *Prophetic Ideal,* all aimed toward the kingdom or reign of God in fullness. With the second and third component the time horizon gets progressively longer, but no less important. Note also the key spaces between these components, and finally the feedback loop from a kingdom vision back to the present.

Here's how it works:

Current Strategic Plan (5 to 10 years). If it doesn't already exist, a strategic plan should be written based on the church or mission's stated purpose and sense of calling or charism (particular grace or gifts for ministry). What is different here from secular models is that this plan, though time-limited, is already looking toward a longer horizon—ultimately the coming of the kingdom of God in fullness, but also a 20 to 40 year vision and a longer-term prophetic ideal (explained below).

Intermediate/Updated Plans. Year by year the plan is reviewed and updated—not only in light of progress, possible setbacks, and new developments, but also in light of growing clarity regarding the longer-term vision.

Vision for the Longer Future (20–40 years?). An inherent and constant part of the planning process is continuing reflection on a longer-term desired future that is consistent with the revealed priorities of the kingdom of God. Every planning session or review should end with this discussion: Are our current plans moving us toward the longer-term vision? Do they need revising in some way? This is an intermediate stage between hard data and larger aspirations.

Unforeseeable Zone. The future is more and more hidden to us the further we look ahead. Even the nearer-term future is unforeseeable to us, no matter how much we rely on prayer, spiritual discernment, and biblical revelation. The space between the longer-term vision and the Prophetic Ideal in particular is the *Unforeseeable Zone* where it is fruitless and foolish to try to plan. However, as we look further down the road, planning gives way to the inspiration of a Prophetic Ideal—what we would *like* to see happen if and as the ministry reflects more fully the wondrous truth of the kingdom of God and as God's Spirit provides inspiration and power. The *Unforeseeable Zone* is a reminder to remain humble, tentative, open-minded and open-hearted as we look into the more misty future. It is thus a crucial part of the planning process. It keeps reminding us that God is sovereign, that redemption doesn't really depend on us, but that even so, we are called to *act* consistently with a kingdom vision, however foolish that may appear to the world.

Prophetic Ideal. Elaborating a Prophetic Ideal is the next crucial step in kingdom-oriented strategic planning.

What is a Prophetic Ideal? It is a *written description* of what our church or mission would increasingly become if it successfully implements plans and takes steps that lead us closer to the kingdom of God while remaining constantly open to the Spirit. It is visionary, heuristic,[1] general, and yet specific enough to be clear, recognizable, and potentially evaluated. It is best written, in most cases, in the form of a *scenario*—that is, a narrative (a kind of imagined

---

[1] *Heuristic*: Using informed guesses to make plausible projections into (not predictions about) the future.

story) about the desired fruitfulness of the ministry in light of the vision of the kingdom of God.

Although this is a "what if" projection, an imagined ideal, it is not so vague or general as to be meaningless. For instance, rather than phrases like "have an increasingly redemptive impact on our neighborhood" it would specify what that might mean concretely—an imagined scenario. *What specifically would actually be different* in terms of kingdom priorities?

Eschatological Horizon. Here the planning process moves beyond history as we know it. The Eschatological Horizon is recognition that we cannot (yet) see over the horizon to the kingdom of God in fullness, even in our own immediate context. This element is a reminder that the full coming of the kingdom of God is beyond our planning or manipulation. It is not for that reason unreal or unimportant, however.

The Reign of God in fullness. This is what the Bible pictures in many prophetic passages. Key examples would be Isaiah 11, Daniel 7, and especially Revelation 21–22. It is useful and prudent for urban churches constantly to hold out before them the full biblical vision of *shalom*, "all things" reconciled and healed through Jesus Christ—and to be constantly looking toward that coming kingdom in hope as ministry and planning go forward. This should be the stuff of preaching, teaching, singing, and all kinds of creative expression. Such a vision helps keep hope and action alive when the inevitable setbacks and heartaches come.

Feedback Loop: Priorities work backward to the present. Note the arrows and the three *Essential Critical Questions.* As part of the planning process, three things continually should happen. Time should be taken to examine these questions:

1. Regarding the Prophetic Ideal: If realized, would this ideal actually contribute to, or move along the trajectory, of the kingdom of God?

2. Regarding the Longer-Term Vision: Is this vision consistent with and shaped by our Prophetic Ideal (on the one hand) and is it a plausible extension of current plans?

3. Regarding the Current Strategic Plan: Is this plan sufficiently open and flexible to allow and facilitate the longer-term vision?

Thus the circle is completed—in fact, a cycle that should be reviewed periodically for new insights and learning. Here the diversity of people's gifts come into play. Some folks will have gifts more for the present, immediate future, and others more for the more distant horizon.

So the strategic planning cycle continues, moving back and forth in both directions: From the immediate and specific to the longer-term and more visionary. Then also back again: From the grand projected future to both our intermediate and current plans. The process comes alive and generates energy as it engages folks with different personalities, gifts, interests, and experiences. So this kind of strategic planning is lively, not dull.

Perhaps the two most strategically important elements in this model are the *Unforeseen Zone* and the *Eschatological Horizon*. Christian planners often are stymied at these points. We assume that the longer-range future is simply beyond the planning process, and thus in practice irrelevant.

The better sorts of strategic planning of course allow space for the "unforeseens." But they have no real way of dealing with these other than by ongoing processes of review, flexibility, and multiple options. In secular models, what I here call the *Eschatological Horizon* is by definition ruled out as beyond the periphery of any serious planning.

As Christians, we must avoid this temptation. We simply must not forget the vision of the kingdom of God in fullness, even (and especially) in our planning. The Eschatological Horizon should be a constant present pressure on us, keeping us from thinking too small, too secular, or two short-term in our plans and projections.

Final Word, Ongoing Process

This approach to Christian strategic planning is qualitatively different from secular planning models in three ways. First, it takes into account the full biblical promise of the kingdom of God—not as mere vague hope or vision, but as strategic pressure back on the present. Second, it maintains an ongoing cycle from the present on beyond The Eschatological Horizon and back again, continuing on repeatedly. Third, the goal is the formation of a redemptive people, not the manufacture and sale of a product or service. The big goal is redemptive Christ-like healing throughout our reachable context, understanding that this often begins with small things, small voices, vital seeds that can grow.

The real goal is to be truly prophetic—to play a part in the grand global project of recovering prophetic Christianity. Ultimately, the final goal of strategic planning for urban mission is nothing less breathtaking than the kingdom of God in fullness.

CHAPTER 6
The Loss of Prophetic Christianity

Since about the year 2000, the Christian Church worldwide has increasingly come to sense it is facing a crisis different in scope and kind from anything ever experienced before.

I will outline the symptoms of this crisis shortly. However I first list four reasons why the crisis Christianity now faces is unprecedented—qualitatively different from anything the Christian Church has ever faced before.

First, this crisis is *truly global*—not just in concept, but in actual fact. The Christian Church is found in more countries and people groups around the world today than ever before. As a result of the remarkable Christian missionary efforts of the 1800s and 1900s, we can now speak of global Christianity in a way that we never could previously.

In his book *The Future of the Global Church,* Patrick Johnstone writes:

> The expansion of Christianity between 1950 and 2000 has no parallel in history. At its heart were the revival of Evangelical and Catholic enthusiasm for missions, and the global growth of Pentecostal denominations and Charismatic networks, all facilitated by global conferences and networking. The result was massive church growth in sub-Saharan Africa and parts of Asia, and the spread of Evangelicalism throughout the Americas. These gains offset the big losses in Europe and the Pacific. The Church truly became worldwide for the first time in history.[1]

Second, the crisis of today's Christian Church is unprecedented because *we are now in the Anthropocene Age* of earth's long history. For the first time in history, the human race has achieved such technological capability and such numbers that it is beginning to have massive impact on the planet itself, particularly on its climate and ecosystems.

---

[1] Patrick Johnstone, *The Future of the Global Church: History, Trends and Possibilities* (Colorado Springs, Colo.: Biblica, 2011), 94.

The Christian Church has hardly begun to grasp the significance of this major shift. Yet it has huge implications for the church's discipleship and mission.

Third, today's crisis is unprecedented because we are now in *the age of instant communication and global social networks*. The most obvious example here is Facebook and similar "social networking" Internet sites worldwide. Facebook was founded in 2004—less than a dozen years ago—and today has nearly 1.5 billion users. Many of us now have Facebook "friends" all over the world, irrespective of national boundaries. This phenomenon adds dimensions, both positive and negative, to the challenges facing global Christianity today.

Fourth, the Christian Church itself has undergone a *major shift in its "center of gravity"* so that the real center of the church is no longer in the West. This is true not only numerically, but also in terms of theology, institutions, and spiritual vitality. Increasingly the church's center is in Asia, though with significant centers of influence also in South America and Central Africa.

Global Christianity is more and more a global network with many nodes rather than having one primary center. Its future growth will look more like an emergent network than like a one-way flow.[2]

These four realities—globalization of the church, dawn of the Anthropocene Age, instant global social networking, and shift of the church's center of gravity away from the West—define the context of the Christian Faith in the today's world. This is the church's new contextual reality.

We should reflect on how different this context is from the situation of the church in 1900 or even in 1950, at the outbreak of the Korean War.

Most of us are well aware of the decline of Christianity in the West—Europe and North America, especially—over the past century. Let us put this fact in the larger context of Christian history since the Day of Pentecost. We need to understand how the Christian Church in the world got to the place where it is today if we would understand how to respond faithfully and effectively.

In this chapter my central thesis is that the Christian Church began as a prophetic movement of biblical faith; and that the Age of Christendom, from about 350 to 1980, produced much good but also often undermined the church's integrity. In the next chapter I show how churches

---

[2] See Sam Law, "Anticipating Change: Missions and Paradigm Shifts in Emergence," *The Asbury Journal* 67:1 (Spring 2012), 4–26.

in urban mission can discern a biblically and theologically sound way out of the present crisis. In these two chapters I trace the route from prophetic early Christianity to our present crisis, and the way ahead to renewal and the recovery of prophetic Christianity. This is a story that moves from life, to death, to rebirth and resurrection. God still says today, as he has in the past, "I will do a new thing" (see Isa 43:19).

I am not proposing a return to an ideal situation in the past. I am talking about finding the way to move forward into God's future—the church moving ahead in witness and testimony to the full manifestation of the kingdom of God, God's will done "on earth as in heaven" (Mt 6:10).

In this chapter we will examine symptoms of critical disease and crisis, compare global civilization East and West, and note the church's loss of ancient wisdom.

Symptoms of Critical Disease and Crisis

It is not hard to find signs that the Christian Church globally is in trouble! Here are the *five most critical signs* or symptoms of this crisis, as I see it.

1. Historic Decline of the Christian Church in the West

The data here are well known. Church attendance and Christian influence have declined steadily in North

America and in Western Europe over the past century, since the early 1900s. Relatively few people in the United States, Canada, and the nations of Western Europe, for instance, now have any knowledge of the Bible or even know who Jesus Christ is.

In the United States, church attendance continues to decline. David T. Olson reports in his book *The American Church in Crisis*, "The percentage of Americans who attended a Christian church on any given weekend declined from 20.4 percent in 1990 to 17.5 percent in 2005." In no state of the United States is church attendance keeping pace with population growth. This means that across the United States, less than one in five citizens attend church regularly.[3] Certainly the number of really committed Christians is much less than that; probably less than one in ten. Further, many American Christians adhere to a kind of church-and-culture blend that is shaped more by American patriotism and nationalism than it is by biblical discipleship.

In general, church attendance in Western Europe is proportionately considerably lower than in North America,

---

[3] David T. Olson, *The American Church in Crisis* (Grand Rapids: Zondervan, 2008), 36-37. Some polls put average attendance at 40%, based on self-reporting, but this likely is considerably exaggerated. In any case, I am not as concerned with specific data as with overall trend.

and continues to decline. Meanwhile the average age of churchgoers continues to rise. This suggests the trend of decline will continue unless there is a major religious resurgence.[4]

This decline does not necessarily mean people are becoming more secular. In fact, today the issue is not so much secularization as it is de-Christianization. Many people claim to be "spiritual," not "secular," but are not Christian. People say, "I am not religious, but I am spiritual."

The mood and worldview in most Western society today is thus neither secularist nor Christian. It is what we might call "secular spirituality."

An important part of this picture is the growth of non-Christian world religions in the West, especially Islam, Hinduism, and Buddhism. According to the *Atlas of Global Christianity,* one-third of the world's population today is Christian, of one sort or another. Just over twenty percent is Muslim, 13.7% are Hindu, and 6.8% are Buddhist. For the past century (since 1910) the proportion of Christians has remained about the same. However the Muslim

---

[4] For the significance of church trends, especially in relation to financial giving, see John L. Ronsvalle and Sylvia Ronsvalle, *The State of Church Giving through 2013: Crisis or Potential?* (Champaign, Ill.: empty tomb, inc.), 2015.

population has nearly doubled (12.6% to 22.4%). The proportion Hindus has grown just slightly, while the proportion of Buddhists has declined slightly. Significantly, the proportion of agnostics grew from less than one percent to almost ten percent today.[5]

The signs of Muslim growth, especially, are highly visible in the West today. Mosques, as well as Hindu and Buddhist temples, are increasingly common in most Western cities. Canada had an ironic television series called "Little Mosque on the Prairie." Since 2007, one of the representatives in the United States Congress has been a Muslim (though by far the majority of Congress is Christian or functionally secular).

Though the United States remains predominantly Christian by profession, the percentage of vital Christians and congregations appears to have declined substantially. Clearly the Christian Faith has less and less influence in society. Opinion polls show continuing decline in what would be considered traditional Christian moral values. Olson projects that weekly church attendance in the U.S. will decline to under 15 percent by 2020. That would be a drop from about one in five to about one in six.[6]

---

[5] Todd M. Johnson and Kenneth R. Ross, eds., *Atlas of Global Christianity* (Edinburgh: Edinburgh University Press, 2009), 6–7.
[6] Olson, 175.

The decline of the Western church is a crisis for global Christianity for several reasons—perhaps most importantly because it creates the impression among many people, especially in media and politics, that the Christian Faith is no longer relevant or influential in the world generally. This, of course, is a silly myth!

On the other hand, the decline of Western Christianity presents opportunities for the church globally. The decline of dominance of the West could mean a more balanced and cooperative Christian presence and witness worldwide, with greater valuing of the contributions of the church's diverse cultures, gifts, institutions, and doctrinal emphases, and a new appreciation of how the Spirit often moves in small ways and quiet voices.

2. Social and Personal Identity Crisis

Second, we face a crisis of human identity.

What does it mean to be human? Where is human identity based? What is the relationship between a single human person and the larger human community in which his or her life is situated?

These are complex but crucial questions. Global society is passing through a major shift precisely at this point.

Throughout history, a person's identity was found in and shaped by family and local community, which were often interconnected. "Who I am" was part of the larger reality of "Who we are" as a family, tribe, or village.

In the West, this connection between person and community broke down with the emergence of modern Europe, from approximately 1500 AD on. There were many contributing factors: The European Renaissance, the Protestant Reformation and the Catholic Reformation (or Counter-Reformation, as it is sometimes called), the Enlightenment, the emergence of European nation-states in the aftermath of the Thirty Years War (1618–1648), the rise of capitalism, the emergence of modern science, the Industrial Revolution beginning in England in the 1700s, and the rise of democratic governments. All these were contributing factors. Another huge factor was of course the global voyages of discovery, coming first from Portugal, Spain, Holland, England, and France, leading to the circumnavigation of the globe and eventually to the age of European Colonialism. These were all important and all interrelated.[7]

A major result of this history was that Western societies developed a culture of individualism—the individual, distinct person, not the larger society or nation, was

---

[7] Each of these can of course be discussed at length. See the discussion under "Civilization East and West," below.

primary. Family and other forms of community became secondary. More and more, personal identity was individual identity rather than group or social identity. Descartes' philosophical formula, "I think, therefore I am," had its social and psychological corollary in the sense of each person being a distinct "individual" rather than a person whose identity was grounded in his or her immersion in the larger group reality of family, tribe, or village. Here we find the rise of Western individualism.

This signaled a *major shift in personal consciousness*, or consciousness of personal identity.[8] The individual person became socially and psychologically primary; the community became secondary. This was true economically, as well. Each person became a consuming unit and less part of a shared and sharing community.

This shift to individualism had positive economic effects but negative social effects. Individualism feeds consumerism and individual entrepreneurship. In these ways it stimulates economic growth. On the other hand it tends to fragment society, tearing apart the social fabric, undermining community solidarity.

---

[8] The Danish philosopher Kierkegaard (1813–1855) was one of the first to recognize this.

A major result is *alienation,* a sense of disconnectedness from the larger society and its traditional values. Combined with economic prosperity, it produces a new *youth culture* that is increasingly alienated from the past and more and more oriented toward materialism, entertainment, and communication technology.

The emergence of this *global youth culture,* so far insufficiently studied and understood, is one of the most important developments of the past forty years. For the first time in history, on a global scale, young people are primarily oriented *toward the present, toward each other,* and *toward global society,* rather than toward their parents, grandparents, and national heritage. Often this global youth culture is however highly individualistic and consumerist, lacking deep interpersonal community and meaning.

This can be overstated, of course. There are exceptions. But this is the macro-trend that began in the West and is increasingly shaping all cultures, East and West, North and South.

Clearly this social and identity crisis has huge implications for the church. I will say more about this shortly. The key point here is that *the church as body of Christ* is precisely God's way of shaping social life and personal identity. As Christians, we find our identity "in Christ"[9] and we find the meaning of our life in Christian community, living out the mission Jesus Christ has entrusted to us.

The church today is faced with the crucial challenge of responding faithfully and effectively to this global crisis of social and personal identity.

3. Global Environmental Crisis

As each year passes, the world becomes more and more aware of our growing global environmental crisis. Fundamentally, this is not a political or economic matter, but an ecological one. Today's environmental crisis certainly has large political and economic dimensions, but the basic issue concerns damage to the earth's ecosystem.

This is a key reason why scientists have begun speaking of dawn of the Anthropocene Age. Human activity, especially in the areas of technology, economics, and warfare, has reached the point where the future of the planet is being forever changed.[10]

The Economist magazine summarized the main realities of the Anthropocene Age:

---

[9] Rom. 8:1, 1 Cor. 1:30, Gal. 5:6, Col. 3:3, and many other passages.
[10] http://en.wikipedia.org/wiki/Anthropocene

Almost 90% of the world's plant activity, by some estimates, is to be found in ecosystems where humans play a significant role. Although farms have changed the world for millennia, the Anthropocene advent of fossil fuels, scientific breeding and, most of all, artificial nitrogen fertiliser has vastly increased agriculture's power. . . . The sheer amount of biomass now walking around the planet in the form of humans and livestock handily outweighs that of all other large animals. The world's ecosystems are dominated by an increasingly homogenous and limited suite of cosmopolitan crops, livestock and creatures that get on well in environments dominated by humans. Creatures less useful or adaptable get short shrift: the extinction rate is running far higher than during normal geological periods.[11]

The ecological implications of this new reality are now broadly recognized by scientists worldwide, and increasingly by national governments and the general public. However in some areas—particularly in the United States—the issue has become so clouded by politics that very little progress is made in addressing the crisis. Meanwhile the rapid economic growth of China, India,

---

[11] http://www.economist.com/node/18744401

South Korea, Brazil, and some other countries is making the ecological crisis drastically worse.

The issues here are well known. The most important ones: Air pollution due to the burning of fossil fuels, deforestation, over-fishing, pollution of the oceans, depletion of available water, growing rate of the extinction of species and decline in biodiversity, and large-scale industrialized agriculture that destroys natural environments and ecosystems.

Today the most obvious sign of this crisis is climate change, which is already producing extreme and unpredictable major weather disasters, particularly tornadoes, floods, droughts, and unprecedented forest fires. We are seeing this now throughout much of the United States. Traditional cycles, such as the coming of seasonal rains and monsoons, have become disrupted.

When I was teaching at the South Asia Institute of Advanced Christian Studies (SAIACS) in Bangalore, India, in 2011, several students from northern India told me of the disruption of natural weather cycles and extensive environmental damage. As one student told me, the crucial monsoon rains arrived three weeks late, completely upsetting the farming cycle.

But there are many other dimensions of the environmental crisis. Gradually we are coming to understand the complexities of earth's billions of ecosystems and the ways these are all connected in one complex *global* ecosystem. The simple fact is: Earth's climate and ecosystems are much more vulnerable to human impact than we had thought.

For Christians, this requires a huge change in thinking; in worldview. We know that God is sovereign, and that he "has the whole world in his hands." Many Christians have thought (or still think) that God will not allow human beings to destroy or significantly damage the earth.

This is a misreading of Scripture. God sets boundaries for his people. He warns us of two ways: the way of covenant faithfulness to God and the way of infidelity to God's covenant. The Bible teaches that if we are faithful to God's covenant, we will care for the earth, and it will flourish. If we are not, the earth suffers. This is a key area of Christian discipleship that the church must not neglect. So this is another matter to which we must return later.

4. Mere Cultural Christianity

Genuine Christian faith means radical commitment to Jesus Christ and thus to his church and mission. Over time, that radical commitment often gets compromised as the church begins to lose its first love (Rev 2:4) or to turn aside to false gods.

Today, the church's major false gods are nationalism, political ideology, materialism, greed (Col 3:5), consumerism, celebrity, and entertainment. Much of the church worldwide is guilty of idolatry in these areas.

The result is *mere cultural Christianity.* The Christian faith becomes just one part of people's cultural identity rather than the center of their life and being. This is what happens when we serve more than the one Lord God. We claim to be followers of Jesus Christ, but often our higher loyalty is to fame, success, comfort, or personal pleasure and satisfaction. And so Christians become functional polytheists.

Although Jesus warned against trying to serve two masters, millions of Christians, and many thousands of churches worldwide, are in fact serving two (or more) masters. What this means, of course—as Jesus made clear—is that we are not really serving Jesus Christ and his kingdom in faithfulness.

Whenever the church puts nationalism, patriotism, wealth, numerical growth, fame, or success ahead of costly fidelity to Jesus Christ and his kingdom, it is guilty of idolatry. It has reduced genuine Christian faith to mere cultural Christianity.

This kind of Christianity may succeed for a time, but it carries seeds of its own decline. It has taken up the weapons of the world rather than the weapons of genuine Christian warfare (2 Cor 10:3–4, Eph 6:4–18). When this happens, the church will eventually fall into crisis, because the weapons of the world ultimately prove ineffective for the kingdom of God.

"But God chose what is foolish in the world to shame the wise; God chose what is weak in the world to shame the strong; God chose what is low and despised in the world, things that are not, to reduce to nothing things that are, so that no one might boast in the presence of God. He is the source of your life in Christ Jesus, who became for us wisdom from God, and righteousness and sanctification and redemption, in order that, as it is written, 'Let the one who boasts, boast in the Lord'" (1 Cor 1:27–31).

Much of Christianity worldwide is in bondage to mere cultural Christianity. In the age of Christendom, this bondage took the form of the alliance of church and state. In our age, it generally takes the form of an alliance between the church and nationalism, or an alliance between the church and popular culture, with its focus on consumerism, individualism, and personal comfort.

5. Major Discipleship Gap

Today the church worldwide is experiencing a major *discipleship gap*. This is the fruit of years of mere cultural Christianity.

What I mean by this is a major gap between what Christians profess and how they actually live. Like the Pharisees in Jesus's day, we have found many ways to make void the Word of God by our traditions.

Jesus said to seek first the kingdom of God, but we believe it is fine to seek first personal success or comfort.

Jesus said we should love our neighbors as ourselves, but we believe it is acceptable to put ourselves ahead of our neighbors' needs.

The New Testament teaches that if we are truly Christians, we are "members of one another" (Eph 4:25) in the body of Christ; all "members of the same body" (Eph 3:6). But many Christians live with little vital connection to the body of Christ and are much more closely connected with their business partners or with non-Christians in various other pursuits, such as entertainment and sports.

The megachurch phenomenon of the past half-century has produced many churches with a yawning discipleship gap. Discipleship has not kept up with numerical growth. They are Acts 2:41 churches rather than Acts 2:42 churches—many added; few discipled, few devoting themselves to discipleship in community. This results is churches with thousands of members, but perhaps with only hundreds of disciples—that is, devout Christians whose lives are really shaped by the gospel, and who are in accountable "one-another" relationships with other Christians so that they are truly together growing up into "the knowledge of the Son of God, to maturity, to the measure of the full stature of Christ" (Eph 4:13). A megachurch of 50,000 members may have only 5,000 or 500 real disciples. And it is the large majority, not the faithful minority, who set the tone and the agenda for the church.

This is the biggest crisis facing the church worldwide, especially in areas of economic prosperity and technological sophistication.

This discipleship gap is the main reason for the historic decline of Christian faith in the West. Why has Western Christianity been in decline? There are many contributing factors, as I have noted. But behind and beneath all these is *one common factor*: The churches have not devoted themselves to the building of disciples, to truly "build[ing] up the body of Christ" (Eph 4:12).

The early church had an effective practice of the catechumenate. Many renewal movements, such as the early Anabaptists, Presbyterians, and Methodists, practiced careful discipleship through various forms of small groups—intimate communities where small voices could be heard. But today such practices have largely disappeared. J. I. Packer and Gary A. Parrett in their book *Grounded in the Gospel* write, "Discipleship impresses us as the key present-day issue, and catechesis as the key present-day element of discipleship, all the world over."[12]

Many churches of course have small groups. But these groups usually are more for therapy or sociability than they are for genuine New Testament discipleship.

We have built church buildings, church organizations, and even church empires, but we have not truly built up the body of Christ—communities of disciples that seek first the kingdom of God rather than some lesser goal.

---

[12] J. I. Packer and Gary A. Parrett, *Grounded in the Gospel: Building Believers the Old-Fashioned Way* (Grand Rapids: Baker, 2010), 17. See also Tory K. Baucum, *Evangelical Hospitality: Catechetical Evangelism in the Early Church and Its Recovery for Today* (Lanham, Md.: Scarecrow Press, 2008), which compares the early Christian catechumenate with the early Methodist class meeting and the Alpha Course today.

It is not evangelism alone, but only evangelism connected with ongoing discipleship, that can bring renewal to the church and make the church effectively God's agent for spreading the kingdom of God on earth.

These then are the five critical signs of the global crisis of Christian faith today: (1) historic decline of the church in the West, (2) social and personal identity crisis, (3) global environmental crisis, (4) mere cultural Christianity, and (5) discipleship gap.

Identifying these factors helps us understand the depth of the church's crisis today, and also suggests directions for a recovery of vitality and faithfulness.

The picture I have painted so far is mostly negative. This is not the whole story, however. I see some bright spots on the horizon, some encouraging signs of God's work in the global church. I will speak of these in the next chapter.

We know of course that the church has grown rapidly throughout the world over the past two hundred years. Much of this growth was sparked by the dynamism of Western Christianity and related Western culture. This raises the question of the connections between Western Christianity and Western civilization generally.

A number of authors have addressed this question. One of the most insightful is the noted British historian Niall Ferguson in his 2012 book, *Civilization: The West and the Rest*. Let us look briefly at his argument.

Civilization East and West

In *Civilization: The West and the Rest,* Ferguson argues that the amazing rise of Western civilization over the past 500 years—politically, economically, and technologically—was due to six main factors. Ferguson says however that today, at the beginning of the twenty-first century, "we are living through the end of 500 years of Western ascendancy." A 500-year epoch in human history is drawing to a close.[13]

Ferguson writes: "What distinguished the West from the Rest . . . were six identifiably novel complexes of institutions and associated ideas and behaviors." These six key factors were (1) competition, (2) science, (3) representative government, (4) medicine, (5) consumer society, and (6) a work ethic grounded largely in Christianity. Ferguson summarizes as follows:

---

[13] Niall Ferguson, *Civilization: the West and the Rest* (New York: Penguin, 2011), xv.

Why did the West dominate the Rest and not vice versa? . . . [It] was because the West developed six [capacities] that the Rest lacked. These were:

1. Competition, in that Europe itself was politically fragmented and that within each monarchy or republic there were multiple competing corporate entities [which, Ferguson argues, added dynamism].

2. The Scientific Revolution, in that all the major seventeenth-century breakthroughs in mathematics, astronomy, physics, chemistry and biology happened in Western Europe.

3. The rule of law and representative government, in that an optimal system of social and political order emerged in the English-speaking world, based on private property rights and the representation of property-owners in elected legislatures.[14]

4. Modern medicine, in that nearly all the major nineteenth- and twentieth-century breakthroughs in healthcare, including the control of tropical diseases, were made by Western Europeans and North Americans.

---

[14] Ferguson shows that this was largely *not* true in Spanish colonies, most notably in South America, which provides an instructive contrast with North America.

5. The consumer society, in that the Industrial Revolution took place where were there was both a supply of productivity-enhancing technologies and a demand for more, better and cheaper goods, beginning with cotton garments.

6. The work ethic, in that Westerners were the first people in the world to combine more extensive and intensive labour with higher savings rates, permitting sustained capital accumulation.[15]

Ferguson believes this 500-year history has now run its course and the West is in danger of substantial decline, particularly given the rise of China.

This is far from being the whole story, of course. We need to be clear about the history and development of Western Christianity, which is not the same as the rise of Western power and influence. The two are related, but the rise of the West was due to other factors in addition to Christianity—particularly to factors of geography and the inheritance of Greek philosophy. Conversely, the growth of the Christian faith does not necessarily produce the kind of

---

[15] Ferguson, 305-06. Ferguson calls these size developments "killer applications," by analogy from the use of computers. These innovations were the "software applications," so to speak, by which the West gained dominance.

economic, political, and cultural dominance that has characterized the West over the past 500 years.

Let us do a quick review of the history of Western Christianity. This history especially since the time of the Roman Emperor Constantine, can be divided into four periods:

Premodernity → Modernity → Postmodernity → New Global Consciousness

Premodernity — from about the year 300 to about 1600. The main features of this period were the rise of Medieval Christendom and of the State Church, in which the connection of church and state came to be assumed and hardly ever questioned. A key development during this period was the rise of Islam, which largely cut off Western Christianity from much of the rest of the world.

Modernity — from about 1600 to 1980. This period was marked by the influence of the European Enlightenment on Christianity and, within the church, an emphasis on church growth and missionary expansion.

Postmodernity — from about 1980 to 2010. Key developments within Christianity were a new emphasis on "emerging" churches and structures, and the growth of "Insider Movements"—that is, Jesus-followers within Islam, and to some degree within Buddhism and

Hinduism, that confess Jesus as Savior and Lord but do not identify with existing Christian churches.

New Global Consciousness — from about 2000, and continuing into the future. The Christian Church is becoming globally conscious as never before. This raises the question of a New Global Discipleship, presenting both opportunities and challenges. What will it mean for the Christian Church to be faithful in both a local and a global sense?

In other words, over 2000 years of history, Western Christianity has moved through three major phases. It has now arrived at the fourth, which I am calling the age of New Global Consciousness. Here the chief challenge is to birth a new global Christian discipleship.

In this process, the Christian Church has gained much but also lost much. In order to get a fuller understanding, we must analyze the church's *loss of ancient wisdom* in some key areas.

The Church's Loss of Ancient Wisdom

The world today is enthralled by *newness*—whatever is current, up-to-date, trending, modern. Today this is true of much of the Christian Church, as well. What is the latest thing? What are the latest innovations in church methodology?

Such thinking lies behind the question I am constantly asked: What will be the shape of the church in the future?

There is, of course, a *counter-tradition* in the church—a tradition that values ancient wisdom. We find this especially in Roman Catholicism and Eastern Orthodoxy. These traditions do value ancient wisdom—largely because of their long history, compared with that of the various Protestant denominations and more recent Pentecostal churches.

Protestants today would do well to ponder the fact that in many places the Roman Catholic and Orthodox churches are growing today. This is due in part to their emphasis on ancient wisdom. In the United States, for instance, Eastern Orthodox churches have grown significantly in the past two decades. Church growth studies in Korea show that the Roman Catholic Church is now doing better in resisting nominalism than is Protestantism. A 2004 Gallup Poll indicated that among Koreans who have changed their religion, nearly half had left Protestant churches, but only 15 percent had left Roman Catholic churches.[16]

For Protestant churches, the way forward is not to abandon what is new and simply return to the old. Vital churches know now to value *both* the new and the old in healthy and creative tension. Jesus himself points the way: "Every scribe who has been trained for the kingdom of heaven is like the master of a household who brings out of his treasure what is new and what is old" (Mt 13:52).

The way forward is not to engage in old battles between the old and the new. Rather, it is to *recover essential ancient wisdom that society and the church have forgotten.* This is the necessary foundation for vitality and redemptive mission today.

The church has suffered a critical loss of wisdom in three main areas. These are:

Loss of personal holism – what it means to be truly human.

Loss of sense of our interdependence with the land.

Loss of authentic discipleship and a kingdom of God vision in the church.

---

[16] Joon-Sik Park, "Korean Protestant Christianity: A Missiological Reflection," *International Bulletin of Missionary Research* 36:2 (April 2012), 59.

In other words, we are speaking here of our relationships as human beings with *each other*, with *the land* or earth, and with *God* as Christians in the body of Christ.

Human health and a healthy society depend on right relationship in these three areas. Loss of ancient wisdom in these areas produces pathology. Human beings and society get sick when these relationships are not in harmony with each other and with God's design. Anthropologist Robert Edgerton in his book *Sick Societies* shows that it is possible for people "who want desperately to live yet [to] adopt practices that threaten their survival."[17] The gospel incarnated in Christian community is the city's best hope for building beliefs and practices that nourish social health rather than undermining it. This means nourishing life-giving relationships in these three directions: Each other, the land, and the Lord God.

Let's look briefly at each of these. Since our relationship to the land is so fundamental, we begin with this.

1. Loss of Ancient Wisdom about the Land

For many centuries, people lived in deep interdependence with the land. This was true of most societies on earth. In the United States, 90 percent of the

---

[17] Robert B. Edgerton, *Sick Societies: Challenging the Myth of Primitive Harmony* (New York: The Free Press, 1992), 187.

population was rural in 1800. One hundred years later, the percentages had reversed: 90 percent were urban. Accompanying this shift was a major transition from agriculture to industry, as well as from farms and villages to cities.

In this process, Native Americans by the thousands were removed from their ancestral lands and placed in restricted reservations. Many thousands died in the process.[18]

Most of us are in a general sense familiar with this pattern of populations shifts from farms to cities. Usually it is described and discussed as "urbanization," with a focus on the rise and development of cities.

We must focus however not just on urbanization, but also on *the loss of wisdom about the land,* as we noted in Chapter One. Earlier generations understood much more about land than do most people today. If they lacked today's scientific knowledge, they possessed generational wisdom that is now mostly lost. Today city dwellers have little sense of the actual importance of the land and the fact that their own survival depends upon it. (Interestingly, Detroit, Michigan, now in recovery after bankruptcy, is

---

[18] Howard A. Snyder, *Jesus and Pocahontas: Gospel, Mission, and National Myth* (Eugene, Ore.: Cascade, 2015).

rediscovering the value of land as vacant lots are being turned into gardens and small farms—"the Greening of Detroit."[19])

But human flourishing requires living in contact with the land, with nature, with the created order. This is built into us, and it is part of God's plan (as I will elaborate in the next chapter).

Today, perhaps we should talk less about urbanization and more about the land—and what has been lost in the transition from the land to the cities. In our discussions about mission, we need to study the land as well as the urban areas. The point is the recovery of ancient wisdom about the land, and thus the recovery of a harmonious relationship between land and people.

This has many implications for the church, for mission, and for society generally, as we will see. No church is healthy if it does not have a healthy relationship with the land—that is, if it pollutes and damages the land, rather than nurturing and caring for it.[20]

Healthy, sustainable society requires living in sustainable harmony with the land. Our forefathers and

---

[19] See for example http://www.greeningofdetroit.com/
[20] See the discussion in Howard A. Snyder with Joel Scandrett, *Salvation Means Creation Healed: The Ecology of Sin and Grace* (Eugene, Ore.: Cascade Books, 2011).

foremothers knew this intuitively. All around the world, we have lost ancient wisdom in this area, however. We must recover ancient wisdom about plants and animals, times and seasons, in order for the church to be healthy sustainably. The great explosion of scientific knowledge about the earth, climate, and ecosystems can help us. We can recover ancient wisdom, then correct and enhance it by incorporating new scientific knowledge.

The recovery of ancient wisdom about the land requires rethinking today's most popular economic models. As Herman Daly and Joshua Farley point out in their prophetic book *Ecological Economics,* today's dominant global economic model fatally misunderstands the relationship between economics and the physical ecosystem. Modern economics assumes that the natural ecosystem is a subsystem with the larger circle of economics. In truth, it is the other way around. Economics is a subsystem within the larger circle of the created order. This means that, in the long run, economies cannot be healthy if they exploit and damage, rather than nurturing and replenishing, the earth—land, seas, and air.[21]

---

[21] Herman E. Daly and Joshua Farley, *Ecological Economics: Principles and Applications* (Washington, DC: Island Press, 2004), especially Chap. 2. From a Christian standpoint Daly and Farley need correction at some points, but on this point their argument clearly is consistent with Scripture.

In today's global economy, we are in grave danger of destroying the very earth that nourishes all life—economic, social, political, or spiritual. We have lost essential ancient wisdom regarding the earth. Today it is urgent that the Christian Church recover this ancient wisdom, based on biblical revelation, and make it an essential part of global mission.

2. Loss of Ancient Wisdom about Being Human: Relationships with One Another

For many centuries, people found their primary personal identity in their own family, clan, tribe, or ethnic group. This was true the world over. "Who I am" was always part of the larger reality, "Who we are" (as noted earlier).

This was true East and West. It was true as much in China as it was in Europe in olden times.

This sense of personal identity based in one's social group can be both negative and positive, of course. We know that tribalism can lead to violence, wars, and even the horrors of genocide and "ethnic cleansing." On the positive side however, relational identity means every person sees himself or herself as part of *a people, a family,* a social group that is essential and constitutive of the person's very identity.

With the rise of globalization, consumerism, urbanization, and the Internet, the sense of group identity has eroded drastically. This is more and more the case with each generation. In our times, we see this happening massively in China, where millions of young people have moved from their villages and families to large cities. There they work in factories and lose much of their contact with their former social network.

What is the result? The major result is *the loss of personal holism*. Life gets cut up into separate parts. People find themselves isolated from the larger webs of relationships that gave them a sense of identity and purpose.

So we have the rise of modern individualism, which now affects today's Eastern nations nearly as much as it does the West.

The results of this are predictable: Increased rates of suicide, unstable families, alienation from parents. People try to find meaning in entertainment, the accumulation of material things, and a constant stream of "experiences" that have little coherence and do not bring a clear sense of personal identity or group solidarity.

Increasingly, we are losing the meaning of being connected with each other as families or as a people. This is a long-term trend that, it appears, will continue.

South Korea experienced this huge transition from group identity to individualism in only three or four generations. This is due largely to its unusual history over the last century: Japanese occupation and its end; rise of Christianity; the Korean War; democratization; the rapid rise of a modern advanced, vibrant economy; and material prosperity. If you are Korean, think about the differences between yourself, your parents, your grandparents, and your great-grandparents. How would each answer these two key questions: "Who am I?" and "What is most important in life?" Yet something similar is happening worldwide.

Humanity today is experiencing a massive loss of ancient wisdom about simply *being human*. This is a loss of personal holism, resulting in fractured identity and a critical loss of a sense of the importance of history.

The Christian Faith, of course, has an answer to this: The church; Christian community today and in history. As Christians, our identity is "in Christ"—in Jesus as only Savior, and in his Body, the church, the community of God's people. "Once you were not a people, but now you are God's people" (1 Pt 2:10).

The Christian Faith has the answer to personal identity, to personal integrity and sense of belonging. But the answer we need is not just church growth or building church community. It is working to rebuild society at the critical levels of marriage and family, and of neighborhood and other forms of small-scale community.

To solve the problem of personal identity, the microstructures of society must be rebuilt: family, neighborhood, community. We need the recovery of ancient wisdom in this area. This is a key part of the church's mission agenda today.

But it is not just human community, or human sociability, that is required. It is human community *in life-giving relationship with the land*. God's promise and God's plan always involve his land as well as his people. So the church must build community that lives in healthy relationship to the land, both locally and globally.

3. Loss of Ancient Wisdom about God

For many centuries, Christians understood that being a true Christian meant being in vital relationship with the Triune God, Father, Son, and Holy Spirit. This meant full commitment to the church, the body of Christ, and to the kingdom of God.

Genuine, vital Christianity means that our commitment to Jesus, his body, and the kingdom of God comes ahead of all other commitments. It relativizes all other commitments, putting them into proper perspective. In genuine Christianity, our commitment to the body and kingdom mission of Jesus has priority over our commitment to family, country, tribe, or ethnic group.

This was the ancient wisdom of the church. In New Testament days, the church practiced close-knit one-another fellowship, or *koinonia.* In the first several centuries, the church maintained a vital practice of *catechesis.* The catechumenate was training in faith and in discipleship and mission; practical godliness.

Throughout church history, times of renewal have generally been accompanied by a new emphasis on community and accountable discipleship. Early Methodism provides a very good example in its use of "bands" and "class meetings," small groups meeting weekly for spiritual encouragement and accountability.

We have already identified the glaring *discipleship gap* in today's church, globally. My point here is that this discipleship gap really testifies to a *loss of ancient wisdom* about who God is and what he both requires and graciously offers. The result is a loss authentic discipleship and of kingdom of God vision in the church.

As the ancient church gradually articulated the doctrine of the Trinity, it understood the connection between Trinity and community. As Father, Son, and Holy Spirit are one in a continual relationship of self-giving and receiving, so the church exists as a fellowship with the Father through Jesus Christ by the Spirit. Because of Trinity, there is community. The Persons of the Trinity are fully, irrevocably committed to and in reciprocal relationship with one another. Some ancient theologians called this *perichoresis,* a mutual interacting and "dancing" together. This then sets the pattern for the church. The members of the body of Christ are called to be irrevocably fully committed to each other in a relationship of mutual, accountable discipleship.

Furthermore, as the ancient church came to understand the radical truth that Jesus Christ is "King of Kings and Lord of Lords," so it lived to proclaim God's kingdom on earth. Its prayer, passion, and program was: "May your kingdom come; may your will be done *on earth* as in heaven."

As the first Christians were radically committed to God, so they were radically committed to each other and to the kingdom of God in the world. It is that simple and that profound. But today's church has lost ancient wisdom about the Trinity and the kingdom of God.

We need the ancient wisdom of the church, reminding us *who God is* and what it means to be his people in the world.

Conclusion

To summarize: Christianity worldwide is in crisis. This is true both East and West. It is true both North and South. The primary reason this crisis is global is that Christianity itself is now global as never before and lives and functions in a world that is globally linked as never before.

Further, we now live in *the Anthropocene Age* in which human action and technology are changing the very nature and condition of the planet.

I have outlined the major symptoms of Christianity's current crisis, analyzing the historic decline of the Christian Church in the West, explaining the roots of today's social and personal identity crisis, highlighting our global environmental crisis, and pointing out the weakness of mere cultural Christianity and in particular the church's huge discipleship gap.

Second, I have tried to identify key factors that explain the rise of Western civilization since 1500 that have produced many of the features of contemporary global society.

Finally, and perhaps most importantly, I have analyzed the church's loss of ancient wisdom in three areas: Our relationship with the earth, with each other, and with God.

And yet—as always with the gospel—there is hope. The next chapter points the way forward from the end of Christendom to vital biblical faith and urban mission.

CHAPTER 7
Recovering Prophetic Christianity

God's people are always on a journey. Hebrews 11 tells us that Abraham, the God-called wanderer, "looked forward to the city that has foundations, whose architect and builder is God." He never quite found it during his life on earth. Yet in another sense he helped build it—"by faith" and thus obedience (Heb 11:10–11).

All the heroes of Hebrews 11 journeyed on and all "died in faith without having received the promises" in fullness. Yet Hebrews assures us, "God is not ashamed to be called their God; indeed, he has prepared a city for them" (Heb 11:13, 16).

The church in the city is on a journey to the heavenly city, fully convinced, paradoxically, that God intends to build signs and models of that heavenly city right here and now in our midst, among us, in our cities and homes and neighborhoods.

God's people are always on a journey, whether we recognize it or not. Sometimes it appears that the church is stopped, or stagnant, or plateaued. Yet whether we see it or not, the church is always changing.

This is the nature of life, in fact, as God made it. It is the nature of the ecology of the created order. It the nature of society as one generation replaces another over time.

So it is today in the nations, cities, and rural areas of the world. The church is changing, always. Faithful urban mission means discerning the changes and the direction of the winds of the Spirit.

As we journey, let us look toward the future and ask where biblical faithfulness should take us—what it would mean to be prophetically Christian in the city today.

It is still true, as always, that God sets before us *two ways*—the way of covenant faithfulness, and the way of polytheistic idolatry as we live among the many gods of this world. This chapter attempts to point the way forward to renewed covenant faithfulness in urban mission that is biblically sound, theologically coherent, sharply relevant to the times, and very practical for church life today.

Six Keys to Prophetic Biblical Faithfulness

The church today, globally, is in the middle of vast spiritual warfare—the kingdom of God versus the kingdom of darkness in its many forms.

So today comes the call to faithfulness, the call for the recovery of genuine prophetic Christianity.[1] Examining Scripture, church history, and today's world, I believe we can identify six keys to recovering biblical faith, especially in urban contexts. While these apply to the church globally, some will be more relevant in some contexts, and some in others.

Here are the six keys to recovering radically prophetic Christian faith today: 1) understanding the earth, 2) uncompromising biblical monotheism, 3) robust Trinitarian faith, 4) defining salvation in a fully biblical way, 5) present hope of the kingdom of God, and 6) living as the body of Christ.

In all these areas, I am appealing directly to Scripture. The answer to the church's crisis today is the Spirit and the

---

[1] Parts of what follows are elaborated in my book, *Salvation Means Creation Healed.*

Word. It is not business methods, education, the Internet, marketing, or "casting visions." It is taking God's Holy Word with radical seriousness.

This means, the *whole Bible*, the Old Testament as well as the New. In its understanding of church and mission, the Christian Church has too often neglected the Old Testament and the full ecological interrelationship between the Old Covenant and the New Covenant. I try here to correct this neglect and imbalance.

1. Understanding the Earth

Most people in the world's major cities today, including Christians, suffer from "nature-deficit disorder."[2] That is, not only do they not understand the importance of the earth to their existence and wellbeing. They (that is, we) also suffer the consequences of the loss of the natural healing effects that come through daily contact with birds and animals, hills and mountains, the trees and the seas—everything that makes up the wonderful created order God has given us.

This is not just a matter of concepts or ideas. It is a matter of emotional and physical wellbeing. For our own

---

[2] Richard Louv, *Last Child in the Woods: Saving Our Children From Nature-Deficit Disorder* (Chapel Hill, N.C.: Algonquin Books, 2008).

health, we need the beauty as well as the resources of nature.

Role of land. It is urgent that Christians come to understand and to experience the importance of the land in God's plan of redemption. We must know the place of the earth in God's plan. For centuries the Christian Church has ignored this crucial knowledge, as I document in my book, *Salvation Means Creation Healed.*

In the Bible, in both Testaments, the words *land* and *earth* are the same word in the original languages, as discussed in Chapter Six. So when I speak here of "land," I mean not only physical soil, but also, by extension, the whole planet earth and in fact *the whole created order* in its vast ecology. Genesis 9 tells us that God established an "everlasting covenant" with the earth (Gen 9:13, 16). This is the foundation upon which all later biblical covenants were established.

God has never revoked his "everlasting covenant" with the earth and all its creatures. It is in fact a three-dimensional covenant between God, the earth, and the human race, as we have seen.

From a biblical standpoint, we may speak of the "ecology" of the earth. I do not mean here, primarily, the ecological understanding that come from modern science. I mean rather the revealed biblical ecology, the biblical foundation of the God-Land-People covenant relationship.

The Bible speaks of the *oikonomia* of God. This means the "plan" or "economy" of God. We may call this the biblical ecological understanding, since both "ecology" and "economy" are based on the biblical image of the "house" (*oikos*) of God. Thus God reveals to us in Scripture the *true ecology* and *true economy* of his plan for humanity and the earth.[3]

God's plan is fundamentally one of *interrelationships*. It concerns God's redemptive plan for human beings in relation to the land and the whole created order. So God's plan of salvation is also a plan for the land, for the earth. If you trace the word "land" or "earth" throughout Scripture, you will see how this is true. Remarkably, the Bible seldom speaks of God's plan of salvation for human beings without also speaking of God's will for the earth.[4]

God's plan is a plan for healing and flourishing, for wellbeing, between people and God and between people and the earth. The key biblical term for this is *shalom*,

---

[3] See especially my book *Liberating the Church,* chapters 2 and 3.
[4] Where this is not explicit in Scripture, it is implicit, based on the language of the Abrahamic and Noahic covenants, which in turn implicitly incorporate the earlier "everlasting covenant" that God makes with the earth in Genesis 9.

which means peace, flourishing, prosperity, wellbeing, and healthy interrelationship according to God's plan.

As Christians, we need to understand the *real ecology* of the earth. That is, we need to understand God's salvific intentions for the relationship between himself, his people, and his land. As Christians, we know that neither Christian mission nor ecological science is complete or holistic if it leaves out the physical and spiritual dimensions of God's creation.

Without this biblical comprehensiveness, we do not really understand the gospel of Jesus Christ or the full meaning of salvation. Without this, we do not properly understand the church and Christian mission.

Economics of land. As I have noted in previous chapters, the question of land is inextricably bound up with the issue of economics. Economics concerns resources and how we use them, and for what purposes.

Nearly all the resources that feed our economy come from the land. Like the foolish man who built his house on sand, or like the farmer who ate up all his plant seeds, our economy is unsustainable if it does not take care of the earth.

Christians must be at the forefront of efforts to teach the world to respect and care for the earth God has made.

This is a necessary component of Christian mission. Urban churches can play a key role here, both in theory and in practice. In a broader sense this truth is part of the message of salvation, since salvation always involves not only people but also land.

We are all economic creatures. We use the earth's resources every day. We buy and sell things. We eat food and discard waste. We consume energy in our cars and trains and in heating and cooling buildings. We use energy, in fact, in everything we do. We use or abuse the land. Perhaps we grow flowers or plant gardens. We use computers and the Internet. We use money and credit, and we are constantly making purchases of clothing, food, and other items.

These are all economic activities. We are all tied into the economy, both locally and globally. Every person, Christian or not, is an *economic* being as well as a *spiritual* being.

As Christians, we need to understand that we are all economic creatures—*and* that *this is part of God's plan*. It is part of the People–Land connection that comes from the hand of God. This is why the Bible talks so much about economic matters—money, food, clothing, economic justice, and the care of the poor, for instance.

Eco-thinking. I emphasize in this book the inseparable connection between economics and ecology. Here Christians have a unique perspective. Since we know that all things come from the hand of God, we know that all our life concerns the "house" (*oikos*) God has given us—the good earth. As Christians, we understand that we are responsible to God and to one another for every aspect of our lives. Everything that affects our life on earth is connected to our relationship with God and with the earth. Thus, biblically speaking, economics and ecology are inseparably linked.

This is a Christian worldview issue. As Christians, we must understand deeply the economic and ecological world God has made. In other words, we must understand the earth in God's plan. Further, we must understand the close interconnection between economics, ecology, and spirituality. This consciousness should be part of our urban discipleship.

The Bible does not permit us to build a wall between spiritual realities and economic realities. Why? Two reasons: because all comes from the hand of the Creator-God, and because spiritual and economic realities are constantly mixed together in each of our lives and in our culture.

This is why we need to *think ecologically* in a broader sense. We need to understand the *real ecology* of the world God has made. Christian mission and Christian discipleship today require comprehensive *eco-thinking*. We should think of "ecology" not just as a matter of the physical environment, or as a matter of natural science. Rather, we should teach a broad and biblical concept of ecology, an understanding that includes spiritual realities as well as physical and social ones. Since the biblical revelation is the story of God, People, and Land, we are actually being unbiblical if we do not include the physical creation in our understanding of salvation and Christian mission.

As already noted, *ecology* deals with the interrelationships between living things, including their relationship with their physical environment. This necessarily includes human interaction with their physical surroundings. As Christians, we know that our environment is more than just the physical, touchable world. It includes the whole creation—things, visible and invisible, in heaven and on earth (Col 1:16, Eph 1:10).[5]

---

[5] A study of the important phrase "all things" in the Bible, especially in Paul's writings, shows decisively that the biblical worldview is an ecological one.

So there is urgent need for biblical eco-thinking in the church today—in our discipleship and in our practice of mission.

2. Uncompromising Biblical Monotheism

A second essential key to recovering prophetic Christianity in the city is *uncompromising biblical monotheism.* We affirm Scripture teaching here, avoiding all forms of polytheism, pantheism, and deism.

The church faces numerous challenges to truly biblical monotheism. The main challenges are Buddhism, Hinduism, Islam, and Secularism. All these are visibly present today in most of the world's cities.

Recently a friend of mine, a Christian sister, was leading a discussion about Jesus Christ in a group of women of varied religious backgrounds. One woman had been raised Hindu. As my friend talked about Jesus, this woman was very impressed. She said, "Yes, I can see that it is good to believe in Jesus. I can believe that Jesus is one of the gods."

Here faith in Jesus was easily swallowed up in polytheism and syncretism.

Buddhism likewise has no conception of the one true God revealed in Scripture and in Jesus Christ. Islam proclaims a radical monotheism, but the Muslim concept of

God is much different from the God of the Bible. It is true that Islam is one of the three great monotheistic faiths that accept the authority of the Hebrew Scriptures, and one true God. But as understood in Islam, God is remote, austere, unknowable, and not revealed uniquely and once-for-all in Jesus Christ.

We face also the challenge of secularism and technological materialism. The technical-materialist worldview is increasingly the worldview of contemporary global culture. In this view, the God of the Bible is not so much denied as ignored. God is irrelevant.

But God is not irrelevant if understood and proclaimed biblically, and if his reality is daily demonstrated in the lives of Christians.

In today's global urban contexts, proclaiming the God of the Bible in all his ultimacy and intimacy is essential to faithful Christian discipleship and mission. We worship "the high and lofty one who inhabits eternity, whose name is Holy"; who tells us: "I dwell in the high and holy place, and also with those who are contrite and humble in spirit, to revive the spirit of the humble, and to revive the heart of the contrite" (Isa 57:15). This wonderful ultimacy and intimacy, together, is the character of our Living Lord.

Uncompromising biblical monotheism is a necessary emphasis today because so many people are conditioned to believe in many gods or no god. Or else people make gods of themselves or of money or sex or power or fame. As Christians, we worship and proclaim the one true God revealed by Jesus Christ through the Holy Spirit.

But it is not an "ism" we proclaim—not monotheism or of any other "ism." Our faith is not monotheism. Our faith is the Good News of salvation and healing through Jesus Christ, the only Son of the Father, revealed to us by the Holy Spirit who teaches us, speaks to hearts, goes ahead of us, and opens the Scriptures to our understanding.

This leads us to the next key for recovering prophetic Christianity:

3. Robust Trinitarian Faith

The Christian faith is unique because it proclaims one God in Three; Three Gods in one. One Triune, Tri-Personal God. Yahweh is no more One than Three, and no more Three than One. God is Trinity, which means not four Gods (Father, Son, Spirit, Trinity), but rather the grand mystery (as it seems to us) of the one Lord God who has revealed himself in three Persons.

The early church hammered out this crucial doctrinal insight, this breakthrough, in an international missional context (as Lesslie Newbigin reminds us). In the first four centuries, Christians had to explain how God the Father, Jesus the Son, and the Holy Spirit could all be one God, not three different gods. The big theological breakthroughs came in the early ecumenical councils and were enshrined in the early creeds, beginning with the Nicene Creed.

The early creeds left many questions unanswered. They are not the last word on how to interpret Scripture, or on the church and mission. But they did solidly nail down the reality of the Holy Lord's personal Triune nature.

For a thousand years the doctrine of the Trinity and its implications for church and mission were largely neglected in the Western Church, with some notable exceptions. Protestant churches have paid far too little attention to the ecclesiological, cultural, and missional implications of this breakthrough doctrine.

The situation changed, however, over the last century. This was due to the development of mission-of-God (*missio Dei*) theology since World War II, and more recently the work of missiologists like Lesslie Newbigin and Christopher Wright. Colin Gunton's prophetic book *The Promise of Trinitarian Theology*, Thomas Torrance's *The Trinitarian Faith*, Leonardo Boff's *Trinity and Society*, and Veli-Matti Kärkkäinen's *The Trinity: Global Perspectives* (among others) show how essential Trinitarian doctrine is for the being and mission of the church.[6] Urban mission leaders should carefully study works such as these as they continue to reflect on their being and mission.

The doctrine and *reality* of the Trinity has huge importance for the recovery of redemptive and creative urban mission today. I cite three reasons:

1. *A biblically sound doctrine of the Trinity safeguards the full reality of Jesus Christ and the Holy Spirit in relation to God the Father and God's redemptive action in history.* Neglecting the doctrine (and fact) of the Trinity and its practical implications runs the risk of an anemic missiology and weak discipleship.

Jesus's incarnation, life, death, and resurrection all took place in real, spacetime history. Jesus continues to work in history through the Holy Spirit, and through his body. A robust Trinitarian theology helps keep our understanding

---

[6] Howard A. Snyder, "Karl Barth's Missional Ecclesiology," Chapter 13 in Howard A. Snyder, *Yes In Christ: Wesleyan Reflections on Gospel, Mission, and Culture* (Toronto: Clements Academic, 2011), 295–21; Colin E. Gunton, *The Promise of Trinitarian Theology*, 2nd ed. (Edinburgh: T. & T. Clark, 1997); Thomas F. Torrance, *The Trinitarian Faith: The Evangelical Theology of the Ancient Catholic Church* (London: T. & T. Clark, 2004); Leonardo Boff, *Trinity and Society* (Maryknoll, N.Y.: Orbis, 1988); Veli-Matti Kärkkäinen, *The Trinity: Global Perspectives* (Louisville, Ky.: Westminster John Knox, 2007).

of salvation grounded in history and constantly reminds us of God's ongoing engagement with his creation.

2. *The doctrine of the Trinity helps us understand the economy of God*—that is, God's overall plan of redemption, his *oikonomia*. The interrelationship between Father, Son, and Spirit is the basis, and in a sense the model, for the Triune God's relationships with people and with the earth. In fact, the ecological nature of all creation reflects the character of the Trinity, as does the creation and full equality of humankind as male and female.

3. *The doctrine of the Trinity is important in bridging cultural and worldview differences.* The key dynamics of the Trinity are unity, diversity, and mutual sharing, or interchange. In this sense the relationship of Father, Son, and Spirit is fundamentally and essentially *ecological*. This fact of the unique reality of each Person of the Trinity in relation to the other two, and to the integral Trinity as one Holy God, gives us a basis for affirming the uniqueness and inherent value of every culture and ethnicity as having its own reality and redemptive possibility. Yet on the other hand, the eternal unity of Father, Son, and Spirit tells us the importance of maintaining "the unity of the Spirit in the bond of peace" (Eph 4:3). It also helps us distinguish the good from the bad in various cultures.

Note that the basis for this unity-in-diversity and diversity-in-unity is not just an *idea* or *concept*. Rather, it is the living reality of the Triune God, Father, Son, and Spirit. This has implications for every dimension of human life and existence, from the nature of human personality to the nature of the church as body of Christ and the church's mission and role in global society.[7]

4. Defining Salvation in a Fully Biblical Way

During the Age of Christendom (in the West, roughly 350–1980 AD), the New Testament understanding of salvation became very seriously distorted. As church and state were joined, discipleship drastically declined. The meaning of salvation became so narrowed down that the church lost most of its dynamism and world-changing vision of the kingdom of God.

Salvation was distorted in five main ways:

1. In much of the church, *salvation became equated with official church membership*, which was equated with infant baptism.

2. In Evangelical Protestantism, *the meaning of salvation was reduced to conversion*. Holiness and discipleship may

---

[7] See the discussion in Snyder and Scandrett, *Salvation Means Creation Healed*, 178–84.

have been taught, but these were seen as secondary, not essential to salvation.

3. *Salvation came to mean eternal life in heaven rather than the whole journey of faithful obedience* from a person's first awakening to God's grace to the final culmination of the kingdom of God. John Wesley properly defined personal salvation as "the entire work of God, from the first dawning of grace in the soul till it is consummated in glory," and including a life of holiness, justice, and discipleship.[8]

4. *Salvation came to be understood as exclusively spiritual rather than holistic*—that is, as involving all dimensions of life and the "all things" of God's creation and redemption (Eph 1:10).

5. *Salvation became individualized rather than experienced as shared life in the body of Christ.* The church came to be understood as "a soul-saving agency" rather than the actual body of Christ on earth, charged with demonstrating and living out all the dimensions of the kingdom of God.

---

[8] John Wesley, Sermon 43, "The Scripture Way of Salvation," *The Works of John Wesley,* Vol. 2 (Nashville, Abingdon Press, 1985), 156. Crucially important here is an understanding of God's "prevenient" or preceding grace. See especially Christopher Payk, *Grace First: Christian Mission and Prevenient Grace in John Wesley* (Toronto: Clements Academic, 2015).

This is not the biblical understanding of salvation. Yet we still suffer the consequences of these distortions. We need to go back to Scripture, both Testaments, and reconceive the whole meaning of salvation in a soundly biblical way.

When salvation is equated with *church membership*, we lose the dynamism and relational accountability of true *koinonia* in the body of Christ.

When salvation is equated with *conversion*, we cut the nerve of the cost of discipleship and the vital motivation for holiness.

When salvation means *the soul's eternal rest in heaven*, we lose sight of God's purposes for the earth and our stewardship mission on earth.

When salvation is understood to be an *exclusively spiritual matter*, we distort God's plan for all dimensions of life and develop a dualistic or gnostic understanding of creation. That is, we come to see spirit as good and material things as bad or at least comparatively unimportant. We actually damage the biblical worldview and undercut the significance of Jesus' incarnation, life on earth, and resurrection.

When salvation becomes *individualized*, it quickly becomes a private matter unrelated to our shared life in the body of Christ and cut off from our civic and environmental responsibility.

The crisis and maladies of the church in the city and elsewhere mostly stem from this fivefold distortion of the biblical meaning of salvation.

We must banish these unbiblical distortions and replace them with the clear teachings of Scripture.

This requires three steps:

First, *recover the biblical doctrine of creation.* In the Bible, "creation" means much more than the fact that God "in the beginning created the heavens and the earth" (Gen 1:1). The biblical doctrine of creation means God's ongoing engagement with heaven and earth—that is, the totality of the world he created and loves. It involves the fullness of God's purposes for the created order.

Much of Christianity still has a very narrow of "low" doctrine of creation. "Creation" means only the beginning of this world, for most Christians. The biblical picture, however, is God's ongoing plan or "economy" (*oikonomia*) for his whole creation, culminating in the reconciliation of all things through Jesus Christ by the Spirit.

We need to see that in Scripture, "heaven and earth" does not mean two separate spheres, irreconcilably different. Rather, the phrase is the Hebrew way of speaking of the totality of the created order.

Second, contemporary Christianity must *understand and affirm the role of the land (or earth) in God's covenantal plan of salvation.* In the Bible, the picture is very clear. as we saw in Chapter Six, it is the story of God, his people, and his land.

Much of contemporary Christianity simply *cuts out* one third of this revealed triangle. In other words, it ignores a key part of revelation! So salvation comes to look like this:

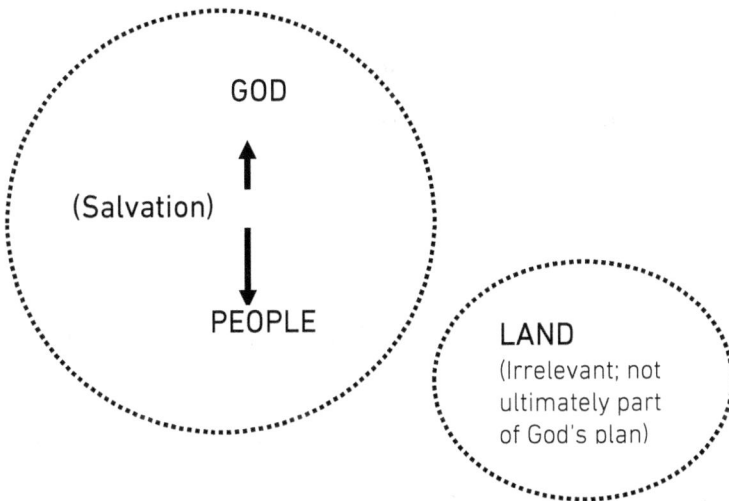

GOD

(Salvation)

PEOPLE

LAND
(Irrelevant; not
ultimately part
of God's plan)

In this understanding, salvation is totally unrelated to the land. The revealed connection between the Creator and his non-human creation is set aside, even denied. The very literal, physical promises of land which fill the Old

Testament are spiritualized into a heavenly "Promised Land" unrelated to earth.

Is it not abundantly clear that this is a gross distortion of Scripture, and thus of the nature and scope of salvation? Let us call this what it is: biblical unfaithfulness in our understanding of salvation.

Third, *the church must understand and affirm the full meaning of Jesus's incarnation, life, and resurrection* and its importance for the church's life and mission.

Evangelicals and other orthodox Christians have always proclaimed Jesus's literal resurrection from the dead. Our faith is in large measure based on the historic fact of Jesus's resurrection and ongoing action through the Holy Spirit.

But the church has often missed the full significance of Jesus's resurrection. The resurrection has been understood as our assurance of eternal life *in heaven, in a solely spiritual afterlife.* This is not what the New Testament teaches.

The Bible teaches the radical physicality of Jesus's incarnation and resurrection. In his incarnation, the Son took on full human physical existence in every sense. In his resurrection he transformed physical existence, bringing "the powers of the age to come" (Heb 6:5) into our present age and experience. We are given new life in Christ, with the assurance of the resurrection of our physical bodies when Jesus returns to "make all things new" (Rev 21:5)—the time when Jesus comes "to restore everything, as [God] promised long ago through his holy prophets" (Acts 3:21 TNIV). Paul insists that "not only the creation, but we ourselves, who have the firstfruits of the Spirit, groan inwardly while we wait for adoption, the redemption of our *bodies*" (Rom 8:23), not just our "spirits" or "souls."

Jesus's resurrection is the certain promise and unshakable assurance that God is bringing a new heaven and a new earth. It tells us that this new reality *has already begun* in Jesus's physical resurrection. Through the Holy Spirit, we now have access to the "powers of the age to come" so that we can be God's "coworkers for the kingdom of God" (Heb 6:5, Col 4:11).

If we take Jesus's resurrection seriously, we will take much more seriously the prayer, and God's desire, that God's kingdom come visibly now; that God's "will be done on earth as it is in heaven" (Mt 6:10).

We need to take much more seriously Paul's assurances in Romans 8 that "If the Spirit of him who raised Jesus from the dead dwells in you, he who raised Christ from the dead will give life to your mortal bodies also through his Spirit that dwells in you" (Rom 8:11). Urban Christians can and should live and testify to the fact that "the creation itself will be set free from its bondage to decay and will obtain the freedom of the glory of the children of God" (Rom 8:21).

With this hope and assurance, we will take discipleship seriously and work effectively to see the "firstfruits" of this reality manifested in every area of life and culture.[9]

Here the work of the Holy Spirit is absolutely crucial! The Holy Spirit draws people to Christ, effects the New Birth, fills and sanctifies believers, builds and empowers the body of Christ, sends the church out in mission, and brings New Creation in all its dimensions. The church must be filled with the Spirit and "keep in step with the Spirit" (Gal 5:25 TNIV), as Paul admonishes.

In other words, the church must be fully Trinitarian, as I have argued.

In sum, we must define salvation in a fully biblical way. We will live and proclaim this Good News of the kingdom in the power of the Holy Spirit.

---

[9] This point, including the important theme of "firstfruits," is fully elaborated in "The Pentecostal Renewal of the Church," Chapter 12 in my book, *Yes In Christ* (259–94).

5. Proclaiming and Embodying the Full Hope of God's Reign

This is the fifth key to the recovery of vital biblical faith. The church exists not for itself, but for the kingdom of God. This is what we are to "seek first" (Mt 6:33).

The church's life and mission should be defined by the sure promise of God's reign. The kingdom of God is both our *hope* and our *agenda*. God's reign through Jesus Christ by the Spirit is both hope to be proclaimed and mission to fulfill empowered by the Holy Spirit.

How do we keep "seeking first God's kingdom" from becoming a mere cliché? In many ways the meaning of the kingdom of God remains complex and mysterious. But three key points from Scripture can help us:

1. *Jesus proclaimed the kingdom of God, and the practical meaning of the kingdom centers in him.* Jesus is King of King and Lord of Lords. We are to proclaim and embody Jesus and his kingdom in our world today, to the ends of the earth and for all global society.

So our primary focus must be on *kingdom growth*, not *church growth*. Church growth is important only as it contributes to kingdom growth.

2. *We proclaim the kingdom as both present and future.* Many times in history the Christian Church has split over whether the kingdom of God is a present or a future reality.

Clearly it is both. It is a mistake to divide up the reality of the kingdom dispensationally, or to adhere to millennial theories that undercut the full dynamism of God's reign among us now. We should expect to see authentic signs of the presence and power of the kingdom in our cities and societies, even as we patiently await the kingdom's full coming.

3. *The kingdom of God touches all areas of life and culture.* Biblically, the kingdom of God promises, and is, a new social order. God's kingdom promises a reconciled humanity and environment based on love, justice, holiness, and peace (*shalom* in the biblical sense). God's reign promises nothing less than radical social reconstruction, "a new heaven and a new earth, the home of righteousness" and justice (2 Pt 3:13). Thus the kingdom involves *all areas and dimensions of life,* from the arts to science, from economics to creation care, from family life to global culture, every aspect of urban and non-urban reality.

The kingdom of God is not a human program. It is not a social, political, or economic theory. It is not an ideology. It is rather *the Christian hope.* It is based on the manifold promises of God all through Scripture. It was announced and demonstrated by Jesus Christ. And its coming in fullness was assured by Jesus's resurrection and his promise to return. In our present labors for the kingdom we may groan. But we are confident because God has given us the Spirit as a guarantee of what is to come—God's kingdom in fullness (2 Cor 5:2–5). In urban mission we remind ourselves continually that in Jesus Christ "every one of God's promises is a 'Yes'" (2 Cor 1:20).

The kingdom of God is the certain hope that God's will shall be done on earth as in heaven; that "the earth will be full of the knowledge of the Lord as the waters cover the sea" (Isa 11:9).[10]

But how can this be? How can it happen?

In one way only. Not by evangelism, important as that is. Not simply by church growth. Not solely by prayer, though clearly prayer is crucial. Not by education or literature; not by marketing or the Internet. Not through politics or economics or urban renewal programs, useful as they may be.

The Bible is very clear here. The only way for the church to be the redemptive agent of the kingdom of God on earth is for it *actually to be the living body of Christ*. This then is the final point, and really the capstone to the whole argument.

---

[10] See further, Howard A. Snyder, *Models of the Kingdom* (Nashville: Abingdon, 1991; reprint, Wipf & Stock, 2001).

6. Being the Living Body of Christ

The Apostle Paul is speaking of the church as body of Christ when he writes, "I . . . beg you to lead a life worthy of the calling to which you have been called" (Eph 4:1). He tells the church to "lead a life worthy of God, who calls you into his own kingdom and glory" (1 Thess 2:12).

The New Testament is very clear that God saves the world *through the body of Christ* by the power of the Holy Spirit. This means first of all, of course, the incarnate and risen Son of God, Jesus Christ. Then secondarily it means *the church*, the living body of Christ. Jesus made it clear that he was forming his special community of disciples to spread his kingdom on earth. The church is to truly, literally, physically be his ongoing work and mission in history. Jesus said: *As* I have loved you, *so* you are to love one another. *As* the Father sent me, *so* I send you—a community of incarnation. *As* I came not to be served but to serve, *so* you are to serve others.

As Jesus had fellowship with the Father and Spirit, *so* the church is to be the Trinitarian community of kingdom witness in the world.

Urban churches must rediscover the powerful, practical meaning of actually *being* the visible, tangible body of Christ in the world.

224

The New Testament reveals what it means for the church to be body of Christ, community of the king, and an accountable fellowship of disciples. The church is called to be the new people of God in the world, transcending all other kingdoms, people groups, or nations.

Since we have this biblical revelation, we do not need a new model of the church. There is no "*new* model of the church"! We should not expect one. All so-called new models are either ideas borrowed from business or secular society, or else the rediscovery of models from earlier periods in history.

The biblical model of the church is the only one that is redemptively effective for the kingdom of God. And that model is the church as body of Christ—the community of Jesus disciples that actually looks and acts like Jesus. For "*as he is, so* are we in this world" (1 Jn 4:17).

The key, then, to the recovery of biblical vitality in urban mission is churches that visibly embody *the vision of the kingdom of God* and that are truly *communities of discipleship*. The church is more than simply a community of believers or an organization of church members. It is to be the authentic body of Christ that practices the discipleship Jesus taught and modeled.

A vision of the kingdom incarnated in a community of faithful disciples is the solution to the church's global crisis today.

Jesus said that any who want to follow him must "deny themselves and take up their cross daily and follow me" (Lk 9:23). That is a call to truly be the body of Christ, a community of authentic disciples.

Being the authentic body of Christ requires an organic life of *worship, community,* and *witness.*[11] To elaborate briefly:

Worship celebrates all God has done in the past, is doing now, and *will do* in bringing his kingdom in fullness. It orients the church toward the reality of God and the character and certainty of his promises.

Community means building a life of visible one-another accountable discipleship through which character is molded according to the life of Jesus and the fruit of the Spirit.

Witness means first of all demonstrating in the world the living Jesus Christ, and then *on this basis*, acting in the world according to kingdom-of-God priorities—proclaiming the Good News; working for justice; serving the poor and suffering; working to heal and nourish God's damaged creation in all dimensions; witnessing to the truth

---

[11] See Snyder, *Liberating the Church,* Chapter 3.

of the kingdom in every dimensions of life, culture, and human endeavor.

Church history gives us some very instructive examples and precedents here. The church of the first two centuries is the primary example. A particularly instructive example is the Methodist movement in England in its first fifty years, during the life of John Wesley. Wesley understood the indispensible link between the New Birth, discipleship, and the hope of God's kingdom in fullness. Based on this understanding, he designed, within the Church of England, a movement that through practical structures embodied the essential organic elements of worship, community, and witness. Much could be learned today from this precedent, adapted to varying cultural contexts.[12]

Conclusion: Prophetic Christianity in an Urban World

In one sense, the challenge facing urban mission today is the same as it has always been: Proclaiming and living out the Good News of Jesus Christ and his kingdom in a world of pain, sin, evil, injustice, and the exploitation of the

---

[12] See Howard A. Snyder, *The Radical Wesley: The Patterns and Practices of a Movement Maker* (Franklin, Tenn.: Seedbed Press, 2014), and Elaine A. Heath and Scott T. Kisker, *Longing for Spring: A New Vision for Wesleyan Community* (Eugene, Ore: Cascade Books, 2010), among other sources.

poor and the land.[13] In another sense, the challenges today are new and unprecedented, as I have tried to show.

Today global Christianity thus faces unprecedented challenges, but also great opportunities amid many signs of hope. Prophetic urban witness today can be enlivened through using the six keys discussed here: 1) understanding the earth, 2) uncompromising biblical monotheism, 3) robust Trinitarian faith, 4) defining salvation in a fully biblical way, 5) present hope of the kingdom of God, and 6) living as the body of Christ.

Perhaps in this unprecedented age, God is about to do a new thing. We have the assurance of God's promises, even as we have sober biblical warnings of judgment.

In his sovereignty, God has placed before us two ways: The way of covenant faithfulness, including authentic Christian witness in all dimensions, and the way of covenant betrayal, which certainly brings judgment on the church and destruction to the earth.

This is a call to prophetic Christianity amidst the challenges of urban mission. Let us fully commit ourselves to the whole gospel for the whole world, with the assurance that if we do so, assuredly "the earth will be full of the

---

[13] Howard A. Snyder, *Jesus and Pocahontas: Gospel, Mission, and National Myth* (Eugene, Ore.: Cascade, 2015), especially Chapters 19 and 20.

knowledge of the Lord as the waters cover the sea" (Isa 11:9).

CHAPTER 8

Renewing the Church, Restoring the Land: The Larger Ecology of Urban Mission

Is the kingdom of God about humans only? Or does Jesus care also about our environment? The places—local, global, cyber—where we live?

Everything in the Bible—from the creation accounts to the covenants and holiness code to the life and work of Jesus Christ to the ultimate consummation of God's reign—tells us that God's plan is to redeem people *with* their environment, not *out of* it. The New Testament stresses this through the repeated use of the key phrase, "all things."

Key to the coming of the kingdom is the Spirit's work in renewal. God renews the church in repeated waves, and each one points ahead to the kingdom of God in fullness.[1] If renewing forces are at work, they will touch people in all their relationships, including those with the land—the physical creation as well as the spiritual and social dimensions of their lives.[2]

This chapter further links ecological issues with God's work in renewing the church, especially in cities. It further expands the perspective of Chapter One, where we examined the ecology of urban mission.

We must look both ways: Examine the impact of contemporary ecological concerns on issues of renewal, and—more fundamentally—ask what the dynamics of revitalization can teach us about revitalization in its largest dimensions. We look especially at renewal in relation to the earth, the physical environment. The renewal of creation and the link between church renewal and the created order is a pressing priority for the church today. Increasingly so, as I will show.

---

[1] Howard A. Snyder, *Signs of the Spirit: How God Reshapes the Church* (Grand Rapids: Zondervan, 1989), 31–63, 245–62.

[2] In Scripture, land/earth (the same word in OT Hebrew, as in NT Greek) has the specific meaning of soil (dirt, ground) and in a more extended sense can represent the whole created universe. Here I am using *land* and *earth* in both senses, as will be clear by context.

The question is this: What is the place of ecological issues within the dynamics of effective urban mission? Or to put it more fundamentally and pointedly: What is the relationship between urban mission and God's intent to "renew the face of the earth" (Ps. 104:30); to "make all things new" (Rev 21:5)? Theologically, it is the question of the relationship between the doctrine of creation and the concerns of soteriology, ecclesiology, and missiology.

Ecological Pressures and Realities

Over the past three decades, the reality of climate change has increasingly affected human society. It has hit economics and politics, as well as human lives directly through droughts, heavy storms, floods, and unprecedented fires. Now climate change is driving up insurance costs.

Climate change touches everything. In February 2011, reports of global food-price increases due to commodity shortages were a major news story. What caused the price rises? Many factors, but underneath were huge environmental issues, mostly related to climate change: Big forest fires in Russia; flooding in China, Pakistan, and elsewhere; drought or other "natural disasters" in many lands.[3]

The world has always experienced fires, floods, typhoons, hurricanes, and so forth. But now a growing international consensus among climatologists, oceanographers, and others in the know tells us that climate change is causing more frequent, less predictable, and more extreme so-called natural disasters.[4]

Among ongoing climate studies, one reported on February 16, 2011, especially caught my eye. Justin Gillis of the *New York Times* reported data showing that the "increase in heavy precipitation that has afflicted many countries" in recent years "is at least partly a consequence of human influence on the atmosphere." Climate scientists used "elaborate computer programs that simulate the climate to analyze whether the rise in severe rainstorms, heavy snowfalls and similar events could be explained by natural variability in the atmosphere. They found that it could not, and that the increase made sense only when the computers factored in the effects of greenhouse gases

---

[3] Climatologists report that the disastrous 2010 flooding in Pakistan was in large part a consequence of the exceptionally extensive forest fires far to the north, in Russia—which in turn were fueled by drought.
4 Among the many sources relating to such issues, see chapter 6, "The Groans of Creation," in Howard A. Snyder with Joel Scandrett, *Salvation Means Creation Healed* (Cascade Books, 2011).

released by human activities like the burning of fossil fuels."[5]

Impartial scientific studies continue to point in the same direction. The only exceptions are a few that are heavily underwritten by the fossil-fuel industry.

Without getting into politically charged debates about global warming and other environmental issues, we can at least note—and verify—that ecological concerns and extreme weather events increasingly occupy the attention of the news media, governments, and the business community. This will increase. Year by year a larger and larger proportion of news reporting will cover extreme climate events such as floods, tornadoes, hurricanes, and devastating storms of snow, wind, ice, hail, and rain. Predictably, the consequences will be severe especially for cities and for the poor. They will threaten political and economic stability in many countries.

These concerns are directly relevant to urban mission. This brief summary of ecological issues is cited mainly to set the context. For from a biblical and theological perspective, pervasive ecological issues are not primarily a matter of current events. They concern, more basically, the biblical perspective on the relation between the land and

5 Justin Gillis, *New York Times* website, February 16, 2011.

humanity. And this in turn has important implications for church renewal and vital urban mission.

The Biblical Picture: God, People, Land

As Christians, we insist on the primacy of biblical revelation in understanding and interpreting the church and its mission. Normative insights from Scripture must inform our efforts to be catalysts for deep renewal.

I focus here on one biblical perspective in particular that is fundamental for urban mission today: the biblical teaching about creation and specifically the relationship, grounded in creation and covenant, that God maintains between himself, humanity, and the land. This is a three-way relationship—God, People, Land—not a two-way relationship between God and humankind only.[6]

Genesis 1 and 2 are foundational, of course. But our first stop beyond the creation account is Genesis 9 and the crucial "everlasting covenant" that God makes with the earth (or land) and "all creatures" (Gen 9:8–17). With repeated emphasis, this key passage speaks of the covenant God establishes "between me and the earth" (9:13). It is an

---

[6] This is elaborated more fully in Snyder and Scandrett, *Salvation Means Creation Healed*, 117–34.

"everlasting covenant between God and every living creature of all flesh that is on the earth" (9:16).[7]

The covenant described here is remarkably comprehensive and enduring. Genesis 9 uses the same "everlasting covenant" language found in later biblical covenants that God establishes. In the background here is the pre-fall description of perfect *shalom* between God, humans, the land, and all living creatures pictured in Genesis 1 and 2.

Note that *the rest of Scripture presupposes this three-way relationship*. It builds upon it, in fact. For example in Deuteronomy 8:10 Moses says to Israel, "When you have eaten and are satisfied, praise the Lord your God for the good land he has given you" (TNIV).

This simple statement is profound. In the first chapters of Deuteronomy, God reveals to Israel what it means to be God's people as they enter the promised land. Moses reminds the people of all he had taught and all that had been revealed at Sinai and through the desert wanderings. Moses is about to depart. So he carefully reinforces the

---

[7] This passage seems to be based on a pattern of sevens: "Covenant" is mentioned seven times, as is "earth"; and the combination "every living creature" (four times) with "all flesh" (three times) also yields the number seven.

revealed truth about who God is and what it means to be God's people in God's land.

The story in Deuteronomy, and in fact throughout the Old Testament, is *the story of God, people, and the earth*. It is the story of God's action through a chosen people to restore harmony to creation by their being a blessing to all earth's peoples (Gen 12:3). This is the larger narrative that lies behind Deuteronomy 8:10.

This one small verse holds all the seeds of the biblical understanding of "holistic" or comprehensive mission. Note the structure of the verse. It speaks of three realities: God, the people, and the land. And it shows the proper relationship between the three:

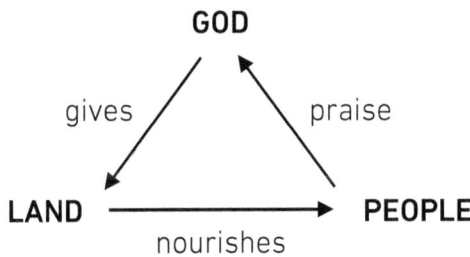

This verse not only mentions God, the land, and God's people. It specifies the *relationship* that God intends between these three realities, these key "subjects." Three fundamental actions are indicated: (1) God *gives the land* to the people; (2) the land *provides food for* or nourishes the people; and (3) the people are to *praise* or worship the Lord. These actions form a perfect triangle, the relationship God intends between himself, his people, and his land. God gives the land, the land sustains the people, and the people in response are to praise God.[8]

In this instance the arrows point from God to the land, from land to the people, then back to God, completing the covenant relationship—perfect *shalom*. In other biblical passages however the action flows the opposite way. God forms and blesses his people; the people are to enjoy and faithfully care for the land (Lev 25 and many other passages); and the land shows forth the glory of God (Ps 19:1 and many other passages). Here the relationships are:

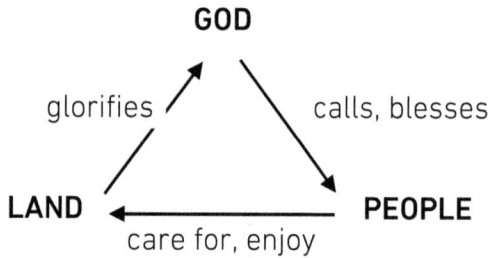

```
                    GOD
                   ↗  ↘
        glorifies ╱      ╲ calls, blesses
                 ╱          ↘
         LAND ◄──────────────  PEOPLE
              care for, enjoy
```

Here is the *biblically revealed, God-intended relationship* between Yahweh, his people, and the land. Since in Hebrew "land" and "earth" are the same word, this is

---

[8] Philosophically and theologically, we note the importance here both of the three "subjects" (God, people, land) and the three relationships. Both the subjects and the relationships are crucial, not one or the other only.

actually a picture of the God-ordained relationship between God, humankind, and the created order. Here is the relationship, the *shalom,* that God purposes. This has been disrupted by sin; salvation heals the brokenness.

Here in the Old Testament, then, we see God through Israel initiating a plan to restore creation to his original intent. God intends *shalom*—a harmonious, reconciled interrelationship between himself, his people, and the land. The action thus flows both ways in perfect ecology. So God's intent may be pictured as follows:

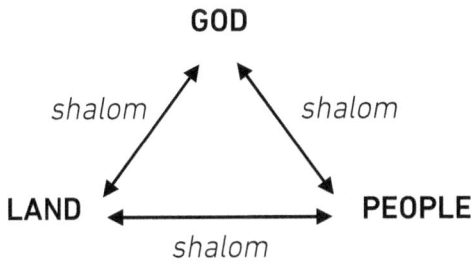

GOD

shalom *shalom*

LAND **PEOPLE**

shalom

To summarize: In the biblical narrative, God creates "the heavens and the earth" (Gen 1:1); he creates humans and places them on earth; and God plants a garden for the enjoyment and sustenance of the human community. This is a perfect picture of *shalom,* the proper covenant relationship between God, humanity, and the earth.

This harmonious balance is shattered by human sin— the fall, then the flood in judgment. But God immediately initiates a series of covenants (beginning in Genesis 9) to bring restoration, salvation, healing. The promise of *shalom* in comprehensive fullness.

This perfect ecology of *shalom* is beautifully captured in a key Old Testament image of Israel at peace: "They shall all sit under their own vines and under their own fig trees, and no one shall make them afraid" (Mic 4:4). In a measure this happened under King Solomon, when "Israel lived in safety, . . . all of them under their vines and fig trees" (1 Kgs 4:25). But that didn't last. So later with Israel's destruction and exile this image becomes an eschatological promise of the kingdom of God in fullness, as in Micah 4:4 and also Zechariah 3:10, "On that day, says the Lord of hosts, you shall invite each other to come under your vine and fig tree."

Here is true *shalom,* peaceful and fruitful harmony between God, people, and the land. Sitting under your own vines and fig trees is an image of creation healed.[9]

The story of the Bible is thus the story of God's perfect purpose, then the disruption caused by human rebellion,

---

[9] Likewise the devastation of vines and fig trees becomes an image of judgment: The enemy "shall eat up your vines and your fig trees" (Jer 5:17); "I will lay waste her vines and her fig trees" (Hos 2:12)—which of course illuminates some of Jesus' actions and parables. See also 2 Kgs 18:31, 1 Mac 14:12).

and finally God's way of restoring the harmonious relationships that were broken and diseased by sin.

This land theme is beautifully interwoven throughout the Old Testament. It recurs over and over. A particularly powerful example is Ezekiel 29–39, and especially Ezekiel 36, where the God-People-Land relationship is central to the vision of Israel's renewal. The parallel with Deuteronomy 8:10 is striking: "Then you shall live in the land that I gave your ancestors; and you shall be my people, and I will be your God. I will save you from all your uncleannesses, and I will summon the grain and make it abundant and lay no famine upon you" (Ezek 36:28-29). The passage goes on to speak of the abundance and fruitfulness of the land.

How does God undertake this mission of healing? We see in the Old Testament that God forms a special redemptive people and gives them a special land—the promised land. God's concern however is not just his chosen people, Israel, but in fact all the nations of the earth.[10] Israel is chosen in order to show forth the truth of God and thus be a blessing to all peoples. God tells Israel, "If you obey me fully and keep my covenant, then out of all

---

[10] "The nations" is a key theme in the Old Testament, for God's plan is to bless all nations and include them in his redemptive work.

nations you will be my treasured possession. Although the whole earth is mine, you will be for me a kingdom of priests and a holy nation" (Ex 19:5-6 TNIV).

So Israel is to be God's priestly people among the nations. A contrast society to show who God is and what God intends. The mission of Israel, then, involves not only Israel's relationship with God but also her relationship with the earth and all its peoples. God is not just the God of Israel; he is the God of all the nations, of the whole earth.[11]

The larger Old Testament picture, then, looks like this:

GOD OF ALL NATIONS

↓

GOD OF ISRAEL

shalom

LAND OF ISRAEL ⟷ **PEOPLE OF ISRAEL**

↓

THE WHOLE EARTH

ALL PEOPLES & NATIONS

As the plan of salvation unfolds in the Old Testament, we thus come to understand four essential truths:

1. Yahweh is God of all peoples, not just of Israel.

---

[11] The theme of "the nations" is commonly emphasized today in urban mission, but in most instances the land is largely overlooked as part of the equation and the discussion.

2. God's plan includes the whole earth, not just the land of Israel.

3. God's plan includes all nations and peoples, not just the Hebrews.

4. God has chosen Israel in order to bring *shalom* to the whole creation.

In the Old Testament we see how comprehensive God's plan is. And yet we do not see the fulfillment of this plan.

But Israel's prophets promised that God would in time send a special servant-king, the Messiah, who would actually accomplish God's redemptive plan. Through the Messiah, God would himself bring perfect *shalom*, as pictured so beautifully in Isaiah 11 and many other passages. The first covenant would be superseded by a New Covenant through which sin would be atoned for, God's Spirit poured out, God's law written on human hearts, and God's purposes finally fulfilled. God's kingdom of justice and *shalom* would come in fullness. This was prefigured already in Abraham's encounter with Melchizedek ("King of righteousness"), who was "king of Salem" (a form of *shalom*) (Gen 14:18–20).

What do we find then in the New Testament? Paul says that through Jesus Christ God is reconciling the world (*kosmos*) to himself (2 Cor 5:19). God has a plan or "economy" (*oikonomia*) "to bring all things in heaven and on earth together under one head, even Christ" (Eph 1:10 NIV). The Lord Jesus Christ has been given the power "to bring everything under his control" (Phil 3:21 TNIV).

Clearly God's plan of salvation as pictured in the New Testament is continuous with the Old Testament revelation. In the older Testament, we see God's concern for all peoples and the whole earth. So also in the New: God is concerned with all peoples and with the whole earth.

In *The Mission of God: Unlocking the Bible's Grand Narrative*, Christopher Wright shows that this is precisely what the Apostle Paul was proclaiming in his mission (comparing Acts 13:17–19 and 17:24–26). Using a triangular graphic similar to the one above, Wright shows how the gospel message expands the Old Testament economy of God, Israel, land to include all humanity and the whole earth, just as prophesied. "All that God did in, for and through *Israel* . . . had as its ultimate goal the blessing of all nations of *humanity* and the final redemption of all *creation*."[12]

---

[12] Christopher Wright, *The Mission of God: Unlocking the Bible's Grand Narrative* (InterVarsity, 2006), 395 (emphasis in the original).

The continuity between the Old and New Testaments is striking. It needs emphasizing, due the tendency in much Christian theology to Platonically over-spiritualize God's saving plan. The New Testament pictures not a divine rescue from the earth. Rather, it shows the reconciliation of earth and heaven—of "all things, whether on earth or in heaven"; things both "visible and invisible." God is "making peace through [Jesus's] blood," shed on the cross (Col 1:16–21). God's plan in both Testaments is to bring *shalom* to all creation. In this sense Christians are still "being saved," because ultimately no one experiences *shalom* in its fullness until the whole creation enjoys *shalom*.

Seeing this progression through both Testaments helps prevent a slimmed-down or distorted understanding of salvation, and thus of the potential scope of mission.

The climax comes in Revelation 21 and 22, and it is urban. We read of the Holy City descending to earth. "God's dwelling place is now among the people, and he will dwell with them. They will be his people, and God himself will be with them and be their God" (Rev 21:3 TNIV). Here is God's plan finally realized, and it is a plan "for the healing of the nations" (Rev 22:2).

The larger biblical picture, then, is of God's comprehensive plan of salvation.

THE TRINITY
THE GOD OF ALL
CREATION

Reconciliation through the work of Jesus Christ

ALL CREATION   ⟷   **ALL PEOPLES & NATIONS**

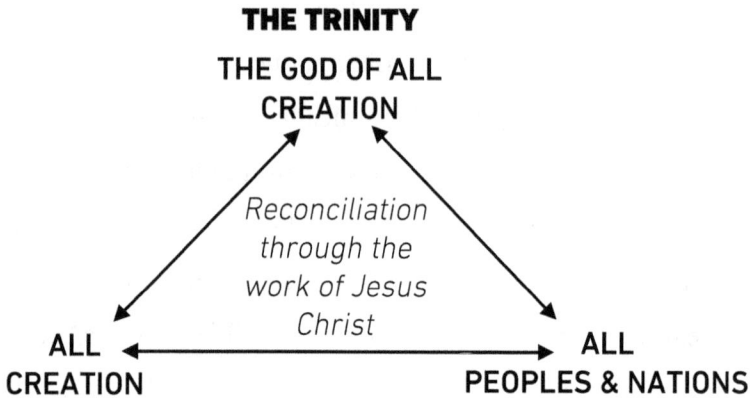

Scripture thus reveals that the holistic mission of God is to bring comprehensive reconciliation to the whole creation. This is the *missio Dei* which God is accomplishing through Jesus Christ in the power of the Holy Spirit. From this comprehensive *missio Dei*, the church derives its mission.

Church history shows that churches often fail to fully embody the gospel's energizing vision and therefore need to experience renewal. Due to a variety of factors and dynamics, movements tend to "run down" or be diverted from their original focus, becoming stagnant or perhaps co-opted by other concerns or projects. Thus urban churches and ministries often need to experience Spirit-led renewal.

In Christian ministry, much depends on the initial vision. The key point here: *The biblical vision in both*

Testaments incorporates the interrelationship of God, People, and Land. Thus any vision or experience of faithful urban mission that does not deeply and integrally incorporate the biblical vision of land/earth will be less than fully biblically comprehensive or "holistic" than it otherwise would be. Any such vision or mission will not only be less comprehensive; it will be less dynamic and less relevant to its social-cultural context—especially in today's increasingly globalized, urban society.

A biblical vision and experience of vital urban mission depends upon and draws much of its energy from the God–People–Land nexus. Without God's presence and action, of course, mission is merely humanism.

In our present context, especially within the Christian church, typically *land* is the missing factor in the God-People-Land relationship. Land itself: The actual physical created order with its abundance of creatures with which human life is inextricably intertwined and upon whose welfare human flourishing depends.

Holistic versus One-Sided Mission

If in fact the biblical vision is one which incorporates God's relationship not only to humans but with the whole creation, then by definition any vision for urban mission will be one-sided—or lopsided, "ec-centric"—if it is blind to creation's essential role in the dynamics of redemption. Respect for and actual engagement with land/earth is essential for at least four reasons.

First and most fundamentally, if land is missing from the vision for urban mission, the vision is not fully biblical (as already argued). This has implications in multiple directions, including ecclesiology and mission.[13]

Second, if land is missing, full missional impact is undermined. To take an example: If a church has a vision for helping the poor, its diagnoses and endeavors will be much less effective if it fails to understand and engage the environmental issues that usually are a major factor in situations of poverty (perhaps air and water pollution in the immediate urban context, but seemingly more remote factors such as deforestation or desertification which impact cities).

Third, if land is missing from the equation, urban mission too easily becomes satisfied with its own internal or institutional success, becoming self-focused, excessively other-worldly, or both. Focus on the land involves us in our

---

[13] For example: a fully comprehensive vision for urban mission will almost by definition engage the spiritual gifts, interests, energies, and professional skills of people who are involved with or have a concern for the full range of land issues, including economics.

common humanity with all peoples and cultures, our mutual interdependence, and out increasingly global interconnects.

Fourth, including the land fundamentally in our missional calculus makes the ministry more prophetic, more socially and ecologically relevant today as environmental issues in multiple ways touch all aspects of our lives. In a world where climate and other ecological issues are more and more the focus of public concern, what does Christian urban mission have to say? What answers can it provide? Urban mission stands mute before many of today's growing global concerns if it misses the full implications of the God-People-Land interrelationship.

With this perspective in mind, I highlight several implications for redemptive urban mission today.

Keys to Comprehensive Urban Mission

If the biblical vision of *shalom* throughout the God-People-Land interrelationship deeply permeates urban mission, the result will be profound. The following three points seem particularly critical.

1. *Urban mission research should investigate the ways "land" has or has not figured in urban ministry.* The "land" theme may be present and dynamic in either a literal or

metaphorical, symbolic sense, or perhaps in some combination of literal and metaphorical. Studies of urban mission in widely diverse cultural contexts and time periods should prove useful here. Cross-referencing between Christian and various philanthropic or development efforts—for example, those concerned with agrarian reform in relation to urban areas, or with addressing particular ecological concerns—might well provide insights applicable to vital urban mission today.

2. *It will become increasingly important to employ an ecological understanding or conceptualization in developing visions and strategies for urban mission.* Theologically and biblically, the link between the New Testament theme of *oikos/oikonomia* (household/economy) and contemporary ecological understandings should continue to be explored.

Vital urban mission today requires a vivid awareness of the spiritual-physical-social-cultural interdynamic which *in fact* exists in the world. We need to study not just the history, sociology, and anthropology of urban mission but also their *ecology* in this expanded and fundamental sense.

3. Students and practitioners of urban mission should *continue to mine the biblical material and the theological implications of the land-and-creation theme for new and timely insights.* The previous discussion already points in this

direction. Other dimensions here include biblical studies of the theme of land, the relation of land in Scripture and theology to other themes of creation, and what the Bible teaches about God's relationship to the created order in terms of sustaining, providentially guiding, and making all things new in Jesus Christ. Trinitarian theological explorations in multiple cultural contexts are relevant here, as are the New Testament themes of the "coherence" of all things in Jesus Christ and of the significance of Jesus's physical resurrection for God's intent to make all things new (e.g., Eph 1:10, Col 1, Rom 8, Rev 21–22).

Here both ancient and contemporary biblical and theological studies can be brought into service in the ongoing study of mission in urban contexts and beyond.

Conclusion

Among many other things, an ecological land-and-creation perspective holds out great promise for bridging Scripture and the Christian tradition and witness, on the one hand, and contemporary global-and-local society, with all its combined economic and ecological concerns, on the other. A vision for healing the city and restoring the land— as fundamental and interwoven themes—is a rich conceptual and practical resource for urban mission today.

CHAPTER 9
Thinking Straight in a Tangled World

Effective, faithful, redemptive urban mission requires thought. Of course it also requires compassion, presence, community, relationships, action, sacrifice—all the things we've discussed in this book.

This chapter discusses the *way* we think about urban mission—that is, our very modes of thought. The city is a mix and often a clash of cultures and therefore of worldviews and ways of thinking. Many conflicts are not only clashes of relationships and values, but also clashes of the very modes of thought we use and assume.

This chapter looks at the ways we think—how we reflect, analyze, and make decisions that we assume are sound because they seem natural to us.

The first part of this chapter discusses four *models of thinking*—the assumed, usually unexamined ways we perceive, analyze, decide, and then take action. We note how culture often plays a key role in how we think.

The second part of the chapter compares logical, analogical, and psychological ways of thinking.

Finally, we apply these insights to the practice of urban mission.

Part One. Four Models of Thought

How do you think? Ever thought about that?

Not everyone thinks the same way. We all tend to think—that is, to reason—in different ways, depending upon influences that have shaped us. Probably genetics plays a role, as well.

Influences that shape our thinking come especially from our culture and family background. We (most of us) have been raised to, unconsciously, think according to one or another set of assumptions.

I call these *models of thinking.* These models shape the ways we think and act, as well as the matters we take for granted.

What are these models or modes of thinking? Four basic ones shape our assumptions and how we act: *Hierarchical* thinking, *linear* thinking, *cyclical* thinking, and *ecological* thinking. As I reflect on these models, I now see how my own thinking has shifted over the years.

1. Hierarchical thinking (and Acting)

Without fully realizing it, many think hierarchically. Their culture has given them a set of assumptions that *precede* the thinking process and thus unconsciously shape it.

In hierarchical thinking, *authority* is the key dynamic. This mode of thinking takes its cues from the structures of authority in the culture and in one's life. Hierarchical thinking can be pictured as a vertical arrow:

↓

As the arrow shows, hierarchical thinking assumes a vertical line from authority (power) to submission; from higher to lower status; from superiority to inferiority. In theology and spirituality, often this is assumed to be a movement downwards from perfection to imperfection.[1]

This mode of thinking places high value on order, stability, and predictability. Theologies which hold to a static, fixed "orders of creation" idea reflect this mode.

Within this model, *ecological thinking* (discussed below) is difficult, if not impossible. This is important for how we view urban mission.

2. Linear Thinking (and Acting)

Here the key is an underlying assumption of *progress*. Or alternatively, in some versions, the assumption of *decline*. So linear thinking can be pictured in these ways:

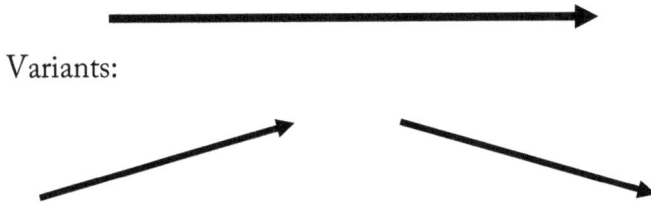

Variants:

The basic dynamic here, as the arrows show, is linear progression from one element or stage to the next, from where we are to where we will be. Inevitable progress (or

---

[1] See for example discussions of the Great Chain of Being. The classic work here is Arthur O. Lovejoy, *The Great Chain of Being: A Study in the History of Ideas* (Cambridge, Mass.: Harvard University Press, 1936, 1964), which because of its analysis of culture and cultural assumptions is still very relevant to urban mission.

decline) is usually assumed. The reversal of the process is considered unlikely or impossible.

This way of thinking easily becomes a philosophy of history (think *Decline and Fall of the Roman Empire*) or perhaps a spiritual worldview. It is in fact a worldview assumption that tends to shape the way we think on a whole range of issues, from spirituality to politics to technology. It affects how we view urban life today, in the past, and prospects for the future.

3. Cyclical Thinking (and Acting)

All life and action is viewed in terms of cycles. The assumed dynamic is *repetition*. What has been is what will be. What will be is assumed to be just another version of the past.

This mode of thinking can thus be pictured this way:

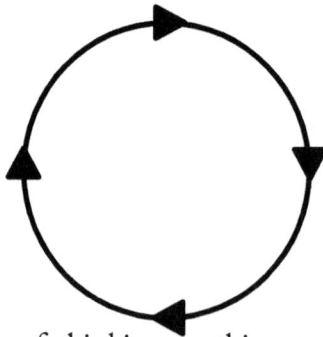

In this mode of thinking, nothing truly *new* happens. (Think of the Old Testament book of Ecclesiastes.) Life is an endless repetition of cycles, with no fundamental progress or real change. If this is our worldview, it will be reflected in the ways we think about life. It will likely influence the way we solve problems and do ministry.

Cyclical thinking is like hierarchical and linear thinking in that there is a sense of movement. But here the movement is cyclical. Life never really goes anywhere totally new. This is reflected in religious worldviews that posit some form of "eternal return."

In cyclical thinking, historical progression and scientific progress are difficult to conceive of. Some historians see this fact as a key reason why scientific and technological progress developed more in the West than in the East, where cyclical thinking has predominated.

This cyclical way of thinking does of course embody truth. We do in fact live within the cycles of nature and seasons, of families and generations. It is easy to see why this mode of thinking has been so powerful over centuries and millennia.[2]

---

[2] For this reason it is not accurate to say the Bible gives us a linear, not cyclical, worldview or view of history. Scripture combines both. God's redemptive revelation breaks the cycle of pagan worldviews but maintains and redeems the cycles of the created order. This in fact is a key aspect of biblical revelation: redeeming the cycles of "nature" (seasons, agriculture, sun, moon, stars, human birth and death, generations) from pagan understandings and idolatry and attempted manipulation through rituals, magic, and sacrifices.

Further, this mode of thinking can be, and often has been, combined with hierarchical thinking. In fact these various modes of thinking are not always mutually exclusive. People may combine various ways of thinking at times. They may use one or another, depending on circumstances. For most people most of the time, however, it seems that one mode predominates.

As leaders in urban mission attempt to build genuine Christian community in the city, they may find that how people function in community is partly shaped by such cyclical assumptions. The more culturally diverse a congregation is, the more this is likely to be true. (Think for instance how dynamics of status or class or caste affect community.)

Here then we have three basic ways of thinking: Hierarchical, linear, and cyclical. But another way of thinking is becoming especially relevant today, as we saw in Chapter One: *ecological* thinking.

4. Ecological Thinking (and Acting)

What is the underlying reality and assumption here? Not authority, not progress, not repetition. Rather it is *life.* And life, while dynamic, is also messy.

So we may picture ecological thinking this way:

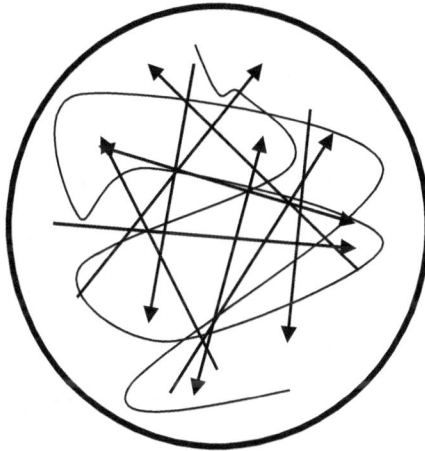

We see multiple interactions in all directions. We encounter multiple feedback loops, often unanticipated. In fact in ecological thinking, very significant but often subtle feedback loops simply cannot be anticipated, as we saw in Chapter One. (Think of the weather or the climate.)

This is because life is highly complex. In ecological thinking, complexity is assumed. Dynamism and continuous flux are expected—the norm.

Ecological thinking means valuing each element (or micro ecosystem) for its own particular role and contribution.

Ecological thinking is *organic*. It understands the importance of organisms; of all living things, and how they interact with each other and with the larger environment. Ecosystems can be either stable or unstable. They are often fragile; vulnerable to disruption. Ecological thinking reflects upon the ways life actually works.

Ecological thinking is compatible *both* with Scripture and (thus) with the actual reality of the created order. It recognizes the partial truth of hierarchical, linear, and cyclical processes and modes of thinking, but is more inclusive. Since it is more comprehensive than other modes of thinking, it is the most wholistic and the most helpful for Christians in attempting to understand theology, mission, urban life, and our own lives. Even the Trinity.

The first three models sketched above—hierarchical, linear, and cyclical—have a key weakness. They make it very difficult to really think ecologically or grasp the dynamism of ecology. Thus they make it hard to think comprehensively and wholistically about salvation and about our own discipleship in relation to each other and to the earth.

When you look at the Bible from an ecological perspective, you see that it is amazingly ecological—ecological in a much more profound sense than secular models of ecology. Our theology and our ethics should reflect this. That is, they should be truly ecological in the biblical sense.

Missional Reflection

All four of these modes of thinking carry big theological implications. Your theology and your ethics (your life and your discipleship) will be different depending on which of these modes of thinking predominates in your life.

Changing from one way of thinking to another inevitably means a *major paradigm shift*. Once you move from any of these models to ecological thinking, for instance, your whole understanding of the gospel and of church and mission changes, expands. I know this from experience.

It is true, as already hinted, that we may combine these thinking modes in various ways or in various areas of our lives. But one will be most basic. It will give us our underlying assumptions—that is, our worldview, our worldstory, our world-feeling. Further, each mode is both shaped by and reinforces existing social structures and arrangements. *Culture conflicts* and *social revolutions* often involve clashes in thinking modes.

In light of this, we may ask some questions as we reflect on our own theology and sense of mission and discipleship.

For example:

> ➢ By which model do we tend to think of or conceptualize the Trinity?

> ➢ The church, in its structure and organization?

> ➢ The city and urban life?

> ➢ Society and culture generally?

> ➢ Our relationships in the body of Christ?

> ➢ Our relationship to the earth and God's other creatures?

> ➢ Do different theological systems tend to assume or favor one of these models of thinking over others?

These modes of thinking might well shape how we tell the story of Jesus Christ. How do we present the promise and the meaning of Messiah's coming?

Hierarchical model: The Messiah comes down from heaven by the Father's authority so that we can know God and eventually be taken up to heaven.

Linear model: Messiah comes in fulfillment of the long, long story of God's redemptive work in history to bring to completion God's plan for the ages.

Cyclical model: The Christian Year is a cycle. Jesus' birth is celebrated as the renewal and celebration of God's promise to send Messiah and bring salvation.

These three all contain truth in their own way. But each is partial, limited. Grand as they are, they may unintentionally distort the fullness of God's economy of salvation.

Ecological model: Jesus comes in fulfillment of God's redemptive promises to bring to glorious fulfillment, to full *shalom* and flourishing, his whole creation when God's kingdom comes fully and the whole earth is truly and completely filled with the glory of the Lord.

Part Two. Thinking Biblically and Missionally in the City

God speaks authoritatively to us through his Word, illuminated by the Holy Spirit. Even so, Christians often disagree on what the Bible really *means*.

Jesus Christ, the incarnate Word, has left us the sacred Scripture, the written Word, to guide Christians on our course through history and culture. God has sent us his Spirit to help us interpret the Bible in light of Jesus Christ, and to understand Jesus Christ in light of the Bible. Jesus himself said to "search the scriptures," for they "testify" of him (John 5:39). Jesus taught the Word to two bewildered disciples on the road to Emmaus. In a remarkable statement we read that Jesus, "beginning with Moses and all the prophets, . . . interpreted to them the things about himself in all the scriptures" (Lk 24:27). This is, shall we say, Jesus' hermeneutical secret, the key to interpreting the Old Testament.

This is good news! Yet from the very beginning, Jesus's followers have struggled to know how to understand and properly interpret Scripture. The book of Acts, the story of Pentecost and the remarkable growth of the early church, itself witnesses to the church's wrestling with Scripture. We see the Apostle Peter's eyes being opened to Scripture through his encounter with Cornelius the centurion. He told the crowd at Cornelius's house, "I truly understand that God shows no partiality, but in every nation anyone who fears him and does what is right is acceptable to him" (Acts 10:35). That was a new learning for Peter—spiritually and emotionally, if not cognitively; no doubt he'd often read as much in the Hebrew Scriptures.

Many things affect how we interpret the Bible. We are shaped especially by our culture and church traditions. But the way we understand Scripture is also partly a function of the *way we think*. And how we think is itself the complex product of temperament, education, and cultural context. Maybe it's even molded by our genetic makeup.

Most of us notice pretty early than not everyone thinks alike! Children learn (or not) how to figure out the thinking of their parents—and vice-versa. Pastors struggle with the different ways their parishioners think—and vice-versa. Theologians think differently not only in content but in styles of thought. Is this part of the difference, perhaps, between (for example) Karl Barth, C. S. Lewis, and Morton Kelsey? Or between John Calvin, John Wesley, and Martin Luther? Or Augustine and Chrysostom? Do we gravitate toward writers who think like we do?

The more basic issue is this: How do we think biblically and theologically? Here are three models that may prove useful. In interpreting the Bible and thinking theologically, we tend to interpret things *logically, analogically,* or *psychologically.* One could consider a number of other modes, but I find this approach especially useful for interpreting Scripture and for gaining insight into different theologians and theologies. They give us some insight into how and why we form our beliefs and understand mission the way we do.

In the first part of this chapter we discussed hierarchical, linear, cyclical, and ecological thinking. These are modes of the thinking process itself. Now we look at logical, analogical, and psychological thinking. These are more like lenses through which we see. The first is highly rational; the second is more figurative (more like poetry); the third is more a matter of feeling and empathy. So these are different categories from the four modes discussed earlier. Cyclical thinking, for example, might be logical, analogical, or psychological.

This becomes clearer as we describe these three perspectives.

How do we reach theological conclusions? The answer is not only a matter of the "data"—the facts and the stories. It is also shaped by our thinking style. Not only the materials, but also the tools. And we may have different tool kits.

People seem to think mainly in one of three quite different ways. Partly because of this, we have different views, different beliefs—sometimes even different churches.

Some of us tend to think primarily on the basis of *logic*. Others think by using *stories*, and some by *intuition*. These are not mutually exclusive; we all use all three much of the time, and according to context. But in most people, one tends to dominate. I would argue that all are good, and even necessary. None should be despised.

Some people's thinking style is *logical*. For others, it is *analogical*. For still others, it may be *psychological*. Imagine a triangle:

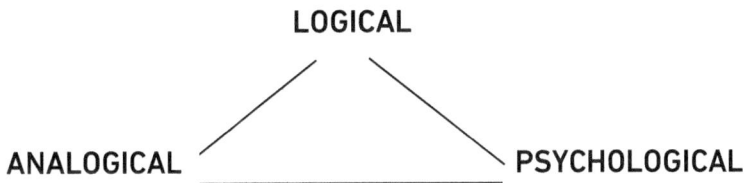

LOGICAL

ANALOGICAL   **PSYCHOLOGICAL**

Three different ways of thinking. One could visualize these also as overlapping spheres or circles, since the three constantly interact with each other.

If someone says you are a "very logical person," is that a compliment or an insult? Most people living in Western societies would probably beam at the compliment. That's because Europe was so influenced by the so-called Age of Reason and the Enlightenment of the seventeenth and eighteenth centuries, and because of the rich inheritance of Greek and Roman philosophy.

But not every culture in the world—and not every Westerner—would think "being logical" is a compliment! In some cultures it would signal higher status if you were said to be one who "tells good stories," or "just has a sense" (intuition) of what is true or right.

Let us examine each of these styles in turn (a logical thing to do): the logical, the analogical, and the psychological. This will help us see which style each of us mainly uses, and how that might be useful in the practice of urban mission:

1. Logical Thinking

Logic is golden in the West, especially in the fields of philosophy, theology, science and technology, and in certain professions, like law. Logic has wonderful strengths. It really is powerful, but it also has key limitations.

The main human capacity that logic uses is *reason*. Logical thinking specializes in *propositions* that declare what is true or not true. In classical logic, a key tool is the *syllogism*—a formal way of stating propositions that helps one construct sound logical arguments and demolish faulty ones. A syllogism consists of two statements or premises, then a conclusion drawn from these. A more formal definition: A syllogism is "An instance of a form of reasoning in which a conclusion is drawn (whether validly or not) from two given or assumed propositions (premises), each of which shares a term with the conclusion, and shares a common middle term not present in the conclusion."[3]

John Wesley (1703–1791), a son of the Enlightenment, was schooled in this way of reasoning. As a young scholar

---

[3]http://www.oxforddictionaries.com/us/definition/american_english/syllogism

he taught logic at Oxford University. Formal and informal syllogisms populate his sermons and other writings. Those familiar with recognized tools and techniques of logic may occasionally smile as they see Wesley's sometimes subtle moves in his more disputatious writings, such as his *Earnest Appeal to Men of Reason and Religion* (1743) and his *Farther Appeal to Men of Reason and Religion* (1745). "We . . . earnestly exhort all who seek after true religion to use all the reason which God hath given them in search out the things of God," Wesley said, but he was quick to recognize its limitations and possible distortions.[4]

Syllogisms can be fun, because they're only as good as their premises. They can be either valid or invalid, and they can be tricky. A valid syllogism would be:

> All normal cows have four legs.
> Bessie is a normal cow.
> Therefore Bessie has four legs.

But this would be an invalid syllogism:

> All cows have four legs.
> Rover has four legs.
> Therefore Rover is a cow.

A logician quickly spots the flaw. The second statement is faulty as a premise because it replaces the more general

---

[4] John Wesley, *An Earnest Appeal to Men of Reason and Religion.* Wesley, *Works* (Bicentennial Ed.), 11:56.

category (kind of animal—cow or dog) with a more limited one (four legs). All normal cows have four legs, but not all four-legged creatures are cows (thankfully, since cows don't make very good house pets or race horses).

The Oxford Dictionary's website gives this example: All dogs are animals; all animals have four legs; therefore all dogs have four legs. Here again we see the more specific contained within the more general category. It would be a simple but invalid move to invert the last two terms so that the formula read: All dogs are animals; all animals have four legs; therefore all animals are dogs.

The logical consistency of syllogisms is much like mathematics, to which syllogisms are logically related.

Syllogisms are useful in theology and in planning, because they help us be precise. They are often abused in theology, however—either by faulty premises or, more commonly, but simply leaving the second premises out and "intuiting" or "assuming" it. For example:

We are saved by faith, not by good works.

Therefore Christians should not do good works.

This leaves out several intervening steps that would need to be examined in order for the conclusion to follow logically from the premises. Theology can be full of this kind of invalid or at least questionable reasoning. We easily make similar mistakes in everyday thinking and planning. A valid syllogism, however, has all the certainty of a mathematical proof. If the premises are valid, the conclusion *has* to be true just as surely as two plus two equals four (at least in our earthly space-time world!). This is because reason is based in God and his character, and therefore is a dimension of the created order and a key capacity of the image of God in men and women.

We might call the logical approach the way of *classical science*, or at least of the "scientific method" that developed especially during the Enlightenment. Good scientific inquiry is logical. Valid scientific conclusions rest not only on the methods and the experiments but also the logic that underlies them.

Some of the greatest Christian theologians have been logicians *par excellence*. Thomas Aquinas constructed highly complex rational arguments. Karl Barth in his great *Church Dogmatics* made extensive use of logic—sometimes using logic even to show its limitations. John Calvin is known for his mastery of logic.

Logical reasoning draws more on the left side of the brain than on the right side. Research into how the brain works suggests that logical functions happen more in the left hemisphere and imaginative functions more in the right. Is systematic theology then mainly a left-brained activity? What about normal everyday life and ministry?

2. Analogical Thinking

Some people inhabit the world of imagination more than the realm of logic. Their thinking tends to be more analogical than logical. Not necessarily illogical; just different.

When we think of analogy and imagination, we think of art and poetry. Rather than using propositions to declare something "is" or "is not," we say something is "like" or "not like" something else. "My love is like a rose." Or we may use "is" but really mean "like." "No man is an island," said John Donne. This is the land of metaphor and simile—as also of story.

The Bible is full of analogical language. Think of Old Testament stories, or of Jesus' parables, or David's poetry. Righteous people are "like trees planted by streams of water" (Psalm 1:3). King Jehoash put down King of Amaziah of Judah with this story: "A thistle in Lebanon sent a message to a cedar in Lebanon, 'Give your daughter to my son in marriage.' Then a wild beast in Lebanon came along and trampled the thistle underfoot" (2 Kgs 14:9).

Much of the Bible, in both its history and its poetry, is in narrative form. In fact, analogical and figurative language is the basic mode of Scripture. Northrop Frye in *Words with Power* notes that "the Bible is, with unimportant exceptions, written in the literary language of myth and metaphor: it is, in short, a work of literature plus. . . . [Thus] within the Bible itself, all the values connected with the term 'truth' can be reached only by passing through myth and metaphor."[5] The point is not that the Bible *is* a myth, but that its most basic linguistic mode is metaphorical and analogical.

Good theology, like good preaching, uses analogies—not just for illustration, but as a way of thinking. Consider John Wesley. Sir Walter Scott when he was boy once heard Wesley preach and years later recalled, "He told many excellent stories!"

Parables and other stories are powerful because they engage more than just the mind. "For a parable is not an explanation. A parable is not an illustration," notes Eugene Peterson. "A parable does not make a thing easier; it makes it harder by requiring participation" of the hearers.[6]

---

[5] Northrop Frye, *Words with Power: Being a Second Study of "The Bible and Literature"* (New York: Harcourt Brace Jovanovich, 1990), xiv–xv. See also his earlier *The Secret Code: The Bible and Literature* (New York: Houghton Mifflin Harcourt, 1981, 1982).

[6] Eugene H. Peterson, *Tell It Slant: A Conversation on the Language of Jesus in His Stories and Prayers* (Grand Rapids, Mich.: Eerdmans, 2008), 59–60.

Some of the most influential theologians and Christian writers of the past century were great storytellers. Think of the Oxford friends, C. S. Lewis, J. R. R. Tolkien, and Charles Williams. It is remarkable how many twentieth-century Christian leaders, such as Charles Colson, owed their conversions or their Christian worldview largely to Lewis's influence.

If logic is the way of science, analogy is the way of art. The genius of art is the role of metaphor and imagination. Artists will tell you they don't try to picture things as they are, but rather as they see or imagine them. Or possibly as they "truly are" at some profound level. Artists resonate with a deeper reality than what appears on visible surfaces.

A key tool of analogical thinking, along with imagination, is *paradox*. This seems almost the opposite of the syllogism. Paradoxes stand propositions on their heads by declaring that two apparently contradictory statements might both be true. Since Albert Einstein's theory of relativity, science has had increasingly to wrestle with paradox, especially in quantum physics. Fritjof Capra and others say scientific investigation is becoming as much art as science.[7]

---

[7] Fritjof Capra, *The Tao of Physics: An Exploration of the Parallels Between Modern Physics and Eastern Mysticism*, 3rd ed. (Boston, Mass.: Shambhala, 1991).

Jesus was a master of paradox when he needed to be, especially when dealing with his critics. Think about the conundrums he posed about his own identity—"If David thus calls him Lord, how can he be his son?" (Mt 22:45).

In contrast with logic, analogical thinking draws more on the right side of the brain. Thus there are even some physiological aspects to whether we gravitate more toward logical or analogical thinking.

3. Psychological Thinking

Finally, there is psychological reasoning. Here the accent is not on reason or imagination, but on *emotion*—that which deeply moves us. We face here the reality and influence of feelings, moods, and attitudes. This is closely related to analogical thinking, yet different enough to require some reflection.

Where reason may employ the syllogism and analogical thinking the paradox, psychological thinking uses *intuition*. Intuition of course plays a role in logical and analogical thinking (often unrecognized), but in psychological thinking it is primary. In this mode, key statements are not about what "is" or what something "is like," but rather about how things "seem" or "feel."

At the end of an impressive logical argument have you ever said, "Yes, but it just doesn't *seem* right"? Or perhaps someone has said to you, "I really can't give my reasons for this, but I *feel* strongly that this is the way things really are." That's psychological thinking.

Instead of propositions (logic) or stories (analogies), psychological reasoning in more fully elaborated form may use myth or allegory—special forms of story. This is not the way of science or art primarily, but is often the way of *games* and *play.* Like analogical reasoning it draws heavily on the right brain, though of course not exclusively.

The Bible is full of psychological insights. We find numerous examples of psychological reasoning in Scripture. Several of the Old Testament writers at times use myth and allegory to communicate God's message. And throughout the Bible—in contrast with much of Western culture—we find the prominence of dreams.

Many of the great mystics and spiritual writers have used psychological reasoning, as well as analogical reasoning. In modern times, one thinks of Thomas Merton. Psychological thinking is found more rarely in systematic theology, which (at least in the West) has tended to value rational thought above all else. Psychological reasoning often abounds in sermons, however, as pastors try to connect with the "felt needs" of their people or give telling or moving illustrations.

One great twentieth century master of this approach was Carl Jung—not a theologian or a preacher, though he thought of himself as some sort of Christian. Jung has had a huge influence on many Christian thinkers and writers, such as Morton Kelsey, in part because of his emphasis on the importance of dreams and symbols.[8]

Here then are three common ways of thinking: logical, analogical, and psychological. Certainly there are others, but we encounter these three constantly in Christian life and thought and in the daily practice of ministry. They abound also in Scripture—another testimony to the comprehensive and holistic nature of the Bible. This is a sign to us that we should value all three approaches as we live out our Christian discipleship.[9]

Recalling the triangle above, we summarize these three ways of thinking as follows

Three Modes of Thinking

LOGICAL	ANALOGICAL	PSYCHOLOGICAL
Reason	Imagination	Emotion
"is" / "is not"	"is like"	"seems" / "feels"

---

[8] For example, Morton Kelsey, *The Other Side of Silence* (Mahwah, N.J.: Paulist Press, 1976), reissued in revised form as *The Other Side of Silence: Meditation for the Twenty-First Century* (Paulist, 1997).
[9] Here again Frye's *The Secret Code* is helpful.

Syllogism	Paradox	Intuition / "sense"
Proposition	Story / Parable	Myth / Allegory
"Science"	"Art"	"Game" / "Play"
Aquinas – Barth?	Lewis, Buechner	Jung, Kelsey, Merton
Left Brain	Right Brain	Right Brain?

Probably we all combine these different modes at different times and in various situations, or perhaps according to different activities that engage us. You often run into all three in the city, both at the level of personal interaction and at the more overarching level of media and public discourse. Yet it seems that for most of us, one mode predominates most of the time. If we think about it, we can see that each has a role to play. We need all three in the Christian life, in our biblical interpretation, and in urban mission.

Who is your favorite doctor? The best physicians combine these three modes. They know how to reason clearly and precisely. They make those more indirect connections that come by analogy and imagination, practicing the art as well as the science of medicine. Plus, they have good intuition and strong empathy. Often they simply "sense" what is wrong and then are able to confirm this through further diagnosis.

Great scientists also combine all three ways of thinking. Maria Popova observes how "scientists traverse the abyss between the known and the unknown, suspended by intuition, adventurousness, a large dose of stubbornness and a measure of luck" in finding scientific breakthroughs. "A good theory is an act of the informed imagination," she notes.[10] The same applies to artists and good pastors and urban workers—except it's not luck, it is God's providence and guidance, the work of the Spirit.

These are sensitivities that people in urban mission can develop. How often we may think that *our* way of thinking is the *right* way, and other ways are defective! How many of our longstanding theological disputes really derive from diverse ways of thinking?

Thinking Out Our Beliefs and Doctrines

For Christians, beliefs and creeds are important. We take theology seriously because we know it makes a huge

---

[10] Maria Popova, Review of *Dark Matter and the Dinosaurs* by Lisa Randall, Sunday Book Review, *The New York Times* (Nov. 29, 2015), BR14.

difference in how we live. We know that Truth is something larger than our personal lives, our own limited experiences. Saving faith is not just a matter of *having* faith, of believing *something*. It is a matter of believing and confessing that some things are true and some are false. Most importantly, saving faith is faith *in someone*—Jesus Christ as Savior and Lord, "for there is no other name under heaven given among mortals by which we must be saved" (Acts 4:12).

But *how* do we think about what is important theologically, important for our faith and life? We can press the above discussion a little further by focusing especially on the ways we interpret Scripture.

We notice that the Bible is full of stories, as well as containing doctrines and history. We tell the stories of Jesus. We recall and teach the stories of Old Testament heroes and scoundrels—David and Goliath, Daniel in the lions' den, Esther and the king. And like New Testament writers, we draw theological lessons from these characters. The church reflects on biblical history and on its own history, and it forms creeds to nail down points of key doctrinal consensus.

Imagine, then, a different sort of triangle or pyramid:

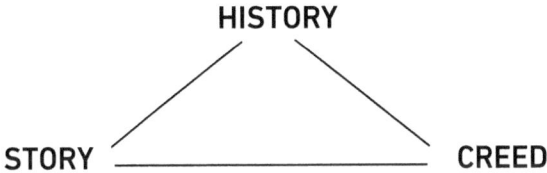

HISTORY

STORY —————————— **CREED**

History is "what really happened," so far as we know. *Story* is how we tell, relate, or imagine what happened or could happen. *Creed* is what we believe or confess about what happened. The Apostle Paul wrote, for example: "I handed on to you as of first importance what I in turn had received: that Christ died for our sins in accordance with the scriptures, and that he was buried, and that he was raised on the third day in accordance with the scriptures, and that he appeared to Cephas, then to the twelve" (1 Cor 15:3–5).

Our life is shaped by history, story, and creed. All three are hugely important for Christians, because ours is a historical faith. It makes a critical difference what really happened in history—that God created the universe; that Jesus Christ actually lived, died, and was raised to life, all within history; that God will fulfill what he has promised to do in history. Our faith is historical, and our mission is historical.

In urban mission, it makes a huge difference how we live in history, in time and space. It makes a difference what stories we *live*, and what stories we tell. We witness effectively by living and telling our stories in the light of "the old, old story" of what God has done and is doing through Jesus Christ in the power of the Holy Spirit. And it is important for our lives and witness what we *believe* about all this—the key truths of the Christian Good News in the context of the nitty-gritty, actual history of the world.

But we ask also: How do we *think* about all this? The point is that we don't all think in the same ways, manners, or styles. Whether we think logically, analogically, or psychologically about the history, stories, and creeds that shape our lives determines in significant measure where we "come out" in our interpretation of events and our understanding of Scripture.

How we interpret the Bible is especially critical. What is our biblical hermeneutic?—that is, our system of interpreting Scripture? Is it logical, analogical, or psychological? Or some mix of all three? And what difference does it make?

The Difference It Makes: Thinking Holistically

How we think does make a big difference. Just as there are values in all three modes of thinking, so there are dangers. How would you like living with a strictly, unbendably logical person, someone moved only by reason and not much in tune with poetry and emotion? It would not be a pretty sight! Or a very livable life. But the same would apply to functioning *solely* by analogical or psychological thinking. People at the analogical extreme might be thought to be "not quite in touch with reality" or "living in the clouds" or "inhabiting their own world." People at the psychological extreme might be viewed as "not really serious" or "more concerned with feelings than truth."

Clearly, we need balance. The church needs holistic thinking as well as holistic living and holistic mission. That is, we need to take into account all of God's truth when we form our doctrines, and we need to live out all God's truths in our witness and discipleship.

Clearly, however, this is an impossible task—*alone*. But it is not an impossible task *in community*. This is partly why God formed the church, to make it very literally the body of Christ in the world, living out the whole, balanced, Spirit-filled life we see in Jesus. We need each other in our thinking and believing, just as we do in our living and loving. In this sense also the church needs to grow up into the fullness of Christ (Eph 3:19, 4:15–16; Col 2:9–10).

Four practical insights can be drawn from the different ways of thinking discussed here. These can help inform and enliven our practice of urban mission.

First, *churches need to think holistically, combining the logical, analogical, and psychological approaches.* We need all three. Each contributes something essential to our lives, our doctrines, and our biblical interpretation.

The Bible teaches that we are created in the image of God. This is a key theological touchstone. In profound ways we as a human race reflect the image of the Holy Trinity, Father, Son, and Holy Spirit. Our capacity to reason and our different modes of reasoning are part of this. Our reasoning gets distorted by sin, just like everything else. But we still have the capacity of reason, to be used for God's good purposes and to God's glory.

God, we may assume, thinks holistically, in fullness! That is, God knows everything that can be known, and he knows the full length and strength of reason, of analogy, of art, of intuition, of feeling. Theologian Clark Pinnock pictured God not as the "unmoved Mover" but as the "most-moved Mover."[11] Yes!

Despite the limitations of our knowledge and ways of thinking, we should try to think like God—to "think God's thoughts after him." This is not audacity or arrogance; it is humble discipleship. We should value all three ways of thinking, benefiting from all of them. Each contributes something to the other. If we combine these three modes holistically then our doctrines, our lives, our communities, and the church's mission will be more whole, healthy, entire, and therefore redemptive.

Second, *the church needs and should affirm all the gifts God gives,* not just some. Paul's teaching to the Corinthian church regarding gifts applies also to our ways of thinking. The church should value and affirm the logical thinkers, the analogical visionaries (some of whom will be prophets), and the psychological thinkers (some of whom will be counselors; others, ecstatics or people with unusual gifts of insight).

How beautiful the church where all gifts are valued and function together to the glory of God and the building up

---

[11] Clark H. Pinnock, *Most Moved Mover: A Theology of God's Openness* (Carlisle, Cumbria: Paternoster, 2001). Although I do not fully endorse Pinnock's "openness of God" theology, certainly on this point Pinnock is fully biblical.

("edification") of the body of Christ! Churches that value people with these various gifts of thinking styles will be more wholesome and more healing. They will look more like Jesus; be a richer reflection and "image" of the Trinity. They will welcome and value children, and learn from them. "A little child shall lead them" (Isa 11:6).

Remember too: The image of God in humanity and in the church is gendered. It exists as male and female. That, strangely and mysteriously but also wonderfully, is God's plan. Historically the church has tended to over-value highly rational ways of thinking and theologizing and under-value more intuitive thinking or so-called "emotional intelligence." One reason for this is that the rational giftings of women often have not been sufficiently affirmed, or their analogical and psychological contributions have been discounted. Holistic thinking in the church requires the full and equal participation of both women and men.

Third and relatedly, *the church needs to be and to build the community of the Spirit.* Holistic thinking requires healthy community, and healthy community fosters holistic thinking. The more we are in touch with each other in the body of Christ—our brothers and sisters in the Spirit—the more we value each other as *persons*. And that in turn leads us to value the way each one thinks, the different modes of thinking. We are likely to find ourselves saying, "Oh, *now* I see what she means!" Or, "*Finally* I feel like I'm beginning to understand him!" In so doing, we will more fully comprehend and embody the Good News of God's reign.

A key reason the church goes to extremes, and sometimes even divides along the fault lines of different thinking modes, is that it often fails to build real community—holistic *koinonia* in the biblical sense.

How in the world did Peter, John, Matthew, Nathaniel, and the other first apostles get along? Not to mention Mary and Martha, Mary Magdalene, Joanna, Susanna, and the "many other" women disciples referred to in Luke 8:2–3. It couldn't have been easy. In fact, they often didn't get along—until after Pentecost. Even then they struggled. Paul locked horns with Peter, Barnabas, and probably a lot of other early believers. He must have had some interesting conversations with Apollos, or with Priscilla in the leather shop in Ephesus, all unrecorded.

How did they do it? How did they remain in fellowship and mission? By complete dedication to Jesus Christ and reliance on the Holy Spirit—and by a strong theology of the church that valued the persons, gifts, and ministries of *all* the people, little regarding distinctions between men

287

and women, rich and poor, educated and uneducated. By affirming all the gifts and recognizing that all believers are priests and ministers of the Good News. In other words, by being a community of the Spirit, the body of Christ.

So also today: Holistic thinking thrives best in healthy community.

Finally, considering these three ways of thinking brings us back to *the importance of the Holy Scriptures and how we interpret them.* Too often biblical interpretation is one-sided or eccentric, depending partly on which mode of thinking dominates. Overly rationalistic biblical interpretation simply skews God's Word. It needs the balance of other modes. But likewise, hermeneutics often suffers from illegitimate intuitive or analogical interpretative leaps that result in what James Sire calls "Scripture-twisting."[12]

Not every word or promise of Scripture can legitimately be applied to us today except through a sound hermeneutic. That means taking the history, stories, and doctrines of Scripture seriously, certainly. It also means combining the analogical, psychological, and logical approaches.

The Bible is amazing. Its holistic message is radical. One testimony to the Bible's Spirit-breathed nature is the

---

[12] James W. Sire, *Scripture Twisting: 20 Ways the Cults Misread the Bible* (Downers Grove, Ill.: InterVarsity, 1980).

remarkable way it combines psychological, logical, and analogical elements. In urban mission today, we dare not slight any of these.

The Bible is basically a story, a divinely-revealed narrative of God's saving intentions and how he has been working these out in history.[13] It projects the story into the future, showing that "history is going somewhere"—namely, to "new heavens and a new earth, where righteousness is at home" (2 Pt 3:13). Story and history, of course, abound in psychological and analogical elements, as well as logical ones, and we see this clearly in Scripture.

Insights for Urban Mission

History—especially salvation history—is a rich tapestry of colorful threads woven together to bring glory to God. Filled with the Spirit, we help weave the threads and in fact are the threads. If we look closely, we see that among those threads are the three we're considering here: logical, analogical, and psychological thinking. We need all three, just as we need each other in Christ's body.

---

[13] The Bible is also, relatedly, the Book of the Covenant for God's people. See "The Book of the Covenant," Chap. 10 in Howard A. Snyder, *Liberating the Church: The Ecology of Church and Kingdom* (Downers Grove, Ill.: InterVarsity, 1983, and reprints), 195–204.

So also, urban communities are often a mosaic of colors and contrasts, people diverse in culture and traditions, but also in personality and ways of thinking. Redemptive urban mission creatively combines the diversity of history, of Scripture, and of people in developing faithful communities of disciples.

Holding up a mirror, we might ask which of these three modes of thinking has been used here, in this chapter. I have tried to combine all three, actually. Since this is a kind of essay—a rational argument, not primarily a story or a picture or a game—the rational mode predominates. But I have signaled the value also of the other two modes.

To fully appreciate the argument, however, we would need now to get up from our chairs, sing some songs, dance, tell some stories, "praise and graze" together, and play some games or go for a walk through the woods or around the neighborhood.

Urban mission leaders can reflect on the usefulness of these insights for their ministry in a tangled world. These different ways of thinking can make for fruitful dialogue and reflection, for example in team ministry—dealing with diversity and cultural differences. These dynamics of thinking and personality touch such areas as personal relationships, decision-making, gender relations, leadership, and community building, both in the church and in larger urban spaces. A fruitful basis for dialogue!

The church is a diverse community and a sacramental community. It is more than it seems to be. When faithful, it is a sign of something much larger, more beautiful, and more ultimate—a sign of the kingdom of God in fullness, of all creation healed.

In the final chapter we look at this "more than" quality of faithful churches, using the language of sacrament.

CHAPTER 10
The Church as Sacrament and Sacrifice in the City

Something strange happens in the church when God's Spirit moves. On the one hand, community and servanthood are rediscovered. With this often comes a new emphasis on the kingdom of God, the social-political-economic-spiritual really not of this world but of God which challenges the present world system. Effective urban churches gain a lively sense of both community and kingdom—of one-anotherness and of global significance.

But another consciousness also penetrates and enlivens urban churches. This is the reality of sacrament. Vital congregations often find that the Lord's Supper becomes an essential focal point of their whole life together. Why?

In part, because of the mystery of symbol and sign. How can we stand it that the kingdom has not yet come and the church is so often unfaithful? We can stand it only through faith in what God has promised. And that faith is powerfully fed, symbolized, and proclaimed in the sacramental reality of the Lord's Supper.

Just as the Lord's Supper points beyond itself, so the very concept of sacrament outgrows the Eucharist to provide a clue and model for understanding the church and the kingdom. At first glance, sacrament and community may appear in tension or even in conflict. Not true. It only looks that way because of the institutional sacramental overtones many Western churches have inherited from medieval Christendom. In fact, at the deepest and perhaps even subconscious level, the reality of the kingdom community draws us to the reality of sacrament.

In Chapter Two we explored the meaning of the church as community: the church is God's servant community on earth for the sake of the kingdom. Now let's see how the reality of sacrament helps us understand and feel just what this means.

The Idea of Sacrament

Saint Augustine (354–430 AD) said that God "has welded together the community of his new people through the bond of the sacraments."[1] But what in the world is a sacrament?

The word *sacrament* isn't found in the Bible. In fact, no New Testament word carries the idea of sacrament in the sense used by most Protestants (baptism and the Lord's Supper) or by Roman Catholics (baptism, the Lord's Supper, confirmation, ordination, marriage, penance, extreme unction). Much of the church's sacramental thinking is inherited post-Augustine, from the medieval church. But the root idea goes back to the church's earliest days.

Essentially, a sacrament is, as Augustine says, a "visible form of invisible grace." More formally, a sacrament may be thought of as "an outward and visible sign of an inward and spiritual grace given unto us; ordained by Christ himself, as a means whereby we receive the same, and a pledge to assure us thereof."[2] This classical Anglican definition is in its essence broadly shared in most Christian churches,

---

[1] Augustine, *Epistle* 54.1.1, quoted in F. van der Meer, *Augustine the Bishop*, trans. Brian Battershaw and G. R. Lamp (London: Sheed and Ward, 1961), 278.

[2] "A Catechism," *The Book of Common Prayer* (Greenwich, Conn.: Seabury Press, 1952), 581.

however interpreted. Properly understood, a sacrament is a
sign and yet more than a sign. It both witnesses to the
operation of God's grace and, in some way not fully
definable, is a channel or means of that grace.

Augustine identified many different things as
sacraments: the Lord's Prayer, the church's feasts or
celebrations, the sign of the cross, as well as baptism and
the Lord's Supper. Hugh of St. Victor (d. 1142)
enumerated as many as thirty sacraments. It was Peter
Lombard (ca 1100–1160) especially who emphasized the
sevenfold set of sacraments that was accepted by Thomas
Aquinas (ca 1225–1274) and confirmed by the Roman
Catholic Council of Trent in 1545–63.[3]

The idea of sacrament started as something flexible and
dynamic. With time, in European Christendom, it became
increasingly technical and mechanical, culminating with
Trent and infusing the Counter Reformation. In the
twentieth century, however, Roman Catholic theologians
began rethinking the whole sacramental idea, culminating
in the Second Vatican Council's more organic, dynamic
understanding of sacrament.

---

[3] "Sacrament," in F. L. Cross and E. A. Livingstone, eds., *The Oxford
Dictionary of the Christian Church,* 3rd ed. (Oxford: Oxford University
Press, 1997), 1435–36; "Sacraments," in Jerald C. Brauer, ed., *The
Westminster Dictionary of Church History* (Philadelphia: Westminster
Press, 1971), 734–35.

From the beginning, the church naturally faced the problem of how to understand itself. The New Testament gave clues which the church gradually developed in various directions, depending on the social context in which the church found itself. Changing sacramental ideas corresponded to the changing circumstances in which the church lived.

In today's urban contexts, sacramental ideas and language can, I believe, be lively aids in the church's self-understanding. But is the concept of sacrament itself valid, viewed biblically? The medieval sacramental system was a distortion of biblical truth in fundamental ways. Is this perhaps true of the very idea of sacrament itself? Is the very concept of sacrament tainted?

Let's look back to Scripture. Four New Testament words and ideas help, offering a dynamic understanding of sacrament: *sign, covenant, mystery,* and *thanksgiving.*

Sign and Covenant. Some of Jesus's miracles were signs that God had come in the flesh, fulfilling his promise (Jn 2:11, 20:30). Jesus spoke of Noah as a sign (Mt 12:39; Lk 11:29). The rainbow was the sign of God's universal covenant with humankind after the flood (Gen 9:12).

The New Testament does not use the word *sign* with reference to baptism or the Lord's Supper, but the idea of sign is present. "For whenever you eat this bread and drink this cup, you proclaim the Lord's death until he comes" (1 Cor 11:26). Both baptism and the Lord's Supper are signs of the new covenant (Col 2:11–12; Rom 6:3–4; 1 Cor 11:25). The new covenant concerns the heart and the spirit, not laws, commandments, and animal sacrifices. New covenant signs must have new covenant meaning. They are not Old Testament signs.

We should guard against falling back into an Old Testament understanding of these signs. Old Testament understanding of these signs greatly enriches their meaning. But an uncritical, un-evangelical return to Old Testament categories undercuts their gospel meaning. This is precisely what happened in the Middle Ages. Old Covenant conceptions undercut New Covenant redemptive dynamism. Old Testament meanings of tabernacle, priesthood, and sacrifice were taken over wholesale, compromising the newness and uniqueness of Jesus Christ.

We insist instead that Jesus Christ fulfills the Old Testament system (Mt 5:17). He is Sacrifice and High Priest. He is the great Sign and Sacrament of our salvation. He fulfills the Old Testament signs. Therefore no signs or sacraments in the church can have their primary Old Testament meaning. Nor should they be permitted to overshadow or displace Jesus Christ as our Sign and Savior, or his presence with us daily by the Holy Spirit. How often human nature prefers a touchable, controllable sign to God's invisible living Spirit.

Mystery. This brings us to the New Testament word *mystery* and, importantly, to the origin of the word *sacrament*.

Paul speaks of "the mystery of Christ" (Eph 3:4), or "the mystery of the gospel" (Eph 3:19) or of the faith (1 Tim 3:9). A key passage is Ephesians 5:32, where Paul speaks about marriage. "This is a profound mystery—but I am talking about Christ and the church." Mystery in these passages refers to God's economy of redemption and reconciliation through Jesus Christ. Clearly it has no special reference to the sacraments of baptism or the Lord's Supper.

Significantly, the Greek word "mystery" (*musterion*) became "sacrament" (*sacramentum*) when the Bible was translated into Latin. As a result, pagan ideas of mystery and sacrament from the Greek and Roman world gradually colored the church's understanding of Christian worship, and especially the Lord's Supper.

Greeks and Romans knew about "mysteries." They knew about, and some practiced, the mystery religions where sacred meals were eaten and sexual immorality was sometimes indulged. This is why early Christians were occasionally suspected of having sexual orgies in their closed worship services and why Tertullian had to say, "All things are common among us except our wives."[4]

With time, and especially after the Emperor Constantine was converted in 323, these pagan understandings filtered into the church and twisted its concepts of baptism and the Lord's Supper. The idea that these observances were mysterious, almost magical rites giving mystical powers began to displace the New Testament understanding of the New Covenant of the Spirit. This led to the medieval view of the mass as a constant repetition of the sacrifice of Christ in which bread and wine literally, physically become Jesus' flesh and blood. It led finally to the whole medieval system of seven interlocking sacraments all keyed to the mysterious power of the priest.

The medieval sacramental-hierarchical system, which reached its climax at the Council of Trent partly in reaction to the Reformation, was highly complex, rational, and consistent. It was both mystical and rational, for the mystical element of faith was captured and routinized by

---

[4] Tertullian, *Apology* 39.

means of religious technique. The sacraments came to constitute the ecology of the church.

In the New Testament, *mystery* has to do with God's kingdom plan of salvation through Jesus Christ— the whole economy of God. Economy (*oikonomia*) and mystery (*musterion*) are closely related, and both point to the kingdom of God and the church as kingdom community. Paul said his commission was "to bring to light the economy of the mystery" of the gospel (Eph 3:9, literal translation). God has made known to us "the mystery of his will," which involves "an economy of the fullness of the times, to bring all things in heaven and on earth together under one head," Jesus Christ (Eph 1:9–10, literal translation).[5]

This is the biblical economy, based in the church as community. But in the medieval synthesis mystery became sacrament, and the sacramental system came to be the economy of the church. The New Testament economy was transmuted by a kind of theological alchemy into the sacramental economy—a system based on hierarchy,

---

[5] *Mystery* and *economy* are associated also in Eph 3:2–4 and Col 1:25–26. In 1 Cor 4:1 Paul and his associates are called "stewards of the mysteries" (*oikonomous musterion*) of God. The association of *oikonomia* with *musterion* in Paul's writings is certainly more than coincidence and is highly fruitful theologically, particularly in the context of the church as kingdom community.

institution, cathedral, law, and technique rather than on community, mutuality, charisms, discipleship, and free grace. It was precisely this system which most of the Reformers protested so strongly.

Thanksgiving. Another word that entered the church's vocabulary was *Eucharist*. The New Testament speaks of "giving thanks" (*eucharstia*). Since thanksgiving was associated with worship and the Lord's Supper became the principal act of worship, the word Eucharist became synonymous with and largely restricted to the Lord's Supper. In much of the Christian church today the Lord's Supper is commonly called *the* Eucharist.

The Sacramental Community

Since sacrament is not a New Testament word and medieval sacramentalism led to a serious distortion of the gospel, should the whole concept of sacrament be dropped in our quest for truly faithful and dynamic urban churches? No. A number of reasons show it is wise to hold on to the notion of sacrament, though applying it in more organic and biblically faithful ways. Sacramental language can in fact spark greater clarity about the church and its mission.

The New Testament use of *sign* and *mystery* (both the terms and the ideas) leads to an understanding of the church for which *sacramental* seems an apt term. If *sacrament* does not mean precisely the same thing as *mystery*, it does help us deal with the meaning of the mystery of the church as a sign of the kingdom in the present age. As a term and concept, *sacrament* is like *Trinity*. It is a legitimate extension and extrapolation from biblical truth, even if not explicitly taught in Scripture. *Sacrament* (understood and controlled by Scripture) is an appropriate vehicle for understanding not only baptism and the Lord's Supper but the Christian community itself.

But can we say that the church is *itself* a sacrament? Can we legitimately speak of the community of God's people sacramentally?

This is precisely what a number of Roman Catholic theologians did in the decades leading up to Vatican II (1962–65) in an attempt to gain a newer and more faithful understanding of the church.[6] Rather than focusing on the sacramental system itself, this approach sees the church as "the primordial sacrament" in which the traditional sacraments are grounded. In the words of Karl Rahner, "As the primordial sacrament, the Church is the constant presence in the world of the saving mystery of Christ and

---

[6] Avery Dulles, *Models of the Church* (Garden City, N.Y.: Doubleday, 1964) 58–59; Eric G. Jay, *The Church: Its Changing Image through Twenty Centuries* (Atlanta: John Knox Press, 1980), 325–27.

his grace." "Since the Church exists in this sense (as the sacrament), there are sacraments in the New Testament sense."[7] This conception found expression in Vatican II. The Dogmatic Constitution on the Church (*Lumen Gentium*) says in its first paragraph, "By her relationship with Christ, the Church is a kind of sacrament or sign of intimate union with God, and of the unity of all mankind."[8] Later the document describes the church as "the universal sacrament of salvation" through which Christ is still active in the world, but which exists now on earth as "the pilgrim Church."[9]

The sacramental conception provides a way of understanding the church in relation both to the world and to the kingdom which is more biblically faithful that the

---

[7] Karl Rahner, "Sacramental Theology," in K. Rahner, ed., *Encyclopedia of Theology: The Concise Sacramentum Mundi* (New York: Seabury Press, 1975), 1486. The sacramental understanding of the church has been explored by Edward Schillebeeckx, Thomas O'Dea, Richard McBrien, Gregory Baum, Henri de Lubac, Yves Congar, and others. It can be argued that both Augustine and Thomas Aquinas saw the church essentially in these terms, but not in a developed sense. Augustine wrote much about the church, but before sacramental ideas were highly developed; Aquinas wrote in a time of highly developed sacramental theology, but wrote comparatively little about the church.

[8] As quoted in Jay, *Church,* 325–26. See Dogmatic Constitution of the Church (*Lumen Gentium*), in Austin P. Flannery, ed., *Documents of Vatican II* (Grand Rapids: Eerdmans, 1975), 350.

[9] Dogmatic Constitution of the Church (*Lumen Gentium*), *Documents of Vatican II,* 407–8.

visible-invisible distinction and more potent for faithful urban witness. As Eric Jay comments, "Here is the seed for a fruitful doctrine of the Church." He continues:

> A sacrament is a gift of God: something earthy is set aside for holy use, a sign and representative of what all things earthly are meant to be, and an instrument of sanctification of all that is earthly. In the idea of the Church as the sacrament of the world, then, we have the concept of a society instituted by God which is itself in microcosm what the world must be, and which exists to enable it to be that which itself is, the body of Christ.[10]

The appropriateness of seeing the church as sacrament can be shown by examining the classical Anglican definition quoted above: "an outward and visible sign of an inward and spiritual grace given unto us; ordained by Christ himself as a means whereby we receive the same, and a pledge to assure us thereof." Note how this applies not only to the church's sacraments but to the very community of God's people itself:

An outward and visible sign. Clearly the church is "outward and visible," not just "inward and spiritual" (though this fact is often slighted). The church is an actual, visible social reality in the world. Its true and proper

---

[10] Jay, *Church,* 326.

visibility, however, is not in buildings or structures but in its gathering in worship and in witness and service to the world. "In face of the *world*—which may or may not understand it—the Church is the living and visible congregation which listens to the divine Word and responds to it, and which proposes it to the world, but by it, inevitably scandalizes the world," as Karl Barth wrote.[11]

While the church takes its life from its "inner and spiritual" relationship to God through Jesus, its life and relationship to God are also outward and visible, just as Jesus' were. And in this outward, visible life in the world, the church is a sign of the kingdom. Jesus said, "Anyone who has seen me has seen the Father" (Jn 14:9); "I am in my Father, and you are in me, and I am in you" (Jn 14:20). "As the Father has sent me, I am sending you" (Jn 20:21). Many biblical passages and images show that the church is not only the community of the redeemed but also a sign of God's presence, activity, and coming reign. And the church

---

[11] Karl Barth, "La nature et la forma de l'Eglise," in *l'Eglise* (Geneva: Éditions Labor et Fides, 1964), 119. Barth however makes almost no use of sacramental language in discussing the church. He uses the visible-invisible distinction and tries to hold the two together, but in a way which is finally ahistorical. The sacramental model is more helpful precisely at this point. Barth does however locate the church's primary visibility in its gathering as a community, not in its institutional structures. See Snyder, "Karl Barth's Missional Theology," Chapter 13 in Snyder, *Yes In Christ: Wesleyan Reflections on Gospel, Mission, and Culture* (Toronto: Clements Academic, 2011), 295–321.

is a sign of these things precisely because it is the community of the redeemed.

Of an inward and spiritual grace. A sacrament signs forth, specifically, the gracious activity of God, his grace that works inwardly and spiritually. This is true of the church itself. It is saved and lives by grace. The church can never be fully explained sociologically, psychologically, politically, or economically. It requires an invisible, inward operation of God's grace to accomplish the new birth and to transform men and women into the body of Christ. The church, when biblically faithful, is an unmistakable sign and witness of God's grace.

Given unto us. It is both the sacramental sign and God's grace which are given to us. The Lord's Supper is a sacrament because it was given to the church by Christ. Human beings didn't dream it up. If this is true of baptism and the Eucharist, it is even more true of the church itself. The church was and is called together and formed by Jesus. In a healthy church believers have the sense of God's gracious gift. We did not earn or achieve this life together. God gave it.

Ordained by Christ himself. Traditionally, an authentic sacrament must trace back in some way to the specific action of Jesus Christ. This is clearly and dramatically so with the church itself. Not only did Jesus say "I will build my church" (Mt 16:18); his very life, death, and resurrection constituted his ordaining the church. The church is ordained specifically to be Jesus' body, his worshiping and witnessing community in the world.

As a means whereby we receive the same. A sacrament, as we have noted, is more than a sign. It is a *means of grace.* A sacrament is a channel and agent of God's grace as God works through it and as persons respond in faith and obedience. On this point, also, the definition of sacrament fits the church. The church is a channel of God's grace, both internally and to the world. This is part of the meaning of the priesthood of believers. We receive God's grace not by the Spirit without the church, but by the Spirit through the church.

A pledge to assure us thereof. A sacrament always points beyond itself to the future. It is a pledge in the sense of a foretaste, firstfruit, down payment, or initial realization. It is not the full reality but a real sign of what God has promised. And the church, animated by the Spirit, is precisely this. Life in Christian community is a promise to all believers that the kingdom will come in fullness, that every knee shall bow and every tongue confess Jesus as Lord

(Phil 2:10–11), that "the earth will be full of the knowledge of the Lord as the waters cover the sea" (Isa 11:9).

A sacrament is both a means of grace and a pledge of grace. It is a promise that God will in fact accomplish what he has graciously promised. In this sense also the church is a sacrament. It has been formed by grace and is a sign that God's kingdom will come by grace—in God's way, not in the ways of the world.

In sum, the church may truly and properly be seen as a sacrament, as sign and microcosm of the kingdom of God. It is crucial however that such a sacramental understanding be applied consistently with the New Testament understanding of the church. The church as sacrament is one model among many, not an exclusive definition of the church, and needs to be balanced by other models. It has both advantages and disadvantages which need to be considered.[12]

---

[12] See the discussion in Dulles, *Models of the Church*, 67–70. As a disadvantage, Dulles notes that the sacramental model "has found little response in Protestant thought" (70). This is understandable but does not attest to the inapplicability of this model to Protestant ecclesiology. The key is maintaining the normative role of Scripture and scriptural models. Dulles seems to prefer the sacramental model because it is useful in relating the institutional model to a more community-centered model; it "supports the best features" of these models "while solving the problems that prove intractable on either of these other two, such as the relationship between the invisible institution and the communion of grace" (68). It is important, however, that the sacramental conception

There are perhaps two primary pitfalls in a sacramental understanding of the church. Such an approach will surely go awry if wedded to an institutional-organizational rather than charismatic-organic view of the church. What might be called the institutional-sacramental view leads straight back to the worst features of medieval Christendom, while an organic-sacramental view can lead to greater freedom and fidelity for the church and points ahead more authentically to the kingdom. The sacramental approach, then, must be joined to and controlled by more explicitly biblical models, such as servant and community of disciples.

A related danger is that the sacramental model may be seen as holding the institutional and charismatic dimensions together in a way that makes more allowance for institutionalism than is warranted by Scripture. The sacramental model is useful in part because it does help us deal with the institutional side of the church without rejecting institutionalization altogether. But the church must always be critical of its institutional side precisely because of the inherent dangers of institutional self-serving, self-righteousness, and self-justification. Properly understood, the sacramental model is not a clever

---

not be applied in a way that uncritically justifies or simply overlooks the problem of the church's institutionalism.

theological excuse or apology for the church's intuitionalism, but a way of showing how the church points beyond itself to God and his future. Precisely this understanding should help the church criticize and correct its institutional tendencies.

In what sense, then, is the church a sacrament? Not in the sense that its institutional form necessarily says anything redemptive in the world, but in the sense that as the community of God's people it is a sign, symbol, and servant of the kingdom of God on earth. The church is, in this sense, truly a means of grace.

Sacrament and Sacraments

The conception of the church as sacrament does not displace the sacraments of the church. Rather, it enhances them. Given the understanding of the church as sacrament, we can view the sacraments of baptism and the Lord's Supper in ways that contribute to transforming witness in the city. Several issues call for comment at this point.

1. The church's sacraments are not magical or mystical rites or spiritual techniques which in themselves transmit spiritual power. They are signs which derive their power from Jesus Christ and his work and from God's grace working in each believer and in the Christian community

so that the signs may be received by faith. Without faith—in God, not in the rites—the sacraments are nothing.

2. Biblical references to the "mystery of Christ" remind us, on the other hand, that God's economy of salvation is beyond human comprehension. It remains a mystery, even though we know its key secret: reconciliation (Eph 3:4–6). In Christian worship there is always more than meets the eye. So even though the sacraments are not mystical rites, they do become channels of God's grace in ways we don't fully understand. This has something to do with God's image in us and with our need for symbols and signs, ritual and mystery. We honor and celebrate these sacraments given us specifically by Jesus Christ and in which he is really present—even though we don't turn them into magical rites or spiritual techniques.

3. Baptism and the Lord's Supper remind us of God's covenant, his promises. God is faithful. He will do what he says. He fulfills his plan in history. In the sacraments we express our faith that God has acted for us in the past, is present now, and will in the future fulfill his plan and manifest his rule. In baptism we find that God does indeed give us new birth and adopt us into his family through faith in Jesus Christ. In the Eucharist we find that, partaking in

faith and unity, we are indeed built up as the body of Christ.

4. The sacraments are acts of Christian community. They help form and feed the flock of God. They build *koinonia*. Every culture has its symbols and signs and cannot exist without them. As God's counterculture in a sinful world, the church is held together, in part, by sacramental signs—even while it knows that "faith working by love" (Gal 5:6) is the fundamental sign of God's presence, and even while it also sees signs in the world, beyond the church, of God's working and of the coming of God's kingdom.

5. Since baptism and the Lord's Supper are part of the church's witness, worship, and community life, how they are observed is important. As acts of community, they should build the church's sense of communion, fellowship, and discipleship. We should avoid observances which over-individualize the sacraments or make them highly formal. The Lord's Supper should be observed with reverence and order, but not with excessive ritual, formality, or mysteriousness. The focus should be on Jesus Christ and his body, the church. The Eucharist should build body life—openness, communication, confession, oneness, reconciliation, sharing, joyful celebration, and dedication to

the God's agenda on earth. Although for the sake of order the church may prescribe who should lead in this observance, the Bible does not restrict the administration of the Supper to ordained persons or to men only.

In the early church, the Lord's Supper was often celebrated as a meal—sharing food and Christian fellowship together, talking together informally. In churches today—especially perhaps in the city—shared meals are important in building and sustaining the reality of redemptive Christian community. Combining the Eucharist with an actual meal can be powerful in creating a sense of community and of the mystery of Jesus's right-now presence with us.

Shared as an act of face-to-face community, the Lord's Supper can be especially prophetic in a digital, remotely-connected world. Social scientist Sherry Turkle notes, purely from a secular perspective, "Conversation is on the path toward the experience of intimacy, community, and communion. Reclaiming conversation is a step toward reclaiming our most fundamental human values." Being "silenced by our technologies," Turkle warns, we in the digitally connected world now experience "a crisis of empathy that has diminished us at home, at work, and in public life." And "the remedy, most simply, is a talking cure."[13]

If this is true sociologically, now much more spiritually and ecclesially?

We of course when we discuss sacraments we have to leave considerable room for the variety of church traditions and liturgies, from highly informal to highly liturgical ("High Church" of various forms). But whatever the form, each congregation should take care to provide clear instruction so the sacraments can be received as genuine means of grace.

6. The Lord's Supper should be observed frequently. In the early church and through much of Christian history, observance was weekly, at least. Because of historical circumstances and reaction against medieval sacramentalism, many Protestants came to celebrate the Supper infrequently, often four times or less per year. Yet some of the great Reformers, Calvin and Wesley among them, celebrated the Eucharist weekly or even daily.

Renewal in the church has often gone hand in hand with a rediscovery and more frequent observance of the Lord's Supper. Christian fellowships today should celebrate

---

[13] Sherry Turkle, *Reclaiming Conversation* (New York: Penguin, 2015), 7, 9.

the Eucharist often, with the minimum probably being once a month and the normal pattern being weekly.

Some argue that such frequent observance cheapens the Lord's Supper, reducing its significance. Curiously, we don't argue this way in other areas. One could argue that the church should keep preaching to a minimum because preaching is so important. Or that since prayer and Bible reading are so important, Christians should engage in these activities only infrequently in order not to cheapen them or make them routine. But the fact is that sacraments are *means of grace*, and means are to be used, not neglected. As John Wesley wrote, "all who desire the grace of God are to wait for it in the means which he hath ordained; in using, not in laying them aside."[14] The church is to feed on God's grace through the Lord's Supper, and it should do so often rather than staying away from the very table to which Christ calls us.[15]

7. We must always keep before us the realities to which the sacraments point: Jesus, the church, the kingdom of God, creation healed. The church is to be the great sign of Jesus' presence on earth and the promise of his return. The

---

[14] John Wesley, Sermon 16, "The Means of Grace," *Works*, 1:384.

[15] In this connection a friend suggests that to abstain from the Lord's Table because it is so sacred is like a married couple's abstaining from sexual relations because sex is so special.

world should be able to look at the church and see Jesus. The love, fellowship, worship, and service of the church can be a sacrament before the world of God's love and reconciliation. Our observance of the sacraments should nourish our understanding and experience of the church as a reconciled and reconciling community.

Sacraments spring from, symbolize, and sign forth the reality of the church as Christ's body. The most important sign of God's presence on earth is not the sacraments but the body of Christ itself—not the bread and wine on the table but the body of Christ, our own flesh and blood, in the world for the sake of the kingdom.

This Is Christ's Body!

This is the point of the sacraments: The church is the *body of Christ.*

A key passage here is 1 Corinthians 10:16–17. "Is not the cup of thanksgiving for which we give thanks a participation in the blood of Christ? And is not the bread that we break a participating in the body? Because there is one loaf, we, who are many, are one body, for we all partake of the one loaf."

The word "participation" here is the New Testament word for community, *koinonia.* In other words, the

Scripture says that our participation in the Lord's Supper is a sharing in Christ himself. It is our community in Christ. In the New Testament, baptism and the Lord's Supper *are* our membership in the body of Christ. In the New Testament church *koinonia* (sharing, community, participation, bonding) was the meaning of church membership. Thus these observances given by Christ are the signs and determiners of the meaning of membership.

This means two things: (1) church membership is highly important and necessary for every believer, and (2) church membership should be understood primarily as participation and community in the body of Christ, rather than as joining an organization or having one's name on a membership roll.

Because of the prominence of organizational-institutional models, Western Christians tend to think of church membership as joining an organization rather than as participating in a community. The sacraments, however, are community acts and make much more sense when understood this way. Biblically, one does not become a Christian and then later join the church. To be born again is to be born into God's family. A Christian is by definition a part of the community of God's people. One can't be joined to the head without being joined to the body. The sacraments, integrated into the worshiping and serving life of the community, are important in order to keep this affirmation from being mere theory or vague idea. Membership in the body of Christ is neither organizational affiliation not an invisible communion. It is a visible participation and sharing in the visible community of God's people.

It is amazing, really, that the New Testament calls the church the body of Christ. The body of Christ is one, and yet in Scripture the phrase "body of Christ" has a threefold meaning. As Barth wrote,

> There are not two or possibly three bodies of Christ: the historical, in which He died and rose again; the mystical which is His community; and that in which He is really present in the Lord's Supper. For there are not three Christs. There is only one Christ, and therefore there is only one body of Christ."[16]

---

[16] Karl Barth, *Church Dogmatics* (Edinburgh: T & T Clark, 1956), IV/1, 666. Barth so closely identifies Christ's physical body and the church as "body of Christ" that he can say the identification church-body is not to be taken merely symbolically or metaphorically. "As His earthly-historical form of existence, the community of His body, His body is the community" (666). While Dulles suggests that herald is the primary model in Barth's ecclesiology, actually Barth's fundamental model is the church as community, or rather community-in-mission, with herald as a secondary model. See Snyder, "Karl Barth's Missional Theology."

Yet the New Testament does give a threefold meaning to "body of Christ": Jesus's physical body, the church, and the bread of the Lord's Supper. The distinction between these three senses is not always clear—precisely because there are not three but only one body of Christ.

The close identification between the church and Jesus's physical body is seen especially in Ephesians. Paul says, "But now in Christ Jesus you were once far away have been brought near through the blood of Christ. For he himself is our peace, who has made the two [Jew and Gentile] one and has destroyed the barrier, the dividing wall of hostility, by abolishing in his flesh the law with its commandments and regulations. His purpose was to create in himself one new man out of the two, thus making peace, and in this one body to reconcile both of them to God through the cross, by which he put to death their hostility" (Eph 2:13–16). "This one body" in verse sixteen may mean either Jesus' physical body, crucified, or the church. Better, and given the way Paul uses such language, it in fact means both. Through his body we are made his body—historically through Jesus's death and resurrection, and sacramentally through the Lord's Supper.

The Physical Body of Jesus

Here we face the mystery of the Incarnation, Word made flesh. This is the mystery of God-in-Man, the Lord God in human person. We can't explain the Incarnation and we can't explain the life of Jesus. Yet neither can we account for the life of Jesus apart from the miracle of incarnation.

Even so, despite and through this mystery, Jesus is our pattern and model. *Because* Jesus is Lord and Savior, and because of the mystery of his presence in us now through the new birth, he is also our example and pattern (1 Pt 2:21; 1 Jn 2:6).

In Jesus's physical body, then, as God incarnate, we have both *model* and *mystery*. While the Incarnation is a mystery, it provides the essential model for the believer and especially for the church's corporate life and mission in the world.

The Church, Christ's Body

Why is the church called Christ's body? In one sense the idea is a mystical one, but it is more than that. The church is the body of Christ in something close to a literal, physical, spacetime sense. It is "the earthly-historical form of existence" of Jesus Christ (Barth). The church is the body of Christ because it is the presence of Jesus in the world by the work and indwelling of the Holy Spirit in the flesh-and-blood bodies of Christ's disciples and especially in the historical social reality of the Christian community.

In this sense, the church as Christ's body is also *mystery* and *model*. To call the church Christ's body is to speak a mystery—the mystery of just how Jesus is joined to the church and the mystery of how the church, in all its imperfections, is a sign of the kingdom. "This is a profound mystery—but I am talking about Christ and the church" (Eph 5:32).

Yet the mystery is consistent with the model. The church *is* a sign of the coming kingdom. It is called to model the age to come which even now is not absent, to be a microcosm of the kingdom. Following the model of the Incarnation, the church's mission is to be the firstfruits of the kingdom, present now, as Jesus was, in humility and service.[17]

Christ's Body in the Lord's Supper

Given this perspective, the church's sharing of Jesus's body and blood in the Eucharist takes on deep significance.

---

[17] The church in fact betrays its identification with Jesus if it fails to be a church of, with, and for the poor—for Jesus has made it clear that he has radically decided for the poor and is present in a special way among them. He stated plainly that service to the poor is service to him (Mt 25:31–46). Here in fact the church as sacrament finds its most real, profound, visible, effective, gracious manifestation.

The bread we break in the Lord's Supper: Is this not our community in Christ? Is this not our membership in his body? Is this not the meaning of the church in the city? In the Lord's Supper, especially, we are the community of God's people—if we feed on the Word by faith and live consistently with it.

The Lord's Supper is an expression of the family of God and a sharing in Jesus Christ. It is both *model* and *mystery*. It is a mystery because we do not know (and the church has never been able to agree) just how Jesus is really present in the eucharistic bread. The Lord's Supper is a mystery of Jesus's presence and a mystery as a means of grace. It participates in the mystery of symbol and sign. It shares in the mystery of the church as the family of God.

But The Eucharist is also a model and sign. As the presence of God in the earthly elements of bread and wine, it symbolizes Jesus's incarnation. It is a model of God's family, for in the Supper we gather together as one, equally dependent on God's grace and all dependent on one another. And it is a model, especially, of the kingdom of God. It signs and signals the future marriage supper of the Lamb (Rev 19:9). In eating bread and drinking wine together the church celebrates and looks ahead to God's new heaven and new earth when every man, woman, and child will be fed and none will lack food either for body or for soul.

The threefold mystery of the body of Christ, then, is a model of the church which lives for the kingdom. The church participates in the mystery and becomes the model when it seeks first the kingdom of God and his justice. In the language of sacrament, biblically controlled, mystery and model are held together so that the mystery does not become mysticism and the model does not become mechanism.

Church, Sacrament, Kingdom, City

Church, sacrament, and kingdom have often been associated in Christian theology, especially in Eastern Orthodoxy and some branches of Roman Catholicism. But this association needs to be animated by the biblical, evangelical spirit. This is the goal here.

As the relationship of God to the world may be understood sacramentally, so the concept of sacrament helps us understand the relationship of the church to the kingdom. The church is not the kingdom; neither is it unrelated to the kingdom. While some sacramental theology has tended to identify the kingdom too closely with the church, some dispensational theology has divorced the two so thoroughly that the kingdom has no present significance.[18]

The church, however, may be understood as the present sacrament (mystery and model) of the kingdom in the world. It both signs, points toward, and by God's grace accomplishes God's rule on earth and God's healing in the city. As sacrament of the kingdom, the church points ahead to what it claims by faith and works for by faith and does not yet fully experience or understand. It prays that the kingdom may fully come on earth, knowing that God by his Spirit must do for us what we cannot do for ourselves, so that we can do for his kingdom what otherwise would remain undone. The sacramental reality of the church will come in fullness only with the historical return of Jesus Christ when the kingdom is finally, fully and definitively established.

Redemptive urban mission means understanding that the church is not the kingdom nor is it unhinged from it. Yet it is free, by faith and by God's grace, to be the kingdom community, a sign of hope in the city, a sacrament of better things to come.

---

[18] Elaborated more fully in Howard A. Snyder, *Models of the Kingdom* (Nashville: Abingdon, 1991; Eugene, Ore.: Wipf and Stock, 2001).

Living and Dying Sacrifice

In the first centuries, the early Christian communities were sacramental signs of God's reign in the cities of the Roman Empire, from Jerusalem outward in all directions. The church was the suffering sacramental sign of God's reign in Rome, Ephesus, Corinth, Antioch, Alexandria, and many other places. To the pagan world this was paradox, mystery, or stupidity. But in fact it was the wisdom of God and the power of God. A key part of that wise mystery was the strange diversity: "both Jews and Greeks" (1 Cor 1:24) —some rich and many poor, women and men, many people of low or no status. Slaves, now brothers and sisters, treated humanely; the lives of children and the newborn protected; marriage respected.

In his remarkable book *The Rise of Christianity,* Sociologist Rodney Stark showed how early Christians in Rome, Antioch, and elsewhere won hearts, minds, and new disciples due to the social impact of Christian virtue. Stark concluded, "*the ultimate factor* in the rise of Christianity" was this: "*Central doctrines of Christianity prompted and sustained attractive, liberating, and effective social relations and organizations.*" It was the social working-out of Christian beliefs "that permitted Christianity to be among the most sweeping and successful revitalization movements in history." The social impact of Christian virtue-in-community—this was the early church's great effective sacramental sign in its first centuries.[19]

It is happening right now in thousands of cities around the world. It can happen even more as communities of urban disciples discover what it means to be, like Jesus, the suffering sacramental sign of sovereign grace in the world's cities.

To the world (and often to many Christians) this sacramental combination of model and mystery, of power and weakness, of outward foolishness and inner wisdom, of joyful suffering sacrifice, is itself a contradiction, foolishness. Wasted effort. But to those who know the public secret of Jesus Christ—the Lamb slain from the foundation of the world—this is the highest wisdom, based upon full confidence that God will fulfill all his kingdom promises.

If it is faithful, the church in the city is not a failure if it fails. It's voice may be small. But it is following the Lamb. Like the many city churches pictured in the Book of Revelation, urban Christians conquer "by the blood of the Lamb and by the word of their testimony, for they [do] not

---

[19] Rodney Stark, *The Rise of Christianity: A Sociologist Reconsiders History* (Princeton, N.J.: Princeton University Press, 1996), "A Brief Reflection on Virtue," 209–15 (quotations, 211; italics in the original).

cling to life even in the face of death" (Rev 12:11). Following Jesus in Jesus's way, the church is the redemptive sacrament of the kingdom of God.

Small voices echo far.

CONCLUSION

This journey exploring larger dimensions of urban mission has brought us full circle. The key question has been: What are the critical challenges facing urban mission today, and how does the gospel meet them?

If there are two big ideas in the book, they are these: The necessity of viewing urban mission with ecological awareness and sensitivity, and the need to ground urban mission in the unique and powerful gospel of Jesus Christ as revealed in Scripture and as incorporating both people and land.

Related to these is the theme of community and discipleship, itself a key biblical focus. The church as a community of Jesus's disciples living, serving, witnessing, thinking, suffering, celebrating, and acting within the world's urban places. I have attempted to connect everything in the book to these fundamental themes.

Long ago the Prophet Elijah, fearing for his life, ran away to the mountains. He hid in a cave in "the mount of God," Mount Horeb. God told Elijah to stand at the mouth of the cave.

> And, behold, the Lord passed by, and a great and strong wind rent the mountains, and brake in pieces the rocks before the Lord; but the Lord was not in the wind: and after the wind an earthquake; but the Lord was not in the earthquake: And after the earthquake a fire; but the Lord was not in the fire: and after the fire a still small voice" (1 Kgs 19:8–12 KJV).

It was *God's* "still small voice," the whisper of the Spirit.

Urban missioners today face strong tearing winds; earthquakes; fires. "Rockets' red glare, bombs bursting in air," whether literal or figurative. All such principalities and powers are ultimately under God's control. All will be judged and all will be reconciled in Jesus Christ.

But God is not mainly in the fires or earthquakes or winds. God is in the "still small voice" of his Spirit who works quietly in people's hearts and communities as they gather around Jesus and live in openness to each other, to the Spirit, and to the alien, the widow, the orphan, the stranger.

Faithful urban mission begins and ends here. Between the beginning and the ending, urban Christians confront urban systems and all sorts of principalities and powers, using their varied gifts to engage all the currents, controversies, and conflicts addressed in this book.

We noted in the Introduction Paul's words to urban Christians in 1 Corinthians, Chapter One. God wisely "chose what is weak in the world to shame the strong" (1 Cor 1:27). "For God's foolishness is wiser than human wisdom," Paul noted, "and God's weakness is stronger than human strength" (1 Cor 1:25).

In his book *Surprised by Scripture,* N. T. Wright observes, "Wisdom is what you need, according to scripture, to become genuinely, fully human." God's wisdom in Jesus Christ is an integrating reality creating wholeness, community, bridging chasms between faith and reason, religion and politics, private and public life.

The Christian worldview is all about wisdom, which in Jesus Christ becomes embodied love. Like the first Christians, faithful urban Christians today believe not only that Jesus rose again, "but that he had, as it were, gone through death and out the other side, leading the way into a new mode of being in which the power of love would defeat the love of power, in which creation and beauty would win out over death and decay, and in which God would become present to people of every shape and type, offering healing and reconciliation, a new start, a new life, a new way of life."[1]

The result is a new community of love, embodied wisdom. Wright observes,

> Love is a mode of knowing all right, but love transcends the objective/subjective distinction that has been inscribed in so much of our thinking in the Western world. In love, the main thing is to admire, respect, celebrate, and take delight in the object of that love, to let it be itself, to *want* it to be gloriously and freely itself, not to snatch it or control it or squash it into another shape. That's not love, but lust. . . . Precisely at the moment when love is celebrating the radical otherness of the beloved—whether it be a star twenty million light-years away or a human being twenty millimeters away—love enters into a relationship with the beloved, a relationship that is defined by the nature of the beloved, but in which admiration is mixed with curiosity, a desire to discover more, respect

---

[1] N. T. Wright, *Surprised by Scripture: Engaging Contemporary Issues* (New York: HarperCollins, 2014), 157, 161–62.

with a longing for intimacy, a desire to know and (so far as is possible) to be known.[2]

This is not the way of the world, nor the way of much city life. But it is the gospel way, the way of truly wise community and witness in the world's cities today.

What cities need, above all, is love and wisdom—the wisdom and love of God incarnate in Christian men, women, children, in Christian community. Jesus is the key to integrated life and an integrated worldview in the city, in the midst of disintegration.

Christians are in the city because they love the city. They don't love its evil and crises, its annoyances and intrusiveness, its false dichotomies. Many would prefer to live elsewhere—perhaps in a peaceful valley or lofty mountain or rural village. And many Christians who don't live in cities pray for them, visit them for cultural events, help support Christians in urban mission in multiple ways.

We love the people in cities, and so we love the cities, even if with deep ambivalence.

But ultimately and wisely, we trust in God, knowing that he is fully able to fulfill all his good promises. We accept the gospel invitation to be coworkers with him in the great work of reconciliation in the city and in the land.

---

[2] Wright, *Surprised by Scripture*, 159 (emphasis in the original).

We remember the assurance, "Perfect love casts out fear" (1 John 4:18). We trust God's Word—his quiet, reassuring, sustaining voice.

AFTERWORD: MISSION THEOLOGY 2.0
The Blogification of the Kingdom

My family and I moved to Detroit in 1966, to São Paulo in 1968, and to Chicago in 1980. This was before computers and emails and blogs, though while in Chicago I bought one of the early Macintosh computers in 1984 (which I still keep as a memento).

Now we're in the Internet age. Over the past five years I've posted a hundred and some blogs on church and mission on my Seedbed site *(http://howardsnyder.seedbed.com/)*. Since many of these are relevant to a theology of urban mission, I close this book with a selection of a dozen short pieces (slightly revised) that serve as further clarification and final reflection on the themes of this book.

Holy, Holy, Holy!

(Seedbed, 4/12/13)

"Holy, holy, holy!" The words resound in praise to the hymned Trinity.

Surprisingly, this phrase occurs only twice in Scripture—once in Isaiah; once in Revelation:

Isaiah 6:3 – "Holy, holy, holy is the Lord of hosts; the whole earth is full of his glory."

Revelation 4:8 – "Holy, holy, holy, the Lord God the Almighty, who was and is and is to come."

Verses so similar that we should mark the differences!

Both passages picture glorious scenes of the Sovereign Lord upon his throne. In Isaiah, six seraphs (*seraphim*, "burning ones") call to each other, proclaiming God's holiness.

Revelation 4 is similar: Four "living creatures" unceasingly sing "day and night." "Holy, holy, holy, [is] the Lord God the Almighty, who was and is and is to come." The seraphs of Isaiah 6 and also the "living creatures" of Revelation 4 have six wings. Pictured here are the glorious angelic beings who ever attend God's throne.

But the passages are different, and the difference teaches us a lesson. In Isaiah: "The whole earth is full of his glory." In Revelation: The Lord "was and is and is to come." Here is the Lord of both space and time. The whole earth (space); all of history (time). Jointly the two passages embrace heaven and earth; space and time! Holy is the Lord.

So in our discipleship, we remember this: The whole earth is full of God's glory, and all time is God's context. Through the promises of God, we see a *story* here. We know that more and more, as God's plan of salvation unfolds, God's glory will be seen in the whole earth. "The earth will be full with the knowledge of the Lord, as the waters cover the sea" (Isa 11:9; see also Hab 2:14).

God's Glory in the Earth

Psalm 33:5 reminds us that the Lord "loves righteousness and justice; *the earth is full* of the steadfast love of the Lord." Psalm 104 sings movingly of God's presence and acts in the earth. "O Lord, how manifold are your works! In wisdom you have made them all; *the earth is full* of your creatures" (Ps 104:24).

Our news channels are full of pain and problems and disasters—not God's glory. We get blinded; we forget that the whole earth is full of God's glory.

The earth shows God's glory in at least six ways.

1. *The beauty, color, and splendor of the creation reflects God's glory.* See a horse run, or stately storks walk, or

graceful birds fly! The last chapters of Job say it over and over. The poet Alfred Joyce Kilmer caught the scent: "I think that I shall never see a poem lovely as a tree."

2. *Each God-imaged man and woman reflects God's glory.* Every person is a God-glory-bearer—in fact, or in potential. God's glory shines in human uniqueness and diversity. Humanity created male and female shows God's glory more than would genderless beings.

3. *The glory of the Lord is seen most fully in Jesus Christ*— incarnation, life, death, resurrection, reign. "The law was given through Moses; grace and truth came through Jesus Christ" (Jn 1:17).

4. *God's glory is seen in the church when it is filled with the Spirit.* His glory shines in the faithful expansion of the church worldwide. Faithful community, vital worship, and diversity of the Spirit's gifts all reveal God's glory. Unfaithful churches tarnish the brightness of God's glory.

5. *God's glory glistens in every act of love, kindness, forgiveness, and reconciliation.* Acting justly and enacting justice shows the glory of the Lord. As God's glory is shown in all his works, so all our works in fidelity to God display his glory.

6. *God's glory appears when we practice creation care, demonstrating God's affection for the earth.* Creation care is

glorious, for it first and foremost honors the Triune God, Father, Son, and Spirit. Honoring God in this way, we bless others now and into future generations.

God's Glory Now and Evermore

Despite the fall and all the problems of sin, the whole earth is still full of the glory of the Lord! Not just *will be*, but *is*! The One who created us and the whole creation to display his glory is still working in the world through his Holy Spirit.

This then is a *fact* we can rejoice in and meditate upon: *The whole earth is full of God's glory.*

Scripture nowhere says explicitly, "Heaven and earth are full of God's glory." Yet that truth shines from nearly every page. The seraphs emphasize in Isaiah 6:3 that "the *whole earth* is full" of God's glory. How easily we forget; fail to see. So easily we feel that heaven is glorious, but the earth is full only of death and disease, evil and woe.

God is the Lord of space and time, of spacetime. Jesus is King of Kings and Lord of history. The Holy Spirit worked in creation, in Jesus's incarnation and full history and resurrection, and is working still. God the Father is, was, and always shall be. Jesus came and is yet to come.

O God, by your Holy Spirit give us eyes to see your glory in all the earth, and grace to manifest your glory in every sphere of our own influence. May we see and reflect and extend your glory. Help us trust your promises for the future as fully as we celebrate your past acts and the resurrection of Jesus, the guarantee and firstfruit of your kingdom in fullness. May your will be done on earth, as in heaven. Amen.

Key implication for urban mission: Focus on God's glory not only in heaven but on earth, now, in our city, in joy and in anticipation of the coming fullness of God's promises.

14 Favorite Ways to Twist the Gospel

(Seedbed, 1/3/14)

It is strangely easy to twist the Jesus gospel so that it means something different from what Jesus actually taught, the truths he stressed. Here are fourteen popular ways the gospel gets subverted.

1. Interpret the gospel primarily through Romans.

Biblical writers, including Paul, tell us to study the whole of Scripture and interpret it through that wholeness. But the persistent tendency to see Romans as the key to all Scripture persists. So the church and the world suffer. *(See my blog, "Misplacing Romans"— http://howardsnyder.seedbed.com/2013 /03/08/misplacing-romans-john-wesley-hermeneutical-corrective/).*

2. Focus solely on "personal salvation."

The Bible does not teach "personal salvation" in the private, individualistic way that phrase has come to mean. Rather it teaches in multiple ways and through many metaphors the reconciliation of all things (for example, Eph 1, Col 1)—though not without judgment.

3. Make heaven the goal.

The Bible and the early Christian creeds say nothing about "going to heaven." Yet that phrase has become virtually synonymous with salvation in many minds. The

Bible focuses on God's will being done on earth as in heaven, and the ultimate redemption of all creation, not some cosmic eternal split between earth and heaven.

4. Split clergy and laity.

This was one of the earliest signs of the "mystery of iniquity" in the church. Once Satan has convinced us that only *a few* (and mainly men of a certain sort) are called into "the ministry," he has reduced the church's effectiveness by ninety percent. The clergy/laity split is thus more debilitating than any other prejudice in the church. It undermines the biblical doctrine of the priesthood of believers, the gifts of the Spirit, and the universal call to *diakonia* (ministry, service).

5. Think economics and politics are not directly gospel concerns.

Walling off economics and politics from the gospel, placing them outside our discipleship, is unbiblical dualism. The gospel is an economic and political reality, so by definition the church is both economic and political. But economics and politics are to be understood in light of the gospel, not the other way round. The kingdom of God is the comprehensive framework.

6. De-prioritize community.

New Testament writers focus much more on community—the body of Christ, our membership in Jesus Christ and thus in one another—than any other topic. The less genuine the community in the mutually-sharing biblical sense of *koinonia*, the more doctrinal disputes become central and the church focuses on everything else but community. This is why I deal so much with this in *Community of the King* and other books.

7. Neglect the Old Testament.

The two most common mistakes here: Neglecting the wholism of God's salvific purposes as revealed in the Old Testament, and buying the myth that all important truths in the Old Testament get "spiritualized" in the New. So "promised land," for example, comes to mean "heaven" or some inner spiritual experience. When this happens, preachers mine the Old Testament looking for "spiritual" nuggets that often have little to do with the biblical historical context and meaning.

8. Limit Justice to personal righteousness.

The Old Testament—Psalms, Prophets, Law, Wisdom—constantly pair justice and righteousness as two sides of the same comprehensive reality. Notice for instance how frequently *justice* and *righteousness* are coupled and used almost interchangeably in Hebrew poetry.

Yet the church often separates them in various ways—for instance making *righteousness* mean personal morality and *justice* something God takes care of by himself through the atonement and/or final judgment. This is flatly unbiblical.

9. Neglect intercession.

The more I read of prayer in the Bible—Moses, David, the Prophets, Job, Jesus's life and example, Acts, the Epistles—the more I am convinced that I and the church generally have neglected the essential ministry of intercession. Through the mystery of prayer and God's Spirit, persistent intercession by God's people can (and often does) change the course of history and relations among nations and peoples and religions—as well as meeting our more immediate and personal needs.

Intercessory prayer is a primary means of seeking first the kingdom of God.

10. Think "believers" instead of disciples.

Jesus calls and forms disciples so that the body of Christ becomes a community of kingdom-of-God disciples. The New Testament rarely uses the word "believers." Today this fact is distorted by the tendency in modern translations to use "believers" in place of "brothers" (in order to be more inclusive) or in place of pronouns such as "them."

What counts is not the number of believers but the number of disciples, and thus the ministry of disciple-making.

11. Substitute heaven for the Kingdom of God.

In the Bible, the kingdom of God is as comprehensive as the reality, sovereignty, and love of God. No spirit/matter dualism. Most people in Jesus's days understood this; they knew that "kingdom of heaven" in Matthew, for example, was just another way of saying "kingdom of God."

In the Bible we see the kingdom of God as both now/future, heavenly/earthly, personal/social, sudden/gradual, inward/outward, in a mysterious dialectic with the church which itself is neither the kingdom of God nor divorceable from God's kingdom.

12. Make faith just one part of life.

We compartmentalize. Our Christian walk gets reduced to just one part of our lives, and that one part is often reduced to simply what we believe.

But now abide faith, hope, and love—and the Bible makes clear which is the "greatest" and most comprehensive. According to the gospel, faith is not the ultimate reality. It is the means to the end of loving God and others and all God's creation with our whole being. And that 24/7, as the saying goes.

The biblical picture is faith working by love; love enabled by faith and powered by hope—full confidence in God's amazing full-salvation-for-all-creation promises.

13. Forget Genesis 9.

There is a huge literature on "covenant" or "federal" theology (from the Latin for "covenant"). Yet oddly, such theology almost always begins with God's covenant with Abraham (perhaps with a passing reference to Genesis 3:15). Yet the first explicit biblical covenant is found in Genesis 9, where God establishes his "covenant between me and the earth" (Gen 3:13).

The emphasis is explicit and repeated: A covenant with humans and all living creatures of every kind. If our understanding of salvation skips from Genesis 3 to Genesis 12, we miss essential biblical teachings about the created order and distort everything else in the Bible.

14. Divorce discipleship from creation care.

When we neglect or distort biblical revelation about the created order, we shrink the gospel to something much less than the Bible promises. We do this to our own loss; we impoverish the church; we over-spiritualize Christian experience and reduce the dynamic of Christian mission.

When we see how discipleship and creation care are *inseparably* connected in God's plan, the church becomes patiently and humbly powerful "to the pulling down of strongholds" (2 Cor 10:4).

There are many other ways to twist the gospel, of course. Anytime we get our focus off Jesus Christ and interpret the gospel through other lenses, we are in trouble.

Use whatever verb you wish—twist, distort, warp, undermine, neutralize, neuter, emasculate, cancel out, undercut—the problem persists and calls for careful Bible-based, Jesus-centered discipleship.

The Holy Spirit was poured out at Pentecost, yet already in the New Testament we see the Apostles battling emerging distortions.

And yet sovereignly, strangely, God's Spirit is at work and will still fulfill the promises and guide the body of Christ into "all truth" (Jn 16:13) until "the earth [is] full of the knowledge of the Lord as the waters cover the sea" (Isa 11:9).

Key implication for urban mission: *Teach and embody the whole gospel.* Watch out for distortions. Ground urban disciples in the Word and the whole plan of God.

What Running Taught Me

(Seedbed, 5/15/13)

Running the race of life! A common cliché. Yet also a biblical image, reminding us of key truths.

Think of Hebrews 12:1–2. "Since we are surrounded by such a great cloud of witnesses, let us throw off everything that hinders and the sin that so easily entangles. And let us run with perseverance the race marked out for us, fixing our eyes on Jesus, the pioneer and perfecter of faith" (TNIV). Jesus is both our example and our goal.

Some of us like to run physically as well as spiritually. Coach Mac McDonald got me running cross-country in high school in Spring Arbor, Michigan, and I've been running ever since—more or less! With time and age, I see more and more connections between physical and spiritual running.

Interesting things happen when I run regularly. If I run faithfully, I lose extra weight, for example. The more I lose weight, the better I run. It's a kind of balance; an equation. Many Christians run, walk, or swim in order to keep a healthy balance of weight and exercise because they want to "glorify God in [their bodies]" (1 Cor 6:20).

Glorifying God in our bodies is Christian virtue. To be

348

spiritual is to be physical. Our Lord Jesus Christ "became flesh and lived among us" (Jn 1:14). In the New Creation our physical bodies will be resurrected to be like Jesus's own body. "For if we have been united with him in a death like his, we will certainly be united with him in a resurrection like his" (Rom 6:5).

Lessons from Running

What do running and other exercise actually teach us? Here are my top learnings:

First, *physical, spiritual, and mental health are all linked.* They reinforce each other. It's hard to be spiritually alert if you're physically ill. If I am sick and unable to run, that affects me mentally and emotionally. Running helps me understand more deeply the intimate ties between spirit, body, and mind. It makes me more alert spiritually and mentally.

Running reminds me just how physical I am! It shows me also the beauty of the world around me; the joy of inhabiting God's good earth, especially if I run outdoors, gadget-free.

A second learning: *Discipline becomes easier the more we practice it.* If I haven't run for awhile, it's hard to get back into practice. But running becomes easier and more enjoyable as I persist. Practice doesn't make perfect, but it makes pleasant.

Same with spiritual disciplines. Prayer, Bible study, devotional reading, generosity, recycling, and participation in Christian community become easier and more rewarding the more we do them. As we exercise ourselves spiritually (in biblically sound ways) we grow spiritually. The more we grow spiritually, the more disciplined we become. A healthy cycle.

This is actually my third learning: *Life moves in cycles; repeated patterns.* We live cycles of days, months, seasons, and years. This is how God made the world (Gen 1:14; Ex 20:8–11, 31:15–16; Ps 104:19; Acts 14:17).

Cycles can work for you or against you. If I've put on extra weight from overeating, I tend to run slower. But if I push against that and run faster, I tend to lose weight. The more I run, the more fit I feel; the more fit I feel, the better I run. That's life.

Many people are not physically able to run, of course, but the principle still holds. We live by cycles that work for us or against us.

The same is true with the physical creation and how we treat it. Humans have dominion over the earth, constructively or destructively. Cycles of life and cycles of death run throughout the created order. Cycles of death, introduced by sin, include the human sin of failing to care for God's good earth and for children, born and unborn.

Cycles of life and death are everywhere—in culture and economics, just as much as in our bodies and spirits. Healthy cycles—for instance, daily and weekly patterns of enough food, rest, exercise, and productive work—increase our health and well-being. But unhealthy cycles— insufficient sleep and rest, too little or too much food, overwork—undermine our health. These are cycles of death.

Life-nurturing cycles are God's way in Christian discipleship and in creation. Consider how Nature cycles and recycles. Empowered by the Spirit and Christian community, cycles of life not only help us grow spiritually. They actually contribute to the coming of God's New Creation in fullness.

Working the Cycles

Some of our most important cycles are grounded in Christian community. As Christians we run *together*, not alone. On the Jericho road there's room for more than just two. Often as Christians we "come to the garden" *together*, not "alone, while the dew is still on the roses." In Christian community we need cycles and disciplines of life together; shared life.

Jesus said, "Where two or three are gathered in my name, I am there among them" (Mt 18:20). This gathering in Jesus's name and presence is essential Christian discipline (Heb 10:24–25). The cycles of daily disciplines, frequent fellowship, weekly worship, and the Christian year remind us how God works in history and of how he put the world together.

We need a healthy biblical balance. We can live by life-giving rhythms of the Spirit. This means respecting and engaging the rhythms of physical as well as spiritual life.

Here is the deeper reason why recycling paper, plastics, leftover food, and other "waste" makes sense. Recycling works *against* cycles of death and *with* cycles of life. The authors of the book *Redeeming Creation* put it this way:

> We extend a Christian response to God's creation when we begin to use less and save more. Those who recycle their own bottles and cans live with integrity. Those who persuade the city council to make recycling part of the normal garbage-collection procedure have changed their world. The reason to recycle materials or to compost leaves goes beyond compliance with local ordinances. It is within compliance of greater ordinances, cycles that

God created for the world in which we live.[1] (Fred Van Dyke, *et al., Redeeming Creation: The Biblical Basis for Environmental Stewardship* [Downers Grove, Ill.: InterVarsity, 1996], 145).

Science tells us that all life is about inputs, outputs, and "throughputs." The technical term is *ecology*—the interconnection of all things in one system, or one "house" (*oikos* in the Greek New Testament, the basis for "ecology"), as created by God. Jesus knew this: "What goes into your mouth does not defile you, but what comes out of your mouth, that is what defiles you"—that is, the "evil thoughts, murder, adultery, sexual immorality, theft, false testimony, slander" that come from the heart. Eating food does not defile, for "whatever enters the mouth goes into the stomach and then out of the body" (Mt 15:11, 17–20 TNIV). That's the normal cycle. "In saying this, Jesus declared all foods clean" (Mark 7:19 TNIV).

We live in interconnected physical-spiritual systems and cycles. Christian discipleship means working *with* all life-giving cycles and *against* those that bring death or evil. Let us then "encourage one another daily . . . so that none of [us] may be hardened by sin's deceitfulness" (Heb 3:13

---

[1] Fred Van Dyke, *et al., Redeeming Creation: The Biblical Basis for Environmental Stewardship* (Downers Grove, Ill.: InterVarsity, 1996), 145

TNIV). These things I ponder as I run.

The Longer Race

Finally, *running even teaches me something about eschatology*, the doctrine of "last things." I'm less tired or winded at the end of the run than halfway through. This is due to the "second breath" or "second wind" runners get once their bodies have adjusted to the pace. So also in our discipleship: Energy actually increases as we catch the pace, as we continue on, as we press toward the goal ahead, ever nearer.

Here is good news! Though we can't all run *physically*, we can all run *spiritually*. As ageing makes us slow down *physically*, we can pick up the pace *spiritually*. So "let us lay aside every weight, . . . and let us run with perseverance the race set before us, looking to Jesus the pioneer and perfecter of our faith" (Heb 12:1–2). The risen Jesus says where he leading us. "In keeping with his promise we are looking forward to a new heaven and a new earth, where righteousness dwells" (2 Pt 3:13 TNIV).

Key implications for urban mission: City life can run us ragged and wear us down. We are forced into its cycles, some of which are destructive or dehumanizing. As Christians and Christian communities we therefore need to 1) establish our own cycles; 2) get the physical and spiritual exercise we need; and 3) work the cycles of life in ways that keep us healthy and bring health and wholeness to others and counterbalance the cycles of death. Run the race in the city, in every sense, including rest.

Jesus-Deficit Disorder?

(Seedbed, 7/15/13)

The poet John Milton described nature as "a wilderness of sweets." I like that.

Richard Louv includes the Milton quote in his remarkable book: *Last Child in the Woods: Saving Our Children from Nature-Deficit Disorder* (referred to earlier in the book).

Richard Louv heads the Children & Nature Network and in 2008 was awarded the Audubon Medal. "Nature-deficit disorder" is not a formal medical diagnosis, he says. However it's certainly a graphic way of spotlighting a big issue.

Here's Louv's concern:

"A kid today can likely tell you about the Amazon rain forest—but not about the last time he or she explored the woods in solitude, or lay in the field listening to the wind and watching the clouds move." Kids today he says "are aware of the global threats to the environment—but their physical contact, their intimacy with nature, is fading."

School kids used to study natural history. Now they study microbiology.

But children, and adults as well, need nature in the raw and the rough. "In nature, a child finds freedom, fantasy, and privacy: a place distant from the adult world, a separate peace."

Three Surprises

Three things surprise me in reading this book.

First, I am surprised how serious nature-deficit disorder really is. Louv writes, "Nature-deficit disorder describes the human costs of alienation from nature, among them: diminished use of the senses, attention difficulties, and higher rates of physical and emotional illnesses. The disorder can be detected in individuals, families, and communities."

Second, I am surprised how suddenly our society has shifted away from daily contact with nature. From 1997 to 2003, the amount of time U.S. children age 9–12 spent playing outdoors or in unstructured ways dropped by half. There was a huge decline in outdoor activities like hiking, walking, fishing, gardening, or playing at the beach.

"In the space of a century," Louv notes, "the American experience of nature has gone from direct utilitarianism to romantic attachment to electronic detachment."

Result: "Today a generation of children is not only being raised indoors, but is being confined to ever smaller spaces." We are raising "containerized kids."

Louv notes that nature, unlike TV, "does not steal time; it amplifies it. Nature offers healing for a child living in a destructive family or neighborhood."

Third, I am surprised at the discipleship implications here.

Louv doesn't write specifically as a Christian, but he dwells a lot on holistic wellbeing. He points to growing evidence that "direct exposure to nature is essential for physical and emotional health" and may actually help children fight depression and "reduce the symptoms of Attention Deficit Hyperactivity Disorder (ADHD)."

Louv cites studies showing that "joggers who exercise in a natural green setting with trees, foliage, and landscape views feel more restored, and less anxious, angry, and depressed than people who burn the same amount of calories in gyms or other built settings."

Let's Get Spiritual!

At this point the traditional "spiritual" response might be: We don't need more nature! We just need more Jesus.

Wrong! That is un-Christian dualism. It is not what Jesus or the Bible teach. Such attitudes are actually part of the problem.

When Jesus said "Consider the lilies of the field," do you suppose he really meant it? Could he have meant much more than just "Get a spiritual lesson from lilies"? Maybe he really meant *consider, think about, ponder, look at, spend time with* the lilies of the field.

That would mean spending time not only with the lilies, but also with the field—which means of course birds, animals, butterflies, trees, the sky and clouds—ultimately, the whole complex ecosystem that the Psalms rhapsodize about.

Our greatest human problem, next to our alienation from God and one another, is our alienation from nature—the creation around us. This is precisely what nature-deficit disorder is about.

We really need to know and appreciate how God's world works. If we don't learn how ecosystems work, we will never learn how the gospel works. This is in essence what Jesus teaches in his parables of the kingdom, as well as in the Sermon on the Mount.

From a biblical salvation perspective, the issue is not just us, of course. It is the place of the created order—and thus all natural ecosystems—in God's plan.

So as part of Christian discipleship, we need to learn how ecosystems work. Pollution, over-development, and deforestation all degrade ecosystems. The degrading of an ecosystem may be invisible at first, but irreversible damage may be happening out of sight.

Louv quotes a naturalist friend, the late Elaine Brooks: "Despite what developers will tell you about restoration, once a piece of land is graded, the biologic organisms and understructure of the soil are destroyed."

Where's the Disorder?

Most Christians, I suppose, believe the greatest human problem is "faith-deficit disorder" or "God-deficit disorder" (to play off Richard Louv's terms). True, perhaps, but one-sided.

God made us to live in an ongoing, life-giving relationship with him but also with his world. Science is showing that we actually suffer physically and emotionally if we don't tend to our nature-relationship.

If you don't do anything else this week, spend two or three hours in a woods, or by a stream, or on a long walk. *Attend* to what you see and hear and smell. *Think about* the relationship God has put in place with plants and flowers and "every living creature upon earth" (Gen 9:15–16).

Your life depends on it. Your children's and friends' lives depend on it. The renewal of the church depends on it.

The flourishing of the earth according to God's plan—and maybe even its survival—depend upon it.

Your sanctity and your sanity depend upon your companionship with the earth. Ultimately, the world depends upon it.

So, go commune with nature. Consider the lilies and the butterflies and the birds and the beetles and the ants.

"Go to the ant, thou sluggard; consider her ways, and be wise" (Prov 6:6 KJV).

Go enjoy nature; let it bless and bliss you. And for God's sake, leave your earbuds behind!

Key implications for urban mission: Design discipleship, Christian community, and urban witness so that it helps heal nature-deficit disorder. This might mean community gardens, walks, visits to parks, retreats in a natural setting, flowers and plants in our homes and worship spaces.

Be creative, and look for people with gifts in this area who can help us all.

Jesus Gets Organized

(Seedbed, 9/23/13)

Now it came to pass in those days, as the number of disciples was increasing, that Jesus went up on a mountain and called his Twelve Apostles to him.

He said to them, "Friends, the time has come to get organized. The crowds are getting too big to handle. Also, I'm thinking ahead; thinking of the future. Thinking of the message, and how people will act when I am no longer with you.

"I am thinking about how to control the message, and about branding. Otherwise this whole movement could go off into the weeds.

"So I now cast a vision for your work. I am appointing each of you to a *strategic task*.

"But first, let me ask: Who do people say that I am?"

The Apostles answered, "Some say John the Baptist. Some say you are Elijah, reincarnated among us. Some say you are some other prophet."

"But what do *you* think?" Jesus asked.

"You are the Messiah!" Peter blurted out.

"Good! I think you've got it," Jesus said. "But we've got to be careful; control the message. We don't want people to get wrong ideas, and we don't want to stir up too much controversy. So keep that under your hats for now."

And then Jesus appointed each of the Twelve to his special role, giving them their job descriptions.

"John," he said, "I appoint you Director of Power Evangelism. James, you will be Coordinator of Signs and Wonders. Your ministries are closely related, and I want you to work well together without quarreling. Figure out a strategy so the healings and other miracles coordinate well with what I'm teaching.

"Matthew, you have a lot of experience with money, so I am appointing you Director of Finance. This includes, of course, budgeting and fiscal management. And be sure to check on tax matters.

"Andrew, you will be Director of Logistics and Crowd Control. I've shown you pretty well how to do it. Five thousand is about as many as we can handle. From now on, you probably should send out several disciples in advance to get things prepared. Look for places that are good for crowds; lots of grass; not too many thistles or rocks or muddy places, and not too hard to get to. Think about food, too. It's going to be a little complicated in Jerusalem, but you can figure things out.

"Judas, I appoint you Director of Publicity and Promotion. You know a lot of key people. I want you to be responsible for branding, for controlling the message, so people don't get wrong ideas.

"Simon, I know you're very zealous about Israel, especially in its relations with the Roman Empire. So I'm appointing you Minister of Foreign and International Relations. You'll have a big job cut out for you in years ahead. We'll keep this movement underground as long as we can, but you will handle political and international matters as they come up.

"Philip and Bartholomew, I hereby appoint you Co-Directors of Spiritual Development. Here's what you do: Keep a record of what I teach, organize it topically, then look up passages in the Jewish Scriptures that will be useful in helping people understand what I mean. Put together a curriculum.

"Thaddeus, I am appointing you Prayer Coordinator. Prayer is very important. I want you to work out a plan to support our whole movement with prayer. Report back to me with your plan in two weeks.

"James Alphie, I appoint you Director of Facilities. I know that will puzzle you, since we don't have any. But I'm looking down the road. Eventually the Jews won't want our small groups in their synagogues any more. So we're going to need our own buildings. I suggest we start small, with houses. We can expand them as necessary—knock out walls or whatever, and when groups raise enough money, they can build bigger special-purpose buildings. I foresee a day when we can have temples just as grand as the Jews have.

"Thomas, I'm appointing you to head up a Task Force on the Future. You and the rest of the Twelve will be my Eschatology Team. Think Big Picture. I suggest you study the prophetic books, especially Isaiah, Ezekiel, and Daniel, to get some ideas. You'll need to look ahead, but also to figure out how best to use a lot of the symbols in the Jewish Scriptures, because we don't want to get into too much trouble. So think of symbols like beasts and turning wheels and trees and rivers and measuring rods, and lots of eyes, and things like that. Work out an outline, and later I'll have John write it up. It's going to be quite a revelation.

"Now, Peter! I know what you're thinking. 'What about me?' You're a big guy, and have a big job for you! I want you to be Director of Evangelism, Missions, and Church Planting. That includes working out strategies for starting new groups of followers. Right now we're working just among Jews, but you need to be thinking ahead.

"Now, finally, I am *not* going to appoint a Director of Theology, because I have someone else in mind who will be good at that. But he doesn't know it yet. It's going to take some big changes before he's ready to write anything that makes sense."

And so Jesus finished his instructions, and each of the Twelve went to work on his assigned tasks.

[Note to readers: This rare document was found in a cave a little ways from Qumran. It is not clear just what happened to all these inspired and visionary plans, but I suspect the document may have been rediscovered about 330 A.D.]

Implication for urban mission: How are we organized? Are we over-structured? Have we put second things first? Where do we get our models? Have we paid enough attention to the New Testament community and the essential priorities of the gospel? What did Jesus *really* say and do?

Church Planting: Five Biblical Ecological Insights

(Seedbed, 3/3/14)

Church planting assumes an ecological process. The very term is organic, not mechanical or architectural.

If we're talking about the body of Christ, not an institution or edifice, we don't *build* the church. We don't *erect* the church. We don't even *start* a church, for that is the Spirit's work.

We plant and grow churches. More accurately: Effective church planters take the lead in planting good gospel seed and become "coworkers" with God (Col 4:11, Phil 4:3, 3 Jn 1:8) in growing faithful, witnessing communities of disciples.

The Bible does of course use *building* language—for example in Ephesians 2 and 1 Peter 2. Jesus said, "I will build my church" (Mt 16:18). These references are clearly metaphorical, though. Peter speaks of "living stones" (1 Pt 2:5). Paul saws the edifice "grows" into "a dwelling place for God" (Eph 2:21–22).

In other words, the root biblical image for the church is a living one—organic, ecological. For the church is grounded in the very life of God the Trinity and the organic world where God has placed us—to which he sent

Jesus in the flesh. So we have images of trees, vines and branches, marriage, and so forth—all images from *life.*

If church planting is organic, then we can learn from ecology. Jesus's parables already point the way. Jesus himself drew on Old Testament imagery of living things and living people.

What then can we learn from ecology? Five things:

1. Church planting is organic, based on principles of life, growth, and reproduction.

So we begin with a paradigm shift away from organizations, physical buildings, machines and technology. We *consciously and consistently* shift to organic insights and images, knowing how powerful such root metaphors can be.

From organic images sprouts a whole crop of insights. Here are two basic ones: *reproduction* and *smallness.* The Bible is full of both accents.

Reproduction: All life grows from other life by a process of reproduction. People give birth to people. Churches give birth to churches. Healthy people and churches give birth to healthy people and churches; unhealthy people and churches birth unhealthy people and churches.

Smallness: Babies are small. Seeds are small. *That's the way life works; how it begins.* Why expect something different with the church?

The institutional, financial, and media advantages of "launching" a large church start are obvious. That's why this approach is popular. But it's not organic or ecological. It produces churches by a different metaphor, and thus from the start has built-in resistance to developing close-knit, face-to-face community as the church's core and the heartbeat.

Sociology backs this up. There are dozens of examples. Early Methodism showed this. In North America, the Methodist movement grew fastest and deepest when it multiplied very small units, often beginning with class meetings. We find an inverse correlation between the size of Methodist churches and overall growth rate. That is, as churches got larger—building larger buildings and professionalizing the leadership—growth declined.

One social, spiritual, and psychological reason is obvious: People feel more personally responsible and accountable in smaller groups.

Small units reproduce other living units with the same DNA. Large institutions slowly form other institutional units with the same institutional DNA—a DNA with inbred resistance to the organic multiplication of small units. This is so obvious from physical life that it's almost a marvel that it's so often overlooked in church life.

Organic DNA produces organic life. Institutional DNA produces institutional life. Why would be expect anything different?

2. Organic church planting thrives on diversity so is inherently more open to crosscultural witness and intercultural community that are more programmatic models.

Since organic church planting is ecological, it is highly sensitive to its environment. Its discernment process is multidirectional, not linear or vertical.

Much of the beauty of creation in Genesis 1 comes from *diversity*. Consider:

"The earth brought forth vegetation: plants yielding seed *of every kind*, and trees *of every kind* bearing fruit with the seed in it. And God saw that it was good. . . . And God said, 'Let the waters bring forth swarms of living creatures, and let birds fly above the earth across the dome of the sky.' . . . God made the wild animals of the earth *of every kind*, and the cattle *of every kind*, and everything that creeps upon the ground *of every kind*. And God saw that it was good" (Gen 1:12–25).

All this with the repeated refrain: "Be fruitful and multiply."

This is a great church-planting text. Living things multiply and over time diversify in response to change. Why should we think this applies to everything else in the world except human life, culture, and organization? Everything except the church?

Diversity, and also *adversity*. Living things constantly face challenges, threats, or barriers that must be overcome. They grow stronger as they wrestle with adversity. Or else they die. We see this in the whole history of God's people, both before and after Jesus's incarnation.

Organic church planting is adaptive. That's how life is. Organisms adapt almost instinctively to changes in climate or relationships. They sense when to make small adaptations early so that change doesn't turn into crisis.

The implications are obvious. Church planting on an organic model will thrive both on internal diversity (personalities, charisms, resources, skills, backgrounds, both genders) and on external adaptivity.

Thus a miracle occurs: "Our kind of people" turn out to be less, not more, homogeneous. Or better: Gospel reconciliation and gospel truth become the operative homogeneous principle. "Our kind of people" turn out to be God's kind of people.

3. Ecology provides key insights for leadership and organization.

This kind of organic logic yields insights for leadership and structure. Neither the New Testament church nor the whole creation is based on theories of leadership, structure, or "best practices." Scripture comes first; creation from the hand of God comes next, before theories.

Here New Testament teachings on spiritual gifts, the priesthood of all believers (that is, the true meaning of *laity*), and Christ-like servanthood come creatively into play. In the New Testament, leadership and structure are organic and charismatic (profound conjunction), not institutional and hierarchical. Whatever institutional models we may inherit (and they have their value), these are *distinctly secondary* to the Spirit's call to *koinonia*, giftedness, and mutual servanthood.

This was the key insight of that liturgical Anglican, John Wesley.

Church planters have a choice *from the first conception* of the idea of planting a church of the model they'll follow. Commitment to biblical community on an organic basis comes first, not somewhere down the line, eventually. You can't change the DNA once the baby is born.

4. Organic church planting is earthy.

Biblical church planting allows no dualism, no split, between the spiritual and the physical. No categorical divide between church and earth, since God's plan and "good pleasure" is "to bring everything together under one head, Jesus Christ—*all things,* things in heaven and things on earth" (Eph 1:9–10).

Since it's part of the larger ecological reality of God's world, church planting *unavoidably and by definition* interacts with all the physical, social, and economic dimensions of the earth's ecology. Every church, whatever its form or tradition, has an ecological impact. It touches people, relationships, money, traditions, politics, birds and flowers and spiritual powers. It engages "the elemental spirits [or principles] of the universe" (Gal 4:3, 9; Col 2:8, 20), of the city, as well as the dirt under our feet, the water we drink, and the toilets we flush.

Ecology is all about energy sources, throughputs, feedbacks, and waste. Organic church planting ponders this.

An example: A particular new church plant is based in a couple home meetings, and as it grows it multiplies home groups. This involves not only leadership, prayer, discipling, coordination, and so forth. It also involves a whole range of other resources: Energy consumed to heat or illuminate houses, transportation from one place to another, perhaps purchasing and consuming food, and dealing with waste. (What happens to food containers? Are they spiritually significant? What do we teach by example? Where does the Bible draw the line on "all things"?)

These varied "things" are not just incidental costs or inconveniences. They are an inherent part of the ecology of the church's life. Everything is related, and everything has impacts, and all belongs to God to be used for his glory and to fulfill kingdom mission.

So we should not send mixed, conflicting signals.

If faithful, organic church planting contributes to the ecological well-being of the whole earth and all its cultures and systems.

5. Organic church planting is eschatological: It aims toward a larger future.

What is the goal of church planting? Conversions? Church growth? Popularity? Crowds? Media attention? "Fully committed followers of Jesus"? The kingdom of God?

All purposeful activity has a goal or end in view, stated or not. All church planting has a default eschatology. The key question is: Do we plant churches for some less worthy goal than the one God intends?

The operative eschatology in church planting will shape the method as well as the goal. The church is to be a disciple-growing community that exists for, is aimed squarely at, the kingdom of God. Immediate purposes always have a longer-range purpose—an eschatological horizon from which light shines to illuminate and guide the present. (See Chapter 5, "Strategic Planning in Urban Mission.")

As I have said before: the church gets in trouble whenever it thinks its in the church business rather than the kingdom business. In church business, people are concerned with church activities, religious behaviour and spiritual things. In kingdom business people are concerned with kingdom activities, all human behaviour and everything God has made, visible and invisible. Kingdom people seek first the kingdom of God and its justice. Church people often put church work above concerns of justice, mercy, and truth.

Church people think about how to get people into church; kingdom people think about how to get the church into the world. Church people worry that the world might change the church; kingdom people work to see the church change the world. When Christians catch a vision of the kingdom of God, their vision shifts to the poor, the orphan, the widow, the refugee, "the wretched of the earth," and to God's future. They see the life and work of the church in terms of the kingdom.

This is where ecology and eschatology meet. Biblical *vision* of creation healed is the goal which shapes our present. Biblical *ecology* reveals the nature of the organism, the church, which is God's primary agent in transformingly carrying forward his purposes to their fulfillment.

I thank God for faithful and effective Church-Planting Movements (CPMs). But CPMs are not self-justifying, for mere growth is not the test. Are they discipling? Are they kingdom-focused? Are they biblically ecological? Ecologically sustainable?

Finally . . .

There is much more to be said. I haven't touched on the question of doctrine or said much about structure, family life, ecologically appropriate technology, and global connections, awareness and responsibility. The point here: View things through the lens of biblical ecology, and new light shines on every angle of church planting.

* * * *

➢ Church planting is organic, based on principles of life, growth, and reproduction.

➢ Organic church planting thrives on diversity.

➢ Ecology provides key insights for leadership and organization.

➢ Organic church planting is earthy.

➢ Organic church planting is eschatological, aiming toward God's future.

We are left then with the master verse for ecological church planting: "Fear not, little flock, for the Father delights to give you the kingdom" (Lk 12:32).

Implications for urban mission: All five of these principles are fruitful for urban witness. The vision of urban mission is not to build a big building or fancy machine in the city. If it finds avenues to create new ministries, microenterprises, organizations, or other ventures, it should do everything *on the basis of organic principles.* In the long run, this proves much more effective and redemptive. But the most important implication: Multiplying communities of Jesus disciples in the city is the most strategic, prophetic thing urban mission can do. This is the root; everything else is the fruit.

When Children and Jesus Suffer

(Seedbed, 4/9/14)

It's possible to get all sentimental and misty-eyed about suffering in general and forget the real pain, tragedy, and injustice involved—the real people.

The biggest problem for the credibility of the Christian faith is the fact of unjustified, capricious, senseless suffering. Especially the suffering of small children. Also of course the suffering of mothers who have lost their own children—maybe even seen them killed. The suffering of prisoners being tortured. The horror of children or teens raped and abused. The suffering of families dying of starvation. The emotional torture of knowing a loved one is being victimized and not being able to do anything. And so on.

This suffering is happening *right now*, even as we think of it. Right now somewhere babies and small children are being killed or maimed or tortured. Depending on who you are and where you live, that might be right next door, or across the street, or even in the next room. Not just halfway around the world.

This is a much bigger conundrum for the Christian faith than the fact that God loves us. Sinful as we may be, humans are created by God in his image. So despite sin, God as loving Creator and Parent *should* continue to love us. Not that great a mystery, compared to the horror of unmerited suffering inflicted on innocents, especially children.

Much writing on suffering treats it as a philosophical issue. But that's secondary. People who suffer don't care much about philosophy, though they often do ask the big "Why?" question. And too often they (maybe especially children) say: "It's my fault. I deserve it." Untrue.

I hesitated to read the novel *The Shack* by William Paul Young because I didn't want to read what happens to the little girl at the beginning of the book. After I'd read the book, however, I was glad I did. Young does an excellent job of putting malicious suffering in a larger redemptive frame.

False Answers

I hear way too many glib, false, irrelevant, or only partial answers to the problem of suffering. Many stock answers sidestep the problem of the suffering of the innocents. For example:

Jesus suffered in our place. Thank God this is true! Jesus suffered and died for the sins of the world. But what does that really mean in light of actual present suffering? If

Jesus suffered in another's place, why does that other person still suffer now? Especially children and the victims of abuse. Especially those with no Christian hope.

Everyone is under God's judgment. Again, true, according to Scripture. But it's no explanation or excuse for the suffering of the innocents, of the little lambs.

All suffering is the effect of sin. This may well be true in some sense; I'm not sure. Everyone's suffering may be the result of *someone's* sin, now or in the past. Yet real suffering continues.

Suffering is God's judgment, or our own fault. In most cases, this is simply not true. Think of Job. Think of Tamar, raped by her brother (2 Sam 13:10–14). So this is a huge and diabolical, self-destructive lie. It doesn't touch, in any case, the issue of unmerited suffering.

Suffering is actually good for us; God uses it to shape and teach us, or to lead us to God. People's stories show that this has at times been true. But it doesn't answer the why question; the larger question of suffering in the world which seems to be purposeless, meaningless, plainly evil.

Present suffering is not really a problem in light future happiness. Paul wrote, "I consider that the sufferings of this present time are not worth comparing with the glory about to be revealed to us" (Rom 8:18).

Ultimately this will be true for the Christian. And for the Christian, this assurance helps relieve present suffering. But it doesn't answer the question of unmerited, often capricious present suffering in the world.

God is impassable; he doesn't feel human or animal pain. Therefore it's not really important. This is unbiblical and, I suspect, heretical and diabolical.

God also suffers. I believe this is profoundly true. Somehow the answer lies in this direction. The reality of Jesus' sufferings—and of the suffering of the Father and the Spirit—is and has been a great comfort to Christians in terrible agonies of suffering. But it does not of course answer the question of the present suffering of children and others.

Don't think about it. Senseless suffering is a mystery we can't solve; better just leave it in God's hands. Focus on God's goodness and love, and trust the rest to God. This option has merit because it affirms a great truth and makes life easier to live day to day. But Jesus certainly seemed moved by all suffering, and can we be insensitive?

We will understand someday. This also is true. We will understand, or it will no longer be a question. But this is not a present answer.

I've spoken here of human suffering; there's also the issue of animal suffering. I won't discuss that except to say that it is part and parcel of the larger moral/ethical problem.

The Big Answer

My conclusion is this: There is no answer to suffering within our present knowledge and experience. We are left with three assurances, however: (1) The unassailable love of God demonstrated visibly in history in Jesus's own incarnation, life, and sufferings. (2) The deep experience of comfort (sometimes even peace and joy) that people who know God often experience in the midst of suffering. I believe this is real, not a psychological trick. (3) Jesus's resurrection and the certainty that he will return to "finish the job," so to speak, putting everything to rights. Jesus followers affirm that one day there will be an answer; that it will be an adequate answer; that it will be an answer expressive of and consistent with God's loving character; and that we will see that it is so.

When Children and Jesus Suffer

But for today, I still wonder about children and suffering and Jesus's love. Is it possible Jesus *actually* takes the place of a child who is horribly suffering? The child who is being systematically burned or maimed, for example, or children left abandoned to die. What happens in their minds and little hearts? I hope—and I suspect—that Jesus *really* comes to them; comforts them; in some way actually takes over their pain by a remarkable mysterious act of substitution. That what the suffering child feels is not pain but the warm embracing arms of Jesus. All children in the world, not just those in Christian homes.

As Christians we *do,* after all, believe in substitution; substitutionary atonement; vicarious suffering.

This is speculation. It is not an answer; it is a hope. I do believe however there is an answer, because God is love.

Meanwhile as Christians we have an ethical commission: "Remember those who are in prison, as though you were in prison with them; those who are being tortured, as though you yourselves were being tortured" (Heb 13:3).

Implications for urban mission: Cities are places of sufferings, and of sufferers. They're often the places not only where suffering is inflicted, but where sufferers from elsewhere—victims of wars or disasters—end up. Urban Christians will make their greatest contribution by working to relieve suffering, to comfort the comfortless, to build communities of healing and safe haven, and to advocate for systemic and policy reforms that reduce the causes of suffering.

The Unfinished Work of Christ

(Seedbed, 4/18/14)

"When Jesus had received the wine, he said, 'It is finished.' Then he bowed his head and gave up his spirit" (Jn 19:30).

Four other times in Scripture we find this phrase or fact of finished finality.

It Is Finished: Creation

"Thus the heavens and the earth were finished, and all their multitude. And on the seventh day God finished the work that he had done, and he rested on the seventh day from all the work that he had done" (Gen 2:1–2). And God pronounced it all "very good."

Creation was finished, but of course in another sense it was just beginning. Now we read of "seed," generations, multiplying life, bursting fruitfulness.

It Is Finished: Tabernacle

Moses "set up the court around the tabernacle and the altar, and put up the screen at the gate of the court. So Moses finished the work" (Ex 40:33).

The echo of Genesis 2:1 here seems deliberate.

Moses was "faithful in all God's house as a servant, to testify to the things that would be spoken later" (Heb 3:5). The tabernacle was finished, according to the pattern Moses was shown on the mountain.

But of course this was the beginning of a new chapter: God's liberated people being formed into a holy redemptive people in the wilderness so God could get on with fulfilling his covenant promises.

It Is Finished: Temple

"Thus all the work of Solomon was accomplished from the day the foundation of the house of the Lord was laid until the house of the Lord was finished completely" (2 Chron 8:16).

This ending was of course a beginning. The kingdom of God was now established on earth (so it seemed). The people of God had a place and form for worshipping God authentically, faithfully, shapingly.

We know that much quickly went wrong, and we note that immediately God's prophets begin to speak of a much greater king and kingdom to come.

So it was. In perfect, remarkable fulfillment of all the Old Testament promises, God himself became king in Jesus Christ.

On the cross God's atoning work was done. Jesus' hour had come. So Jesus gasped, or rather shouted, his last: "Finished!" Earlier, in his High Priestly prayer, Jesus said, "I glorified you on earth by finishing the work that you gave me to do" (Jn 17.4). Atonement finished, yes—but a new chapter and history is beginning.

It Is Finished: New Creation

Nearly at the end of the Bible in the great capstone book of Revelation Jesus shouts: "It is done! I am the Alpha and the Omega, the beginning and the end. To the thirsty I will give water as a gift from the spring of the water of life" (Rev 21:6).

Jesus is not only the end but also the beginning. In how many senses and dimensions, we don't fully know.

The water is flowing; the river is surging.

Today we live between the "It is finished!" of the cross and "It is done!" of creation healed. By the Spirit we live out the atonement as Jesus's discipling body in the world.

It seems that with the Lord God, Holy Trinity, every ending is a beginning.

There is no end to what God, together with his willing, loving creatures, can do in the continuously unfolding glory of God's creative design and history.

Charles Wesley famously wrote: "Love's redeeming work is done!" But—yes and no. Jesus finished his atoning work on the cross. He has not yet finished his redeeming work. The Holy Spirit, the Spirit of Jesus, is still at work in the world. Jesus is still working to bring the kingdom of God in fullness, the New Creation, all creation healed, in which God's will is done perfectly on earth as (echoing, reverberating, uniting) it is in heaven.

Salvation is still an unfinished painting, an unfinished symphony, uncompleted history. An ongoing mission.

Implications for urban witness: The already-but-not-yet dialectic of "it is finished" continues, and we are in the middle. What Jesus has done for us in the past is our basis; what he yet will do to bring his kingdom in fullness is our confidence and hope and joy and strength. Urban mission draws strength, courage to continue, from both dimensions of God's "It is finished" actions.

Revolution in Theology: Six Ecological Facts

(Seedbed, 6/21/14)

Say *ecology*, and eyes glaze over. People think: Science – technical stuff – boring, difficult, irrelevant.

I argue: Say *ecology*, and people should think of the Bible. This could revolutionize theology.

Why think Bible? Because ecology comes from the hand of God and reflects his glory. God created a world of immense beauty, variety, and complexity which is most fully understood through ecological categories (and perhaps most fully appreciated through poetry and music).

For many Christians, such an ecological shift would be a worldview shift. I suspect many Christians would say: Ecology has nothing to do with the gospel. Wrong!

Here are six spiritual-physical facts about ecology. Combine them with Scripture, and you have a fuller biblical worldview than in traditional theology.

What Is Ecology?

Ecology is popularly defined as "the branch of biology that deals with the relations of organisms to one another and to their physical surroundings." Since life is more than physical, I expand *ecology* to mean the study of all life forms in relation to each other and their surroundings, both physical and spiritual. Christians know that the realities and influences on our lives are spiritual as well as physical.

An *ecosystem* is "a biological community of interacting organisms and their physical environment." Expanded Christian version: An ecosystem is the totality of all living things within a particular context in their interdependence with one another and with their physical and spiritual environment.

Ecosystems range from cosmic to microcosmic: All that God has created. But not even the tiniest is inconsequential, for ecology is all about the interrelationship of *everything,* no exceptions. Nothing excluded.

Six Spiritual-Physical Facts

1. Life and energy. Ecology is about life, and life is about energy.

Physical fact: Ecosystem are living systems. Whenever any life form is born or dies, the ecosystem changes in some manner.

Spiritual fact: All energy comes from God. In creation God mysteriously infuses his own life into the created order—initially and continuously.

Spiritual-physical fact: Humankind is a combination of matter and spirit in constant interaction. Not one or the other. We are physical-spiritual-social beings. In God's reality, spirit and matter are not opposites or aliens. Physical reality is a dimensionally limited part of spiritual reality.

2. Constant change. Every ecosystem is in flux, slowly or rapidly. Tomorrow is different from today and yesterday, even if minutely. This gives rise to history.

Physical fact: All living creatures have a life cycle. Meanwhile the inert parts of creation also change due to time, weather, and the action of living things. Tomorrow that beautiful mountain or seacoast will be slightly different.

Spiritual fact: As part of the created order, humans are constantly changing spiritually. Change may be gradual or sudden; perceptible or hidden. This fact derives from God himself, Triune Creator, who in one sense is changeless but yet is dynamic, full of transformative energy.

Spiritual-physical fact: We're always changing both physically and spiritually—interactively between body, mind, spirit, will, other people, earth and its atmosphere and its creatures. Food or lack thereof affects your spirit as well as the earth and its creatures, from which food comes. And so on. This necessarily shapes how we understand "holistic" spirituality, community, and ministry.

3. Input > Throughput > Output. To be alive and thrive, every being and every ecosystem requires ongoing energy input. The energy is processed, nourishing or otherwise affecting the organism or system (throughput). Work and waste result: always there is output.

Physical fact: Every living thing requires continuing energy inputs: Food, water, air, solar energy (indirectly, if not directly). Energy is absorbed, used, and discharged in some form. (Jesus commented on this.)

Spiritual fact: The same is true spiritually. Spiritual life also requires input, grows (or not) by throughput, and produces output in ways healthy or unhealthy, destructive or innocuous. (Jesus commented on this, also.)

Spiritual-physical fact: All dimensions of our lives are constantly shaped by input, throughput, and output physically and spiritually—which means (among other things) economically, esthetically, emotionally, socially, and so on. A constant cycle: physical and spiritual inputs, throughputs, and outputs interacting.

4. Complex interdependence. The complexity of even tiny ecosystem is nearly beyond belief. Multiply that by billions of other ecosystem, and you get some idea of the world *on earth* which God created, let alone that "he made the stars also" (Gen 1:16)!

But it's not just complexity; it's interdependence. Every ecosystem, even the tiniest, is constantly in complex interaction with others—and thus with the whole. In the ecological sense, there is nothing that doesn't matter.

Physical fact: It is so. Everything you touch, see, use, consume, appreciate, invest, love, or ignore is woven into the earth's complex ecology.

Spiritual fact: The same is true spiritually. We can only imagine the complex ecology of prayer, meditation, good intentions, acts of love and self-giving, worship, prevenient grace, angels and demons, and God's Spirit. Yet the Bible beautifully images it. "My word . . . shall not return unto me void" (Isa 55:11). Do not despise "the day of small things" (Zech 4:10).

Spiritual-physical fact: Physical and spiritual ecosystems interconnect. They are part of one larger whole, since all comes from the hand and energy of God's Word and Spirit. Affirming this is still a huge worldview shift for most people. What you do with a soda can affects you spiritually, and affects in a tiny but not insignificant way the whole spiritual-physical ecosystem.

What you pray about can have physical effects beyond your knowing. (Now begin multiplying that.)

Yes, spraying chemicals on your lawn *does* harm the poor in Mali. Probably the prayers of the folks there help us.

5. Feedback loops. Ecological science emphasizes feedback loops. This is a key way of explaining and clarifying the complex interdependence described above. "Feedback loop" refers to the dynamic by which every action cycles back on itself to produce and often amplify further change. Think of feedback in an audio system. If a microphone is too close to the loud speaker, the sound cycles and reverberates and amplifies into a horrid screech until it is interrupted.

Physical fact: Every action or change in nature has an effect which bounces back and affects the source. "You can never do just one thing." But this is complex, not simple, for feedback loops cycle through other feedback loops, multiplying themselves. Such loops can be helpful or devastating. A good example is your physical body. The most pressing broadscale example today is the climate and climate destabilization.

Spiritual fact: Feedback loops are spiritual as well as physical. Think of prayer, worship, and Christian obedience and example. Healthy churches and healthy families flourish through healthy feedback loops.

Spiritual-physical fact: Feedback loops are no respecter of the supposed material-spiritual split. Quite the opposite! Toss that soda can, and it joins complex feedback loops—to your own hurt, and especially to the hurt of the poor and vulnerable. Feedback loops operate complexly in all directions, so naturally they are found in business, economics, the arts, family systems, and all the spiritual-physical dimensions of culture.

6. Entropy and extropy. Entropy is the inexorable tendency of all systems to run down. It describes the move from order to disorder. (It is easier to mess up your room than to straighten it up!) More technically, entropy is a measure of a system's disorder. Science calls this the Second Law of Thermodynamics.

Physical fact: Every system gradually moves from order to disorder as energy is spent. This is true in an overall, physical-cosmic sense, and it carries through to the smallest ecosystem. Without continuing input of new energy, a system will become dead or inert. Our physical bodies are good examples: We keep them renewed or refreshed, but not forever.

Spiritual fact: Our spiritual life is affected by what happens to our bodies and to the physical world around us. We live in an entropic world.

Spiritual-physical fact: While we are in this timebound life, there is no full escape from entropy. However prayer, Christian *koinonia*, and communion with God do lift us out of the entropic dynamic to some degree.

I suspect that spirit is not subject to entropy—rather, that entropy is a dimension of spacetime existence only. Satan has an interest in seeing us succumb to entropy spiritually as well as physically, however—that is, in our whole being, as well as in the decay of creation.

So I use the term *extropy* as the opposite of entropy. Extropy means the effect of God's creative and sustaining energy on matter, including our own lives. Extropy is the process by which God overcomes creation's "bondage to decay" (Rom 8:21), renewing the church by a dynamic which is not simply its own and by the Spirit preserving the created order and drawing it toward the kingdom of God in fullness. Creation healed, restored, and freed for further flourishing.

I suppose extropy in this sense is another word for God's love and grace. The wonder of love is that in loving, new energy is created and released. So, for example, a loving church is a powerful church. A church energized by love is a living witness to the inbreaking of God's Spirit in the present, and an inbreaking of the ultimate reality of the kingdom of God. Here extropy is at work, not just entropy.

This is part of the ecology of the church, of our own lives, and of the interface between spirit and matter.

The End and the Beginning

Bottom line for Christians: *Everything*—creation, grace, awakening, justification, sanctification, discipleship, giftedness, ministry, mission, the kingdom of God, creation care, history—should be understood ecologically in this physical-spiritual way.

This could creatively shake up theology, discipleship, mission, and the church's impact on the world.

Eventually, it will.

Mission and the Big Culture Lie

(Seedbed, 9/18/14)

There's a big problem with Christian mission—not only in North America, but worldwide. The problem is this: Most Christians, and Christian missionaries and pastors, have only the foggiest notion of what *culture* really is.

Happily, I have encountered a few inspiring exceptions! But let's talk about the fog. I want to expose a Big Culture Lie.

First, a little background.

Gospel and Culture

From beginning to end, from creation to new creation and beyond, the Christian story is the story of culture. The significance of this is often missed. It's overlooked in our own lives, very often, and in the history of church and mission.

Christian mission is inseparable from the realities, issues, and dynamics of culture. But what is "culture," actually?

By *culture* I mean all the ways human beings interact with each other, with their physical environment, and with the unseen environment—and the cumulative fruit of these interactions over time. This is my definition.

Culture is first of all physical objects and ecologies, because on these all human life rests. Every cultural artifact comes first from the earth. It is made of physical things—objects and living creatures found in the particular environments where humans live. Wood, rocks, shells, paint, glass; ants, worms, eagles, microbes, whatever.

Human cultural artifacts result from human engagement with such physical things. Symbols, thoughts, music, buildings—these are the fruit of our interaction with the physical universe, plus interaction with each other and with the unseen world. Written language, including the alphabet and Chinese characters, apparently developed from pictographs—that is, symbolic drawings of physical things and their relationships.

Consider music. In *The Great Animal Orchestra,* Bernie Krause describes the myriad sounds arising from creation—from the air, land, and waters. "The planet itself teems with a vigorous resonance that is as complete and expansive as it is delicately balanced. Every place, with its vast populations of plants and animals, becomes a concert hall, and everywhere a unique orchestra performs an unmatched symphony." Listen, and you will hear "the tuning of the great animal orchestra, a revelation of the acoustic harmony of the wild. . . it is likely that the origins of every piece of music we enjoy and word we speak come, at some point, from this collective voice."[2]

Culture is Physical

Earthly culture is physical-thing-dependent. This is why it varies with weather, terrain, and available food and building materials. Is there anything more cultural than food? Yet music is close behind.

This is also why earth's climate is so critically important.

We easily forget the physicality of culture. Say "culture" and we think of art and ideas and orchestras, or science and philosophies and customs—not dirt and microorganisms. But culture mostly rises from the earth.

Physical things like hills and fruit and rocks and animals become the raw material of language, which builds up analogies and metaphors and ideas, which shape thought and stories, which grow into literature, music, dance, religion and more, and thus over time arise as culture.

---

[2] Bernie Krause, *The Great Animal Orchestra: Finding the Origins of Music in the World's Wild Places* (New York: Little, Brown, 2012), 9–10.

Take away material things and the "natural" world, and culture collapses.

Culture grows like a tree; sings like a bird; rolls like thunder; uses tools like hoes and violins all made from the stuff nature provides. From the earth.

The physical, material side of culture is so omnipresent that it disappears from our view. The physical becomes invisible. Yet it never really disappears. Which is why it is always present in the gospel and in church and in mission and in cities, just as it is present from the first to the last page of Scripture—from "Let there be light" to "tree of life."

In our reading of Scripture the visible easily becomes invisible. We get so used to sheep, fig trees, sandals, fish, wheat, and so forth that we stop really seeing them.

Looking for the invisible, we miss the visible. Really a form of dualism. So we think Jesus's parables teach only spiritual lessons; have only heavenly meanings.

Christian mission always happens within one or many cultures. So we'd better get used to it. Figure out how to work with culture, not against it—and within culture, seek to cooperate with the Spirit's work of bringing all things into conformity to Jesus Christ. Not to ignore culture; not to commodify; not to exploit nor dominate. But to appreciate, redeem, enjoy, enrich.

The Big Culture Lie

The Big Culture Lie is that you can redeem culture without healing the earth. The big lie is that culture exists and can be interacted with without dealing with its physical, earthy basis.

Just as you can't have a healthy civilization on a sick planet, so you can't have holistic mission without working to heal the earth.

This is why the Bible is so physical; why earth is earthy. It explains much about the Incarnation—which in turn points the direction of mission. "*As* the Father has sent me . . . ."

Jesus the Mud-Maker

(Seedbed, 6/23/15)

Jesus did many symbolic acts. Here's one: Healing a blind man one Sabbath day in Jerusalem, recorded in John 9.

"As [Jesus] walked along, he saw a man blind from birth. His disciples asked him, 'Rabbi, who sinned, this man or his parents, that he was born blind?' Jesus answered, 'Neither this man nor his parents sinned; he was born blind so that God's works might be revealed in him. We must work the works of him who sent me while it is day; night is coming when no one can work. As long as I am in the world, I am the light of the world.' When he had said this, he spat on the ground and made mud with the saliva and spread the mud on the man's eyes, saying to him, 'Go, wash in the pool of Siloam (which means sent). Then he went and washed and came back able to see." (Jn 9:1–7).

This story has multiple meanings. But let's focus on the mud.

Jesus made mud from his own spit and smeared the mess on the blind man's eyes—and the man was healed. Strange!

We learn that this happened on a Sabbath. So in making mud Jesus was "working" on the Sabbath—said the Pharisees, whom Jesus was intentionally provoking. Jesus says, provocatively, "We must work the works of him who sent me while it is day [even on the Sabbath]; night is coming when no one can work. As long as I am in the world, I am the light of the world." Something and someone greater than the Sabbath is here.

God, People, Land

Jesus needed no mud or spit to heal the man. So something more is going on. The story comes to life when viewed through an Old Testament lens. Sabbath . . . healing . . . land (mud) . . . questions of "work," and of rest and *shalom*. Hmmm.

Why the mud? Look at all Jesus's healings, and you see that his "method" (so to speak) varied. Sometimes a touch; sometimes a word; sometimes something more dramatic, as here.

The most obvious reason for this variety in Jesus's healings is that Jesus wanted to undercut any ideas of magic or surefire formulas.

But in the case of the mud, there's a deeper purpose: To symbolize and signal reconciliation —God, people, land.

Jesus intentionally brings mud into the healing process, setting up all kinds of symbolic resonances. Mud is dirt; dirt is land; land is earth. The Bible is all about God, people, and land.

What is Jesus doing here? Once again he is reenacting the Old Testament Messianic and covenant narrative and promise. He is again showing aspects of his Messiahship. Jesus the great healer, as prophesied.

The muddy healing act is thus triple: Immediate and physical (the man is healed); historical and prophetic (referring back to the Old Testament covenant); and future or eschatological: The coming of God's kingdom in fullness, when everything in heaven and earth is reconciled in the New Creation. And all this in continuity, not only discontinuity, with today's actual physical mud.

Old Testament references to mud and spit are generally negative. Jesus turns the reference to a positive one, as he often does.

The Muddy Kingdom

Jesus sanctifies the mud as he heals the man. He redeems the image and the physical reality. Of course the mud does not need sanctifying, except in our unbiblical misunderstandings.

Jesus's use of the mud was symbolic, yet much more than symbolic. It was real and actual at two levels, at least: the physical healing of the man, and the certainty and physicality of the coming kingdom of God in fullness according to the order of Jesus's incarnation and resurrection.

There is gobs more to this healing story, having to do with physical and spiritual blindness and the question of who really was blind—the man or the Pharisees. That's part of the ecology of the story, so not unrelated to the mud. But this is enough for now.

My Fourth Conversion

(Seedbed, 4/19/15)

My fourth conversion came about five years ago.

First Conversion: Jesus

I was a child, and there was no one datable experience. But before I was twelve it was clear to me that I wanted to and must follow Jesus Christ. I claimed Jesus as my Savior and Lord, and through ups and downs have grown in that commitment and relationship and surety.

I became a member of the Free Methodist Church in Spring Arbor, Michigan.

The key Bible verse would be 1 John 1:9, "If we confess our sins, he is faithful and just to forgive us our sins, and cleanse us from all unrighteousness" (KJV). That's only one of many biblical passages that shaped my life, but it perhaps best encapsulates the central truth.

Eventually I learned that Jesus wanted to show me something bigger and better than my own conversion.

Second Conversion: Jesus's Body, the Church

About a dozen years later, when I was in seminary, I was converted to the church, the body of Christ. Of course I was already a church member and was on my way toward ordination. But I misunderstood. I did not "discern the body." My understanding was mostly individual and organizational.

Through the influence of Prof. Gilbert James (a sociologist) and others at Asbury Seminary, and through my experiences and Bible reading, I began to understand the social-spiritual nature of the body of Christ. I came to see the organic and ecological nature of the church. One could not be joined to the Head without being joined to the Body. That fact wasn't (and isn't) primarily about organization. It's about relationships, about community.

So when we went to Brazil in 1968, I had to spend the next year or two working through Ephesians to figure out what I was now a part of (church, body, family, "member").

My 1975 book *The Problem of Wineskins* was mainly my report on this discovery.

One of the Scriptures that best encapsulate this truth is 1 Corinthians 12:12, "Just as the [human] body is one and has many members, and all the members of the body, though many, are one body, so it is with Christ." Paul writes that we are "co-membered together," "members of each other"—and not just in a mystical or symbolic or "spiritual" sense. In the New Testament, "member" has neither an organizational nor an abstract sense. It is an organic reality.

But eventually I learned that Jesus wanted to show me something bigger and better than the church itself.

Third Conversion: Jesus's Reign – The Kingdom of God

In a few years, studying and living the church led to a surprise: The church exists not for itself, but for the kingdom of God. After the 1974 Lausanne Congress I began exploring this in *Community of the King* (1977), *Liberating the Church* (1983), and especially *Kingdom Manifesto* (1985) and eventually *Models of the Kingdom* (1991). (Thanks to Jürgen Moltmann's *Theology of Hope* and other providential circumstances.)

During the 1974 International Congress on World Evangelization in Lausanne, Switzerland, suddenly it hit me: In our theology, why do we *end* with the kingdom of God ("eschatology"), when Jesus *began* with it? This was my reflection on the order of topics treated at the conference.

So when we were at the Irving Park Free Methodist Church in Chicago, my question was: What does it mean for this little part of Jesus's body to exist for the kingdom of God, not for itself?

Two key verses: "Fear not, little flock, for your Father delights to give you the kingdom" (Luke 12:32, my translation), and "Seek first the kingdom of God and its justice, and I'll take care of everything else" (Mt. 6:33, my paraphrase).

Churches which are outposts of the kingdom of God are restlessly kingdom-mission-driven with a global vision, pledging allegiance to nothing that competes with kingdom priorities. (Aware of the problems with "kingdom" language, I explored that question in *Models of the Kingdom*.)

A vision for the kingdom of God here and now. But eventually I learned that Jesus wanted to show me something bigger and better than my understanding of the kingdom of God.

Fourth Conversion: Jesus's Creation – The Earth

When the United States and some other nations briefly discovered the physical environment and ecology in the 1970s, before promptly forgetting about it for two decades in suicidal amnesia, I started to wake up to broader dimension of God's reign.

This was evident already in *Liberating the Church*. But it was a long process. Only in the last few years, actually, has it dawned on me that God is really serious about his will being done on earth as in heaven. Long ago the Lord God made some startling promises: "They will not hurt or destroy on all my holy mountain; for the earth will be full of the knowledge of the Lord as the waters cover the sea" (Isa 11:9 – one example among many).

I explored some of the meanings of this in *Salvation Means Creation Healed*, with Joel Scandrett (2011). But I'm still learning what this means. I tried to imagine it in my book *Jesus and Pocahontas* (2015).

Now my life verse has become Isaiah 6:3, "Holy, holy, holy is the Lord of hosts; the whole earth is full of his glory."

For years I missed the second part of that. The verb is "is," not "will be." I believe and hope the Lord is teaching me what it means that "the whole earth *is* full" of God's glory, and how that changes everything in our mission and discipleship and relationships.

In Isaiah 6 and in all the Bible, holiness and the earth belong together. So gradually, little by little, I think I'm coming to understand more fully Ephesians 1:10, that God has "a plan for the fullness of time to bring everything in heaven and on earth together under one head," Jesus Christ. (my translation). And why Irenaeus (c. 130–202 AD) spoke of "recapitulation" in his reflection on this verse.

Other Dimensions

I should add that the roots of each later conversion were already present in earlier ones. Each reality and dimension is embryonically contained—"nested"—in the previous ones. Jesus starts us on an expanding road of discipleship and discovery. We are talking about multidimensionality, after all; about the full economy and ecology of salvation.

Also, woven into all these conversions was a growing awareness of the significance of the fact and doctrine of the Trinity—that salvation is a Trinitarian drama. Also, the surpassing significance of God's assured covenant promises.

Today I am fully persuaded that within the next quarter century or so, Jesus will show me yet bigger, better, brighter dimensions of his liberating, healing, redeeming, restoring plan.

Eventually I will disappear, but I won't go away.

About the Author

Howard A. Snyder currently serves as Visiting Director of the Manchester Wesley Research Centre in England. He has taught at Tyndale Seminary in Toronto (2007–2012), Asbury Theological Seminary (1996–2006), United Theological Seminary in Dayton, Ohio (1988–1996), and in Chicago and São Paulo, Brazil. His two dozen books include *The Problem of Wineskins, The Community of the King, Salvation Means Creation Healed* (with Joel Scandrett), and most recently *Jesus and Pocahontas: Gospel, Mission, and National Myth* (2015).

References

Ali, A. H. (2010). *Nomad: A Personal Journey Through the Clash of Civilizations*. London: Simon & Schuster.

Ali, A. H. (2015). *Heretic: Why Islam Needs a Reformation Now*. New York: HarperCollins.

Banks, R. (1980). *Paul's Idea of Community: The Early House Churches in Their Historical Setting*. Grand Rapids: Eerdmans.

Barth, K. (1956). *Church Dogmatics*. Edinburgh: T & T Clark.

Barth, K. (1964). La nature et la forma de l'Eglise. In *l'Eglise* (p. 119). Geneva: Editions Labor et Fides.

Baucum, T. K. (2008). *Evangelical Hospitality: Catechetical Evangelism in the Early Church and Its Recovery for Today*. Lanham, Md.: Scarecrow Press.

Boff, L. (1988). *Trinity and Society*. Maryknoll, N.Y.: Orbis.

Brauer, J. C. (1971). Sacraments. In *The Westminster Disctionary of Church History* (pp. 734-735). Philadelphia: Westminster Press.

Capra, F. (1991). *The Tao of Physics: An Exploration of the Parallels Between Modern Physics and Eastern Mysticism* (3rd. ed.). Boston, Mass.: Shambhala.

Collins, K. J. (1985). The Scripture Way of Salvation. In *The Works of John Wesley* (Vol. 2). Nashville: Abingdon Press.

Daly, H. E., & Farley, J. (2004). *Ecological Economics: Principles and*

Applications. Washington D.C.: Island Press.

DeYmaz, M. (2007). *Building a Healthy Multi-Ethnic Church: Mandate, Commitments, and Practices of a Diverse Congregation*. San Francisco, Calif.: Jossy-Bass.

Dulles, A. (1964). *Models of the Church*. Garden City, N.Y.: Doubleday.

Dyke, F. V. (1996). *Redeeming Creation: The Biblical Basis for Environmental Stewardship*. Downers Grove, Ill.: InterVarsity.

Eastman, M., & Latham, S. (Eds.). (2004). *Urban Church: A Practitioner's Resource Book*. London: SPCK.

Edgerton, R. B. (1992). *Sick Societies: Challenging the Myth of Primitive Harmony*. New York: The Free Press.

Ellul, J. (1971). *Propaganda: The Formation of Men's Attitudes* (original French 1962 ed.). New York: Alfred A. Knopf.

Enoch Wan, e. a. (2014). *Diaspora Missiology: Theory, Methodology, and Practice, 2nd ed*. Portland, Ore.: Institute of Diaspora studies of USA.

Fallows, J. (2015, November). The (Planet-Saving, Capitalism-Subverting, Surprisingly Lucrative) Investment Secrets of Al Gore. *The Atlantic*, pp. 85-96.

Ferguson, N. (2011). *Civilization: The West and the Rest*. New York: Penguin.

Finney, J. (1996). *Recovering the Past: Celtic and Roman Mission*. London: Darton, Longman and Todd.

Flannery, A. P. (1975). Dogmatic Constitiution of the Church. In
   Documents of Vatican II. Grand Rapids: Eerdmans.

Francis, P. (2015). *Encyclical on Climate Change and Inequality: On Care
   for Our Common Home.* Brooklyn, N.Y.: Melville House.

Frasier Institute. (n.d.). Retrieved February 6, 2016, from
   https://www.fraserinstitute.org/

Freedom House. (n.d.). Retrieved February 6, 2016, from
   https://freedomhouse.org/

Friedman, H. S. (2012). *The Measure of a Naton.* Amherst, N.Y.:
   Prometheus.

Fry, N. (1990). *Words with Power: Being a Second Study of "The Bible and
   Literature".* New York: Harcourt Brace Jovanovich.

Frye, N. (1981,1982). *The Secret Code: The Bible and Literature.* New
   York: Houghton Mifflin Harcourt.

Garrison, D. (2004, Winter). Church Planting Movements vs. Insider
   Movements: Missiological Realities vs. Mythiological [sic]
   Speculations. *International Journal of Frontier Missions, 21*(4),
   151-154.

Gibbons, D. (2009). *The Monkey and the Fish: Liquid Leadership for a
   Third-Culture Church.* Grand Rapids: Zondervan.

Gillis, J. (2011, February 16). Retrieved from New York Times online.

Global Compact Cities Programme. (n.d.). Retrieved February 6, 2016,
   from http://citiesprogramme.com/aboutus/the-cities-

programme.

Global Mapping. (2015, December 3). Retrieved February 6, 2016, from http://www.gmi.org

Global Witness. (n.d.). Retrieved February 6, 2016, from https://www.globalwitness.org/en/

Gornik, M. R. (2011). *World Made Global: Stories of African Christianity in New York City.* Grand Rapids: Eerdmans.

Grigg, V. (1992). *Cry of the Urban Poor.* Monrovia, Calif.: MARC.

Grigg, V. (2009). *The Spirit of Christ in the Postmodern City.* Auckland, New Zealand: Urban Leadership Foundation.

Grigg, V. (2012, November). Hovering Spirit, Creative Voice, Empowered Transformation: A Retrospective. *New Urban World Journal, 1*(1), 18.

Grigg, V. (2014). *Companion to the Poor: Christ in the Urban Slums* (3rd ed.). Auckland, New Zealand: Urban Leadership Foundation.

Gunton, C. E. (1997). *The Promise of Trinitarian Theology* (2nd ed.). Edinburgh: T. & T. Clark.

Heath, E. A., & Kisker, S. T. (2010). *Longing for Spring: A New Vision for Wesleyan Community.* Eugene, Ore.: Cascade Books.

Heitzenrater, R. P. (2005). *The Works of John Wesley* (Bicentennial ed.). Nashville: Abingdon Press.

Hoefer, H. E. (2001). *Churchless Christianity.* Pasadena, Calif: Wm. Carey Library.

Hooft, W. V. (1956). *The Renewal of the Church.* Philadelphia:
Westminster Press.

Hunter, G. G. (2000). *The Celtic Way of Evangelism.* Nashville, Tenn:
Abingdon.

Jay, E. G. (1980). *The Church: Its Changing Image through Twenty
Centuries.* Atlanta: John Knox Press.

Johnson, T., & Ross, K. (Eds.). (2009). *Atlas of Global Christianity
1910-2010.* Edinburgh, Scotland: Edinburgh University Press.

Johnstone, P. (2011). *The Future of the Gloabal Church: History, Trends
and Possibilities.* Colorado Springs, Colo: Biblica.

Karkkainen, V.-M. (2007). *The Trinity: Global Perspectives.* Louisville,
Ky.: Westminster John Knox.

Keller, T. (2012). *Center Church: Doing Balanced, Gospel-Centered
Ministry in Your City.* Grand Rapids: Zondervan.

Kelsey, M. (1976). *The Other Side of Silence.* Mahwah, NJ: Paulist Press.

Kimball, D. (2003). *The Emerging Church: Vintage Christianity for New
Generations.* Grand Rapids: Zondervan.

Krause, B. (2012). *The Great Animal Orchestra: Finding the Origins of
Music in the World's Wild Places.* New York: Little, Brown.

Latourette, K. S. (1941-1944). *A History of the Expansion of Christianity*
(Vols. 4-6). New York: Harper & Row.

Lausanne Creation Care Network. (n.d.). Retrieved February 6, 2016,
from http://lwccn.com/

Law, S. (2012, Spring). Anticipating Change: Missions and Paradigm Shifts in Emergence. *The Asbury Journal, 67*(1), 4-26.

Lewis, R. (2007, Summer). Promoting Movements to Christ within Natural Communities. *International Journal of Frontier Missiology, 24*(2), 75-76.

Livingstone, F. L. (1997). Sacrament. In *The Oxford Dictionary of the Christian Church* (3rd ed., pp. 1435-1436). Oxford: Oxford University Press.

Louv, R. (2008). *Last Child in the Woods: Saving Our Children From Nature-Deficit Disorder.* Chapel Hill, N.C.: Algonquin Books.

Lovejoy, A. O. (1936,1964). *The Great Chain of Being: A Study in the History of Ideas.* Cambridge, Mass.: Harvard University Press.

McIntosh, G. L. (2004). *Evaluating the Church Growth Movement: Five Views.* Grand Rapids: Zondervan.

Meer, F. v. (1961). *Augustine the Bishop.* (B. B. Lamp, Trans.) London: Sheed and Ward.

Nelson, G. V. (2008). *Borderland Churches: A Congregation's Introduction to Missional Living.* St. Louis, Mo.: Chalice Press.

Olson, D. T. (2008). *The American Church in Crisis.* Grand Rapids: Zondervan.

O'Malley, J. S. (2013). *Revitalization Amid Diaspora--Consultation Three: Explorations in World Christian Revitalization Movements.* Lexington, Ky: Emeth Press.

Ortiz, M. (1996). *One New People: Models for Developing a Mutiethnic Church.* Downers Grove, Ill: InterVarsity.

Packer, J. I., & Parrett, G. A. (2010). *Grounded in the Gospel: Building Believers the Old-Fashioned Way.* Grand Rapids: Baker.

Padilla, C. R. (1985). *Mission Between the Times.* Grand Rapids, Mich.: Eerdmans.

Park, Joon-Sik. (2012, April). Korean Protestant Christianity: A Missiological Reflection. *International Bulletin of Missionary Research, 36*(2), 59.

Payk, C. (2015). Grace First: Christian Mission and Prevenient Grace in John Wesley. Toronto: Clements Academic.

Peters, R. E. (2007). *Urban Ministry: An Introduction.* Nashville: Abingdon.

Peterson, E. H. (2008). *Tell It Slant: A Conversation on the Language of Jesus in His Stories and Prayers.* Grand Rapids, Mich.: Eerdmans.

Pinnock, C. H. (2001). *Most Moved Mover: A Theology of God's Openness.* Carlisle, Cumbria: Paternoster.

Piper, J., Corwin, G., Travis, J., & Travis, A. (2005, Jan.-Feb.). An Extended Conversation about 'Insider Movements'. *Mission Frontiers*, 16-23.

Popova, M. (2015, November 29). Review of Dark Matter and the Dinosaurs. *The New York Times; Sunday Book Review*, p. BR14.

Rahner, K. (1975). Sacramental Theology. In *Encyclopedia of Theology:*

The Concise Sacramentum Mundi. New York: Seabury Press.

Ranking the Rankings. (2014, Nov.8). *The Economist.*

Rhodes, S. A. (1998). *Where the Nations Meet: The Church in a Multicultural World.* Downers Grove, Ill.: InterVarsity.

Rifkin, J. (2000). *The Age of Access: The New Culture of Hypercapitalism Where All of Life is a Paid-For Experience.* New York: Tarcher/Putnam.

Ronsvalle, J., & Ronsvalle, S. (2015). *The State of Church Giving through 2013: Crisis or Potential?* Champaign, Ill.: empty tomb, inc.

Roszak, T. (1969). *The Making of a Counter-culture.* New York: Doubleday Anchor.

Sider, R. J. (1977). *Rich Christians in an Age of Hunger.* Downers Grove, Ill.: InterVarsity.

Sire, J. w. (1980). *Scripture Twisting: 20 Ways the Cults Misread the Bible.* Downers Grove, Ill.: InterVarsity.

Snyder, H. A. (1975). *The Problem of Wineskins: Church Structure in a Technological Age.* Downers Grove, Ill.: InterVarsity Press.

Snyder, H. A. (1983). *Liberating the Church: The Ecology of Church and Kingdom.* Downers Grove, Ill.: InterVarsity Press.

Snyder, H. A. (1989). *Signs of the Spirit: How God Reshapes the Church.* Grand Rapids: Zondervan.

Snyder, H. A. (1991). *Models of the Kingdom.* Nashville: Abingdon.

Snyder, H. A. (1995). *Earth Currents: The Struggle for the World's Soul.* Nashville: Abingdon.

Snyder, H. A. (2004). *The Community of the King* (rev. ed.). Downers Grove, Ill.: InterVarsity.

Snyder, H. A. (2011). *Yes in Christ: Wesleyan Reflections on Gospel, Mission, and Culture.* Toronto: Clements Academic.

Snyder, H. A. (2014). *The Radical Wesley: The Patterns and Practices of a Movement Maker.* Franklin, Tenn.: Seedbed Press.

Snyder, H. A. (2015). *Jesus and Pocahontas: Gospel, Mission, and National Myth.* Eugene, Ore.: Cascade.

Snyder, H. A., & Runyon, D. (2002). *Decoding the Church: Mapping the DNA of Christ's Body.* Grand Rapids, Mich.: Baker Books.

Snyder, H. A., & Runyon, D. V. (1986). *Foresight: 10 Major Trends That Will Dramatically Affect the Future of Christians and the Church.* Nashville: Thomas Nelson.

Snyder, H. A., & Scrandrett, J. (2011). *Salvation Means Creation Healed:The Ecology of Sin and Grace: Overcoming the Divorce Between Earth and Heaven.* Eugene, Oregon: Cascade Books.

Stark, R. (1996). *The Rise of Christianity: A Sociologist Reconsiders History.* Princeton, N.J.: Princeton University Press.

Stott, J. R. (1978). *Christian Counter-Culture: The Message of the Sermon on the Mount.* Downers Grove, Ill: InterVarsity.

Tennent, T. C. (2013, January-February). The Hidden History of

Insider Movements. *Christianity Today, 57*(1), 28.

Tertullian. (n.d.). *Apology 39.*

The Book of Common Prayer. (1952). Greenwhich, Conn.: Seabury
Press.

The Economist Pocket World in Figures. (n.d.). The Economist.

The Greening of Detroit. (n.d.). Retrieved February 6, 2016, from
http://www.greeningofdetroit.com/

Torrance, T. F. (2004). *The Trinitarian Faith: The Evangelical Theology
of the Ancient Catholic Church.* London: T. & T. Clark.

Transparancy International. (n.d.). Retrieved February 6, 2016, from
http://www.transparency.org/cpi2011

Travis, J. (n.d.). The C1 to C6 Spectrum. *Evangelical Missions
Quarterly, 34*, 407-408.

Travis, J., & Travis, A. (2005). Appropriate Approaches in Muslim
Contexts. In C. H. Kraft (Ed.), *Appropriate Christianity.*
Pasadena, Calif: Wm.Carey Library.

Travis, J., & Travis, A. (2005, Sept.-Oct.). Contextualization among
Muslims, Hindus, and Buddhist: A Focus on Insider
Movements. *Mission Frontiers*, 12-15.

Turkle, S. (2015). *Reclaiming Conversation.* New York: Penguin.

U.S. Department of State. (n.d.). Retrieved February 2016, 2016, from
Human Rights Reports: http://www.state.gov/j/drl/rls/hrrpt/

U.S. Department of State. (n.d.). Retrieved February 6, 2016, from

Countries and Regions: http://www.state.gov/countries/

Wallis, J. (1980, January). Rebuilding the Church. *Sojourners, 9*(1), p. 12.

Wallis, J. (1981). *The Call to Conversion.* New York: Harper & Row.

Wan, E. (2014). *Diaspora Missiology: Theory, Methodology, and Practice* (2nd ed.). Portland, Ore: Institute of Diaspora Studies of USA.

Welcome to the Anthropocene. (2011, May 26). Retrieved February 6, 2016, from The Economist: http://www.economist.com/node/18744401

Wikipedia. (n.d.). Retrieved February 6, 2016, from List of Freedom Indices: https://en.wikipedia.org/wiki/List_of_freedom_indices

Wikipedia. (n.d.). Retrieved February 6, 2016, from Anthropocene: http://en.wikipedia.org/wiki/Anthropocene

World Christian Database. (n.d.). Retrieved February 6, 2016, from (http://www.worldchristiandatabase.org/wcd/)

World Values Survey. (n.d.). Retrieved February 6, 2016, from http://www.worldvaluessurvey.org/wvs.jsp

Wright, C. (2006). *The Mission of God: Unlocking the Bible's Grand Narrative.* Downers Grove, Ill.: InterVarsity.

Wright, N. (2014). *Surprised by Scripture: Engaging Contemporary Issues.* New York: HarperCollins.

Young Evangelicals For Climate Action. (n.d.). Retrieved February 6, 2016, from http://www.yecaction.org/

GENERAL INDEX

INDEX OF NAMES

Scripture Index

The Old Testament

The New Testament

www.ingramcontent.com/pod-product-compliance
Lightning Source LLC
Chambersburg PA
CBHW062356090426
42740CB00010B/1299